Arabian Satire

Letter from the General Editor

The Library of Arabic Literature series offers Arabic editions and English translations of significant works of Arabic literature, with an emphasis on the seventh to nineteenth centuries. The Library of Arabic Literature thus includes texts from the pre-Islamic era to the cusp of the modern period, and encompasses a wide range of genres, including poetry, poetics, fiction, religion, philosophy, law, science, history, and historiography.

Books in the series are edited and translated by internationally recognized scholars and are published in parallel-text format with Arabic and English on facing pages, and are also made available as English-only paperbacks.

The Library encourages scholars to produce authoritative, though not necessarily critical, Arabic editions, accompanied by modern, lucid English translations. Its ultimate goal is to introduce the rich, largely untapped Arabic literary heritage to both a general audience of readers as well as to scholars and students.

The Library of Arabic Literature is supported by a grant from the New York University Abu Dhabi Institute and is published by NYU Press.

Philip F. Kennedy
General Editor, Library of Arabic Literature

ديوان

حميدان الشويعر

LIBRARY OF ARABIC LITERATURE
المكتبة العربية

Arabian Satire

Poetry from 18th Century Najd

Ḥmēdān al-Shwēʿir

Edited and translated by
Marcel Kurpershoek

Reviewed by
Saad Sowayan

Volume editors
Clive Holes
Philip F. Kennedy

NEW YORK UNIVERSITY PRESS
New York

NEW YORK UNIVERSITY PRESS
New York

Library of Congress Cataloging-in-Publication Data

Names: Shuwayʿir, Ḥamīdān, active 18th century author. | Kurpershoek, P. M. editor translator. | Shuwayʿir, Ḥamīdān, active 18th century. Poems. Selections. English. | Shuwayʿir, Ḥamīdān, active 18th century. Poems. Selections.
Title: Arabian satire : poetry from 18th-century Najd / Ḥmedan al-Shwe'ir ; edited and translated by Marcel Kurpershoek.
Description: New York : New York University Press, 2017. | Series: Library of Arabic literature | In English and Arabic. | Includes bibliographical references and index. | Description based on print version record and CIP data provided by publisher; resource not viewed.
Identifiers: LCCN 2017024578 (print) | LCCN 2017025519 (ebook) | ISBN 9781479811199 (Ebook) | ISBN 9781479818730 (Ebook) | ISBN 9781479878062 (cloth)
Classification: LCC PJ7765.S58 (ebook) | LCC PJ7765.S58 A2 2017 (print) | DDC 892.7/14--dc23
LC record available at https://lccn.loc.gov/2017024578

New York University Press books are printed on acid-free paper, and their binding materials are chosen for strength and durability.

Series design by Titus Nemeth.

Typeset in Tasmeem, using DecoType Naskh and Emiri.

Typesetting and digitization by Stuart Brown.

Manufactured in the United States of America
c 10 9 8 7 6 5 4 3 2 1

Table of Contents

Introduction

Najdī Fascination with Ḥmēdān al-Shwēʿir

None of the early poets who composed their verses in the vernacular of Central Arabia has remained more in vogue than Ḥmēdān al-Shwēʿir.[1] Across a distance of three centuries, his voice and words are immediately recognizable to a large audience of cognoscenti in Riyadh and beyond.[2] There are many reasons for this. Perhaps it is simply because Ḥmēdān's plain way of talking and the folksy tone of his often satirical tableaux—from his domestic life to the political struggles of his day—seem to epitomize the quintessential Najdī spirit. Through his poetry he emerges as the embodiment of the plucky, headstrong, yet intensely socially committed oasis farmers who have ensured that Najd remains the only Arab land never to be colonized by a foreign power and who later provided the backbone of the nascent Saudi state. Often harsh, and even coming across as rude to a more refined taste, Ḥmēdān's Najdī spirit is reflected in the large number of proverbs, sayings, and words of gnomic wisdom coined in his verses or deployed in his work. In Najdī circles, therefore, Ḥmēdān's verses are frequently quoted to make a point or illustrate an argument.

Neither particularly religious nor irreligious, Ḥmēdān is mostly concerned with wordly matters. In his poetry religion is present as a natural part of the cultural environment. The same applies to the religious establishment, the ulema, who come in for a fair amount of his tongue-lashing for their venality. One would be hard pressed to find a similar picture painted of them in later literature. This emphasizes the fact that Ḥmēdān's poetry is perhaps the most important source for insight into the mental outlook of townspeople in Central Arabia before the reform movement launched in 1745 by the preaching of Muḥammad ibn ʿAbd al-Wahhāb in conjunction with the expansion of Saudi state power. After that date, the dominance of this movement in the Najdī heartland, and its intolerance of dissenting views, inevitably colored the cultural mindset, especially among the sedentary population of the towns where it held sway.

Ḥmēdān is also admired for the fear he inspired through his *hijā'*, his invective poetry. As he put it, "I give judicious counsel, expose scandals, and apportion blame with no fear of censure" (see §26.3). However, his poetry describes the price he was made to pay for his invective. In one famous case, he felt obliged to compose a lengthy poem of apology to the most powerful ruler of his time, 'Abd Allāh ibn Muʿammar, emir of the town of al-ʿUyaynah.

What sets Ḥmēdān apart as a poet is his self-deprecation. The intrepid poet who boldly takes aim at the mightiest rulers of his day cuts a rather sorry figure in the bosom of his family. His own marriage is presented as a case in point: he tries to mollify his bully of a wife, until he has had enough and threatens her with divorce (§1.11). But Ḥmēdān's self-mockery is mostly situational. Somewhere in his tableaux he will paint himself in a less than dignified position. When he and his four friends are attacked by two louts, the piece ends with the line: "I do not know the name of the fifth brave hero; he scrammed, firing farts from his ass." It is generally assumed that Ḥmēdān means himself as the fifth of the group (§31.13).

In short pieces like these Ḥmēdān is a master of buffoonery. His ribald humor exposes how society's chivalrous ideals in many cases are merely a façade and sham. One way he achieves this is by bringing himself on stage as an antihero. He takes delight in depicting himself as a man down on his luck, held in little regard by those closest to him, and the target of his enemies' wrath. We should not take this literally. The diminutive form that so frequently occurs in his choice of words, including his moniker al-Shwēʿir, is a deliberate stylistic device. When it is applied to his own person, it seems to reduce him in size—not in order to belittle his status but rather to ridicule more effectively those who have puffed themselves up and exaggerated their own self-importance.[3]

The fascination with Ḥmēdān in his native Najd has to do with the way he put his art and personality at the service of affirming traditional values in an unconventional and sometimes provocative way. He saw himself as an artist whose outrage at false pretensions drives him to tear off masks. Ḥmēdān translated the idea of the world as a stage into a set of characters and situations as part of a poetic morality play, in which his sons Māniʿ and Mjalli are stock characters and he and his wife are shown in almost Punch and Judy-like scenes.[4] This theatrical approach, the emphatically down-to-earth and conversational tone of his narrative, and his involvement in the political struggles of his time make him an outstanding artist in the eyes of his compatriots—modern and old alike. He experimented with the tools handed to him by convention and created something new. He also cuts a lonely figure: no one in his native Najd has been able or daring enough to follow in his footsteps.

Ḥmēdān's Life and Times

Little is known with certainty about Ḥmēdān's life, though he is named more than any other poet in Najdī chronicles. All we have are stories that once circulated orally and the poems attributed to him.[5] What we do know for a fact is that Ḥmēdān was born in the small town of al-Qaṣab, about 165 kilometers northwest of Riyadh. The date of his birth is unknown and widely varying dates for his death are given. It is generally assumed, however, that he was born in the late seventeenth century and flourished as a poet in the first half of the eighteenth century. If one combines events and personalities in the poetry and the information from the chronicles, most of his work was probably composed in a period roughly from 1705 to 1740.

He lived in the region that was of the greatest interest to the Najdī chroniclers; a region that stretches from al-Dirʿiyyah and Riyadh, as well as some locations further south, over roughly four hundred kilometers north to ʿUnayzah, Buraydah, and other towns of al-Qaṣīm Province. While Najd is conspicuous for its combination of sedentary and Bedouin lifestyles, this region of al-Yamāmah is decidedly sedentary.[6] Agriculture was once the mainstay of its economy, principally the cultivation of date palms and wheat. Irrigation water came from ancient wells that tapped into large underground reservoirs accumulated from the torrential streams that course down the wadi channels during sporadic downpours.

The towns of al-Yamāmah at that time can be compared to ancient Greek or medieval Italian city-states, each with its own ruling classes in perpetual competition, internally as well as with other city-states. Geographically, these little city-states are grouped in clusters that were separated by both distance and natural barriers. Warfare was often triggered by the expulsion or flight of one of the factions in a town, which would seek asylum in a neighboring town. Inevitably, after some time the exiled faction would return in force, supported by the town of its temporary residence, and sometimes in alliance with other towns or tribes. Upon its victorious return, this faction would be installed in power by its friends, and the other factions would either have to submit or flee the town. In some cases, this pattern would play out over decades.[7] Usually one town would emerge in each of the regional clusters as hegemonic and would start to play the role of kingmaker in its neighborhood, as is evident from Ḥmēdān's poetry and from the chronicles.[8] Most of the ruling families and clans from Ḥmēdān's day continue to enjoy their preeminent status. They constitute a kind of sedentary aristocracy, now intimately tied to the Saudi state. This continuity, stretching back to pre-Saudi times, explains why Ḥmēdān's praise, or more often lampooning, of these families' hometowns is still a sensitive subject in Saudi Arabia.

Ḥmēdān's native town of al-Qaṣab is situated in a somewhat remote corner of al-Washm, equidistant from Sudayr and more powerful towns in al-Washm. What set al-Qaṣab apart were the evaporation ponds at the foot of the sands that were exploited by its people, and still are today.[9]

The town seems to have been left relatively undisturbed for most of the time. Not so Ḥmēdān, who at some point felt compelled to seek refuge in the little town of Uthayfiyah.[10] His poem on the subject mentions a dispute with his kinsmen in al-Qaṣab. Uthayfiyah was a dependency of the town of Tharmadā', which, like Julājil in Sudayr, played the role of kingmaker in al-Washm. Ḥmēdān caused major trouble by exhorting his hosts to stop paying tribute and instigating Uthayfiyah to rise up against its overlords.

It was to the south of Tharmadā', in Wadi Ḥanīfah, the pre-Islamic center of al-Yamāmah, that the most influential power in the region had its base. The princely lineage of Ibn Muʿammar of al-ʿUyaynah was preeminent until it was destroyed by the house of Saud.[11] Al-ʿUyaynah reached its apogee under ʿAbd Allāh ibn Muʿammar, whose court fostered Islamic scholarship.[12] The religious reformer Muḥammad ibn ʿAbd al-Wahhāb rose to prominence in al-ʿUyaynah until he was asked to leave—a fateful decision as the preacher was to become instrumental in the downfall of the Ibn Muʿammar dynasty. As a result of an unfavorable comment, probably in verse, Ḥmēdān fell foul of ʿAbd Allāh ibn Muʿammar. Having incurred the ire of the prince, his position had become sufficiently precarious for him to feel obliged to compose an extensive apology (poem 21).

ʿAbd Allāh ibn Muʿammar's long reign from 1684–85 until his death during the plague epidemic in 1725–26 provides a terminus ante quem for Ḥmēdān's poem of apology.[13] In the poem Ḥmēdān solicits advice from his kinsman ʿUthmān ibn Sayyār. In 1725 ʿUthmān killed his son, even though he had voluntarily stepped down from his position earlier in favor of his son.[14] It seems likely that the poet's self-imposed exile from al-Qaṣab occurred when ʿUthmān was no longer in a position of influence, perhaps not long after his family tragedy.

In a poem that still enjoys wide circulation, Ḥmēdān describes his departure from al-Zubayr, not far from Basra in Iraq, to return to his home country (poem 15). At the first well on the borders of Najd he encounters Famine, in the person of the scantily clad Abū Mūsā—a reference to the knife, *mūs*, wielded by hunger thus personified. Abū Mūsā informs the poet of the state of affairs in Najd, and the poet heads southwest. On his way he delivers judgment on the towns and rulers of Sudayr, some of it in words of praise but mostly with derision. The poet's artifice consists of simply repeating the judgments confided in him by Famine, Abū Mūsā. This poem may have established Ḥmēdān's notoriety as a master of *hijā'*, invective poetry.

Oral sources report that Ḥmēdān worked as an agricultural laborer in Iraq.[15] Given these circumstances and the poem's tone, it seems probable that Ḥmēdān was still quite young when he composed it. It combines rakish daring and mockery with the innovative framing of his satire within a narrative of travel. Ḥmēdān's encounter with famine thus personified is entirely realistic. There were two severe droughts that most likely occurred during Ḥmēdān's youth: one in 1702–3 and the second in 1715–18.[16] The chronicles recount that in those years people died in vast numbers from starvation and that many of the survivors escaped to al-Zubayr, Basra, and al-Aḥsā'.[17]

Conceivably, Ḥmēdān joined the stream of refugees to Iraq during one of these droughts. If so, the drought of 1702–3 would best fit with a hypothetical chronology of Ḥmēdān's life and work. If Ḥmēdān went to Iraq as a young man, and composed this poem in 1705, one might suppose a date of birth not long after 1680. But this is just one possible construction of a rough timetable for the poet and his work.

The Poet's Kin and Artistic Milieu

Ḥmēdān is said to have been born Ḥamad ibn Nāṣir al-Sayyārī.[18] Ḥamad ibn Nāṣir's moniker became Ḥmēdān al-Shwē'ir (Humaydān al-Shuway'ir). Ḥmēdān is a diminutive of Ḥamad, and al-Shwē'ir of *al-shā'ir*, "the poet." It is said that the diminutive al-Shwē'ir was given to him by his enemies as a scornful epithet.[19] If so, Ḥmēdān probably took it as a suitable nom de guerre and the name stuck. In Saudi Arabia his descendants have the plural al-Shawā'ir as their family name.[20]

Like 'Uthmān ibn Ibrāhīm al-Sayyārī, who became the headman of al-Qaṣab, he belonged to the clan of al-Sayāyirah that is part of al-Du'ūm (sg. al-Da'm), a branch of al-Jubūr, one of the tribes of Banū Khālid.[21] ʿUthmān's father had been installed as headman of the town by the famous poet Jabr ibn Ḥazmī al-Sayyārī. Jabr seemed more interested in poetry than in leadership. He survived his successor to the town headship and passed away in 1708.[22] His great age notwithstanding, he retained his playful spirit right to the end, if we are to judge by a poem he received as late as 1703 from Khalīl ibn ʿĀyiḍ, dubbed "Muṭawwaʿ of al-Maskūf" (i.e., of a mosque in the old alleyways of ʿUnayzah).[23] In it, the Muṭawwaʿ—a term now synonymous with the Saudi religious police—speaks about how lovelorn he is. He complains that his temptress leads him like a lamb to the slaughter. And worse: "You made me remiss in the performance of supererogatory prayers; I even fall short in the regular prayers to the Lord; / when reciting the Lord's graces, I instead utter my greetings to you, for my heart has gone rushing off toward you."[24] If people were but mildly scandalized at how the Muṭawwaʿ passed his time, it indicates that a relatively lighthearted culture prevailed before a sterner version of the creed was imposed in 1745.

Ḥmēdān must have known Jabr's poetry and evidence that Jabr may have influenced him has been set out in convincing detail.[25] Jabr was in regular communication with poets elsewhere in Najd and much of this "poetic correspondence" has been preserved in manuscripts. The most famous examples are the poems exchanged by Jabr with Rumayzān ibn Ghashshām, his son-in-law and politically more important colleague, the chief of al-Rawḍah in Sudayr.[26] While Jabr was first and foremost a poet, Rumayzān's poetry shows him to be a man of action primarily concerned with the exercise of power.[27] He was killed in 1668–69, in one of the internal struggles in al-Rawḍah.[28] Ḥmēdān exhibits some of the traits of both men.

However, why exactly Ḥmēdān left his hometown of al-Qaṣab for Uthayfiyah is not known. A story is told about it in the rich oral lore surrounding the poet's exploits, but as with so many others that feature Ḥmēdān as their protagonist, this one has all the characteristics of folk legend.[29] According to the poem on this episode, other towns declined his request for asylum before he was accepted by Uthayfiyah (§§22.45–48). Some locations connected with his stay in this town are still known and can be visited. In the abandoned old town of al-Qaṣab, a small mud house, now in ruins, next to one of the gates, is said to have been Ḥmēdān's.[30] Apart from such exiguous traces, the only other source is Ḥmēdān's poetry itself.

Ḥmēdān the Poet

Ḥmēdān speaks in different guises: as paterfamilias at the helm of the family boat with its unruly crew; as a picaresque antihero who revels in taking potshots at the hypocrisy and moral failings of the established order; as a peasant who toils in his grove, often to no avail and with no guarantee of success; and as poet, his primary vocation, recording in verse what he sees as the meaning of life.

His verses distinguish poetry as his main claim to fame—unlike some predecessors such as Rumayzān ibn Ghashshām for whom poetry was an appendage to a political career.[31] Ḥmēdān vaunts his poetic achievements in the style of time-honored *mufākharah*, self-glorification in hyperbolically boastful verse: "My ambition is harder than the hardest rock, and fires my determination with passionate zeal: / It has shot my fame beyond Arcturus" (§§20.16–17); or: "My renown shot higher than Sagitta" (§26.28). Poetry also provided him with a refuge from life's vicissitudes. He regarded poetry as his comrade in solitude, and he believed in the power of poetry to make people see things in the same way he did and to help them keep their bearings: "Useful and pleasant words slake a heart's thirst as irrigation quenches dry crops; / When spirits sag for lack of company, solace lies in befriending my peerless verse" (§§20.11–12).

There is no indication in his poetry that he was financially rewarded for his compositions. Ḥmēdān speaks of men always on the edge of starvation: collectors of firewood in the sands and laborers in the nearby evaporation ponds—their mouths grimy and ever thirsty, so poor that all their lives they could not even touch a single date (§§18.2–3).

Though he complains of penury, Ḥmēdān did not fall into that category. He contends that he joined a failed raid simply to be able to meet the needs of his family and little children (§11.5). As with his family life, his self-presentation as a peasant of modest means is part of his theatrical mise-en-scènes, but also has the ring of lived experience. So he speaks of the location of his grove; of how its irrigation keeps him toiling so late that he must combine the sunset and evening prayers; of disappointing harvests and months of work in vain (poems 1, 22, and 33). He mocks peasants who work al-Qaṣab's cultivable areas before a flood has replenished the wells (§33.2). He even prays to be spared the fate of being a peasant (§33.8). Nevertheless, he expresses enormous pride in his rows of magnificent trees with their heavy bunches of dates that make his grove a paradise of shade. His farewell speech to them is a remarkable soliloquy, delivered while the audience of trees listens in silent shock to his voice, which quivers with emotion as he steels himself to abandon a treasure he had invested so much in (§22.22). But this railing against a peasant's fate does not stop him from advocating unflagging labor as the best guarantee of success: "If your son's hands are daubed with mud from digging a trench around his date palms, / Before long, you'll see, your boy will start a business and make it thrive" (§§14.8–9).

This example is taken from a long poem in *rajaz*.[32] The four poems in this meter (poems 10, 11, 12, and 29) as well as one in the kindred *hazaj* meter (poem 14) comment scathingly on types of person and behaviors. Like a Najdī philosopher wielding a hammer, Ḥmēdān tests them and finds many of them hollow. In two poems, his discussion of human categories are heralded by the marker "some men," with his most incisive criticism reserved for pious cheats and men of religion who fleece their customers, and he demolishes the pretensions of would-be leaders (*shēkhin mitshayyikh*; §12.6). The poem in *hazaj* categorizes people by behavior: "so-and-so is notable for acting in such-and-such a way." One of the other poems in *rajaz* is remarkable for its viciously effective invective. In it, the notion of raiding for booty as a chivalrous sport is torn to shreds, and the poet takes special delight in mauling the reputation of the raiders' chief ("We went on the raid but the coward shirked the task: he sat with folded wings, like a lice-ridden raptor"; §11.13) whose words did not match his deeds.[33]

Literacy

In the final poem in this meter Ḥmēdān warns against ever putting any trust in a hereditary enemy. It ends with a remarkable admission: "Listen, once upon a time Moses was a murderer. We have followed suit, no different. / This I know from a tradition on which all agree—Bedouin and settled folks my witness, both" (§§29.16–17).[34] It is one of many references in his poetry that make us wonder whether Ḥmēdān was literate. Saudi experts do not rule out the possibility, but point out that, in the settled towns of Najd, literacy was never a precondition for being cultured. It is known for certain that some masters of Nabaṭī poetry who flourished later than Ḥmēdān were literate and were well versed in classical Arabic literature.[35] It was not unusual for at least some members of the community to have memorized the Qur'an. Works on Arab and Islamic history and literature were found in most towns of some significance in Najd.[36] This knowledge was also circulated orally and absorbed by illiterate men with cultural interests.

In the poem of apology to Ibn Muʿammar the poet swears by several suras of the Qur'an and compares the subject of his laudatory verses with famous generals, leaders, and poets who lived a thousand years earlier (§§21.53, 21.61). In another poem, the compact between the "false" prophetess Sajāḥ and her male colleague Musaylimah is adduced as proof of the futility of mendacious opportunism. Ḥmēdān also compares someone to the Samaritan in the Qur'an (§19.65).[37] The poet pictures himself as he pores over "works of genealogy," to ferret out the truth about the chief whose spurious claims he will soon unmask (§11.22). He scoffs at the self-importance of a religious scholar who cannot read or write (§12.13). Yet all such references to the world of literacy in this type of poetry are fully compatible with functional illiteracy.[38] This also applies to the poet's reference to letters, ink, and paper (§20.3).[39] The transition marker "enough of this" (*daʿ dhā*), followed by a desert journey and the messenger's delivery of the message, harks back to early Arabic poetry (§28.34), as does the use of *mudām* for "wine" in the poetry of Jabr al-Sayyār.[40] But such use of archaic words and expressions is widespread in the predominantly oral milieu of Nabaṭī poetry. Therefore the question of Ḥmēdān's literacy, illiteracy, or semiliteracy must remain open, though it is quite possible that he had at least some ability.

Self-Portrait

The closest thing Ḥmēdān offers by way of a consistent self-portrait is found in the seven wisdom poems (poems 2, 7, 16, 19, 26, 30, and 33) composed in *mutadārik*.[41] One of these poems, seventy-four verses of marriage counsel, is addressed to his son Māniʿ, while the others are addressed to Mjalli—in one poem the phrase "my boy" must mean him. Mjalli is presumably a younger son because the poet refers to himself as an old man in all these poems. Traditionally, wisdom is the purview of men who command a wealth of experience to be mined for valuable lessons. These nuggets of wisdom are provided to those who seek the sage's guidance: a shortcut to knowledge that would otherwise take a lifetime to garner. This poetry is similar in function to the many thousands of Najdī proverbs, but it has the advantage of being integrated into a lively poetic narrative. Ḥmedān compares it to indicating signposts in the wilderness of life that would remain invisible to men less tried and tested than he (§26.4).[42]

The poems addressed to Mjalli portray the poet as an old man (*ʿōd*, or the diminutive *ʿwēd*) who is treated with disrespect in his own household, is frail and weak, and has trouble getting to his feet and walking. Again, we should not take this portrait literally.[43] After a few verses this plaintive tone gives way to the boast of his skillful navigation of life's pitfalls: a clever sage who, while "weak of limb," is "endowed with a strong mind" (in Arabic, *aṣgharih*, "his smaller part," i.e., his tongue; §30.6). His mental faculties also receive fulsome praise: "Learn from a man clever, tested, and wise, a penetrating mind, prescient about the blows of fate" (§2.2). When the sage launches into his sermon, he expects not to be contradicted or interrupted. The listener is admonished (the imperative of the verb is used) to listen and pay close attention.

The decrepitude that the poet laments must therefore be taken with a pinch of salt. The feisty graybeard is yet another member of the cast of characters that act out the script written by the poet. In terms of mental capacity at least, the poet-sage is capable of remarkable acrobatics: "Listen carefully, my boy, to this wise old man, for I have swum in the deep waters of thought. / I tame rhymes with sound meanings, subduing refractory ones without use of reins. / I give judicious counsel, expose scandals, and apportion blame with no fear of censure. / I can read hidden traces and sand-covered trails, find wells without help of landmarks" (§§26.1–4) These four verses capture in a nutshell the poet's self-image: a brilliant artist, adept at ferreting out life's secrets, and ready to assist those who deserve his advice. He is also the implacable enemy of falsehood, savaging charlatans, self-important pretenders, and anything that smacks of the humbug that tarnishes the world and obscures truth. The poet as fearless and blameless knight brandishes his poetry without paying heed to the displeasure caused by his revelations. Such intrepidness is especially important because a poet's profession depends upon it: he speaks truth to power. Should the poet flinch and compromise his standards, he will slide into mediocrity or worse. The poet wears his adversaries' taunts as badges of honor: "These are the words of a learned and discerning poet: Ḥmēdān, who has a reputation for irreverence. / My verse is readily understood by thoughtful minds that can navigate the peaks and troughs of meter" (§§14.1–2).

The Poetry

Ḥmēdān and Literary Convention

The upward and downward course depicted in this line can be construed in the context of the deep waters of thought evoked in another verse, in which the poet tends to his craft: "Melodic verses that swell and roll like roaring waves on a pitch-black sea" (§20.4). He tames the assault of inspiration with skill: "I am the expert craftsman who forges verses, working the meter effortlessly. / I pick intricate rhymes from memory's store, with a hand that reaches into the inner recesses of art" (§§20.5–6). The poet's "peaks and troughs of meter" is linked to the surge of waves, a metaphor for the succession of long and short syllables of the metric scheme. When spoken aloud, the meter creates an impression of a bobbing movement, like a ship riding on the sea (though we should make an exception of those meters with mostly long syllables.) After all the Arabic word for "meter" is *baḥr*, "sea."

The meter of these verses on the art of poetry is *ṭawīl*, "the long meter," one of the best-attested meters in Arabic poetry. It befits the four poems that are among Ḥmēdān's most serious endeavors (poems 20, 21, 22, and 28). They deal with political developments—including his own involvement in them—set against a background of the general condition of society. All four run to considerable length: on average, fifty-seven verses. They are multi-thematic, in the tradition of the Arabic *qaṣīdah*, but bear little resemblance to its classical form. One of the four articulates Ḥmēdān's view of himself and his poetic ethos. In the other three the poet follows his immediate predecessor Jabr ibn Sayyār and other early Najdī poets in arguing his case in a flowing, narrative manner, uninhibited by a framework of classical *qaṣīdah* structure.

But Ḥmēdān largely dispenses with earlier convention. Jabr and his poetic correspondents stuck to the conceits of their genre—mostly in the guise of a stereotyped love affair. In spite of their flashes of originality, they remain wrapped up in a poetic world closed in upon itself. Ḥmēdān threw the doors of poetry wide open and allowed entry to the political and social realities of his day, which he worked into his vision. His awareness of the audacity of his enterprise is also evident in quasi-nonchalant throwbacks to literary cliché: tongue-in-cheek reminders of how far behind he had left tradition as he cut his own path. For example, a prayer for rain to fall on the land of "the buxom girl" sent by him as a present is as much a cliché as the description of the girl itself (§1.19). In the same poem the poet pokes fun at convention by hinting at a financial reward for these "gifts." The poem is obviously not meant to solicit remuneration (poem 1). A similar wink at tired cliché is contained in the request to his son Mānīʿ to climb a high lookout "And see if you can spot a caravan's tail at al-Ṭēri, carrying our folks away down Wādi Khlayyif" (§22.15): this is the primeval image of the forlorn lover who watches his amour being carried away by the departing tribe.

Women and Family Members in the Poetry

Women feature prominently in Ḥmēdān's work. He depicts his own marriage as initially happy—a genuine love affair—but no longer so at the moment of the poem's composition. In his sole poem rhyming on the letter *hamzah,* his wife nags him for money and complains of his lack of "erotic prowess."[44] The poet in his turn reminds her that the days of youth and romance have gone forever, and that if she keeps making impossible demands she can get her divorce from him.

The longest poem in the collection, seventy-four verses, shows the practical side of Ḥmēdān's poetry. It reads like a catalogue of different types of women; it proffers advice on how to select those with desirable characteristics, and especially how to avoid falling into the trap of marrying types like Sārah, the spoiled wife of his son Māniʿ. Ḥmēdān concludes by saying that the right choice guarantees a successful and enjoyable life in all circumstances: "Make sure you are respected at all times, be you affluent or scorched by drought" (§19.74).

It is no surprise, therefore, that love poetry as such (the genre of *ghazal*) is absent. Images of buxom girls are sparingly used and when they are they are used as clichés in vignettes with caricatures of silly men and situations or in parodies of conventional models. Ḥmēdān repeatedly paints old women as hideous hags (§§2.3–11; 11.32; 19.56). As with other motifs, the poet seeks to create a binary antithesis with young girls. Such extremes may in turn stand for the intrinsic unfairness and fickleness of a "world" (*dunyā*) in which values are turned upside down and shamelessly prostituted.[45]

Ḥmēdān voices disgust at domestic violence and the despicable men who commit it (§23.5). The poet curses men who beat or otherwise mistreat their wives. His warning against marrying such brutes is repeated in another poem, which pictures a miser who cudgels his mother-in-law and damages his mother's ribs for being too generous with the food (§§16.27–28). He also seems to take delight in acting in a manner entirely opposed to how a male chauvinist behaves, as when he humorously recounts how in his search for a wife he was rebuffed by women in whom he showed an interest. He tells his wife that if she is looking for a more suitable husband she can go ahead.[46] This makes some of the bias expressed against old women look incongruous—even though similar bias is found in Najdī collections of proverbs and Najdī poetry in general.[47] We can speculate that in some way the violent opposition in Ḥmēdān's poetry between an *ʿajūz,* a woman past the reproductive age, and a *bint rahūz,* a buxom girl, bears some relation to the effect worked on the Najdī outlook by the binary experience of years of drought followed by years of plenty that come with copious rainfall. But this does not reduce the jarring effect of these verses: "Once a woman has passed the mark of forty, and her black tresses are streaked with gray, / The moment has come for you to dig a trench six feet deep: throw her in with a rope around her knees! / Bury her there as you would a rotting corpse; don't be scared: no one will come to seek revenge" (§§2.9–11).[48]

These lines are from a poem composed in *mutadārik*, a meter with a relatively quick succession of long and short syllables.[49] In Ḥmēdān's work this meter is exclusively reserved for wisdom poems in which the poet is generous with advice based on his rich experience.[50] In four of the seven poems in this meter Ḥmedān addresses his son Mjalli, who does not feature with any great distinctiveness or prominence in his other poems and is not given a "character" of his own (because he is only used as a foil, the obedient and passive listener, in the poems where he is mentioned by name; poems 2, 16, 26, and 30).

Ḥmēdān's other son, Māniʿ, probably his firstborn, has a more complex relationship with his poet father. He plays the principal or a supporting role in ten poems—all but three of them in the meter of exclusively long syllables in the satirical mode (poems 4, 8, 9, 13 [though not named, clearly this son or someone like him is meant], 17, 18, 19, 22, 24, and 28). Often Ḥmēdān expresses exasperation with his passively rebellious son. He describes a particularly galling moment when Māniʿ returns from a spell of work in al-ʿĀriḍ, the area of present-day Riyadh, in the company of a wife, without having first sought his father's approval for this marriage. Ḥmēdān always calls Sārah by the derisive diminutive Swērah. This utterly impractical luxury doll opens his longest poem, the encyclopedia of marriage advice: "Our plowmen labored in the fields while he was distracted by little Sārah. / Our folks struggle to tend palms and raise children while he busily buys musk and ambergris" (§§19.1–2).

From the poem we learn that Māniʿ took her as a second wife, a practice that Ḥmēdān ridicules as a luxury; a sheer waste for someone in his son's social position. Judging by this and other passages we might infer that the poet did not take more than one wife. Māniʿ is scolded for indulging himself while at the same time falling far short of filial duty toward his aging father: the poet is aghast that his son cannot even spare a simple cloak to cover his father's back. The son's new wife is depicted as a useless nuisance to the family, a woman without shame or scruple, and adept at bossing others around. Māniʿ is at her beck and call, especially when summoned to satisfy her sexual desires, a subject described in graphic detail in two of the poems (poems 17 and 18). Ḥmēdān compares her, and the type of woman she stands for in his poetry, to "a hyena struck by rabies" (§19.5).

In the universe of Ḥmēdān's poetry, Māniʿ is a stock character who serves as a foil for his views on what is good and bad. The verse quoted above implies several meanings at once. Ḥmēdān positions himself on the side of the frugal, hardworking, inherently skeptical and wary ethos of the Najdī peasantry. It is an ethos born from the harsh conditions of the country itself—an environment where scarcity of resources makes for constant civil and military strife. In such a setting Māniʿ's behavior spells ruin for him and those around him.

Put differently, the poet's warnings and his criticism, whether aimed at Māniʿ or other targets, are a manual for survival in the extreme conditions of Najd at that time. It also explains why his advice is still considered relevant in Saudi Arabia—perhaps because of a lingering awareness that the affluence brought by the oil boom may one day turn out to have been just one more turn of the "world's" wheel of fortune (§§4.4, 5.14, 20.35, 20.38, 28.3), and that society would do well to prepare at least mentally for the shock of renewed hardship ahead.

At first glance Māniʿ appears to be the black sheep of the family. But upon closer scrutiny it becomes clear that his father secretly has a soft spot for him and his independence of mind. Perhaps in his son he may even recognize his own youth, as in the verses: "I am no stranger to passion and love's temptations; in my halcyon days I plucked their flowers at night: / We swam in a sea surging with sinful rapture, enjoying our nights while the guards slept" (§§26.5–6).[51]

Contrary to initial impressions, we come to suspect that Māniʿ, in spite or perhaps because of his frivolous escapades, is the son closest to his father's heart. He is self-willed, but also strong, and can be depended on in a crisis. It is to Māniʿ that he turns in the greatest crisis of his life, the conflict that made him leave his native town of al-Qaṣab. It is to him that he explains his motives for spurning his kinsmen, even at the price of abandoning his beloved grove of date palms. Then he instructs him to spur on his mount and seek out possible places of asylum: "I appealed to the honor of my courageous son who abstains from food for a week if rebuked. / My boy, if guided by fear, you will not sally forth: villains will not willingly make way for you" (§§22.27–28). It is to Māniʿ that the poet confides how much he loathes the headman of a certain town as well as the parasitic religious establishment. And in another poem he feels close enough to him to ask for this favor: "Māniʿ, say this prayer for my guest: 'May a viper bite you on the way!'" (§8.1). Māniʿ is not so much his father's prodigal son as the poet's alter ego and first comrade in arms.

Poet of War and Peace

Three of the four poems in *ṭawīl* meter begin in a key charged with foreboding: "Time is pregnant, events are its midwife. Are there things that cannot be, yet are?" (§28.1). Najdī chronicles maintain that the fateful events these verses allude to were instigated by Ḥmēdān when he called on Uthayfiyah to throw off the yoke of nearby Tharmadā' and stop paying tribute. It is of course possible that this claim was based on the poetry itself. But extant texts leave no doubt that Ḥmēdān applauded this act of disobedience that was a declaration of independence. It inspired the poet to elaborate on the theories of war he had expounded in other poems. As an example, he holds up his own refusal to accept dishonor: "I'd rather have a slab of rock for a pillow than sleep on a soft carpet in a land of ignominy. / Even if I have to drink brackish water mixed with bitter apple, I value self-respect more: / More than owning Baghdad and its territories, sweet-scented Basra, and the shores of Oman" (§§28.12–14). So Uthayfiyah should not grovel before Tharmadā', just as Ḥmēdān preferred to abandon his palm gardens rather than suffer humiliation at the hands of his kinsmen.

The first chords of the other two poems set a similar tone. The poem to Ibn Muʿammar opens with a lament about the corrosive effect of money: "Wealth elevates the children of the vulgar herd as penury fells the lofty, crashing down like tall trees" (§21.1).[52] When times are out of kilter and the wrong people accumulate wealth, the forces of evil are given a free rein. It is precisely in times such as these, the poet argues, that one may expect to hear this sort of calumny at the ruler's court.

The third poem contains the poignant narrative of Ḥmēdān's self-imposed exile from al-Qaṣab to Uthayfiyah. The elegiac first verse, borrowed from the classic abandoned camp scene,[53] voices his grief at having to leave everything behind: "No use praying for the return of the days that snatched away our friends and kin" (§22.1). Without the protection of one's kinsmen, one must expect the worst: "What the dark nights carry in their bellies is unknown, inseminated at dusk, giving birth at dawn" (§22.4).

Scattered throughout Ḥmēdān's work we find pithy sayings, proverbs, maxims, and similes. These often involve a bestiary of animals and birds that symbolize opposite ends of the moral universe: the noble falcon is contrasted with insignificant sparrows or despicable birds that peck the gutters for food; pedigreed steeds are worlds apart from dull oxen, as are the hideous hyena and the gracious gazelle, the vulnerable rabbit and the fearsome lion, and especially the Arabian spiny-tailed lizard, also called the dabb lizard after its Arabic name, *ḍabb*.

In Najdī lore the dabb is a creature fabled for its longevity, toughness, and ability to defend itself against intruders by hiding in underground chambers, as inaccessible as Najdī towns with their walls and fortress-like houses made of mud. Ḥmēdān teaches us that we should not put our trust in fortifications only, but rather in a united, well-trained body of men able to confront the enemy on the battlefield. In a famous extended simile, Ibn Nḥēṭ, the ruler of al-Ḥuṣūn in Sudayr, is compared to a dabb lizard coaxed out of its burrow by the ruler of Julājil, who shouts that there is nothing to fear, and that swarms of locusts have settled all over the ground—a delicious meal waiting to be gobbled up (§§16.30–35). Enticed out into the open, the dabb is captured, its jaws tied and hamstrings cut, and then slaughtered. Indeed, the chronicles inform us that ʿUthmān ibn Nḥēṭ was ousted from power by his own sons in collusion with the ruler of Julājil.[54]

Ḥmēdān's rule for political survival is that attack is the best defence: "Hit him with steel, by hook or by crook. Thus are grave affairs settled with ease" (§28.33).[55] While we should proceed with deliberation, confiding our plans only in those in whom we have the utmost confidence, a preemptive strike will keep enemies at bay. By keeping the enemy in a state of fear and by wrongfooting him, a ruler will buy respite from aggression and deter all his enemies. Other forms of defence, such as trying to fend off a menace by appeasing an enemy and paying protection money, only serves to whet his appetite. "Mind you don't appear meek or ready to settle, or you'll pay more than half of your wealth" (§34.10). And "If you pay protection money every day to keep them at bay, they say, 'A soft target'" (§28.23).

Time after time Ḥmēdān stresses that fear is a poor counselor. Instead, one should remember that: "Caution cannot save you from the arrows of fate, as al-Shwēʿir Ḥmēdān has warned you so often"(§16.36).[56] In addition to the weakness of caution as a form of defense, he argues that women, who spend their lives in the safety of home, nevertheless fill up the cemeteries as much as men do. In any case, dying by the sword is more honorable than, and preferable to, dying in bed; and survival in battle will reap the fruits of glory (§§30.33–34).

Ḥmēdān is no warmonger. In many poems he expresses his dislike of bloodshed and deplores the grief that armed strife brings. He speaks scathingly of rascals who set fire to a conflict and scamper, leaving others to deal with the consequences. He mocks fools who believe that war means "supping on meat and broth, / Or sleeping with delicious damsels," (§§24.8–9) and who "think that war is all sword dancing and merry songs, with shapely, cow-eyed coquettes for company" (§6.5). Ḥmēdān warns against mass psychosis created by an excited crowd: "His head is easily turned by the sight of patterned breeches and the beating of drums in the streets" (§24.18). His verdict on those who stir up trouble and armed strife is severe: "Break his bones and seize his wealth, and let his children weep and wail" (§24.14). To the poet's mind war is inevitable and necessary: "He who wishes to rule with his sword in its sheath is like a wingless bird trying to fly" (§7.15). But going to war is a matter of the utmost gravity that requires responsible decision-making and the ability to execute those decisions.

As always, Ḥmēdān balances his concepts. Problem-solving and peacemaking are among the endeavors he rates highest: "If I could make a wish, I'd ask that three types of men never die—for the rest I do not care; let them die in peace: / The knight of valiant deeds, the generous spender, the mediator who helps people resolve their disputes" (§§12.26–27). He wants to have no truck with negotiating from a position of weakness or seeking at all costs to avoid armed confrontation. He is resigned to the reality that, once started, war must run its course, or keep burning until its flames subside and an opportunity for mediation arises. Only when "Graves are crammed with fresh corpses, and the laments of the bereaved ring loud and long," (§24.20) does peace become possible: "No truce lasts unless it is preceded by funerals, with heads rolling and hands tied behind backs. / That is the moment to start your mediation, when hotheads make room for calmer men" (§§29.13–14).

Ḥmēdān's verse makes no mention of any attempt to create a less destructive system of relations among Najdī city-states. Such a system only came about gradually as the Saudi state tightened its grip on its neighbors through application of the austere interpretation of Islamic Law ushered in by Muḥammad ibn ʿAbd al-Wahhāb. Ḥmēdān's take on events reflects the tribal spirit of his society. As a modern historian puts it: "The Najdī settler was no less rigorous in his tribal outlook than his fellow countryman, the nomad."[57] Ḥmēdān champions this spirit, as when he vaunts his clan's relentless pursuit of revenge no matter how much time has elapsed: "We dug up the well of revenge when it had over time become filled with the drifting sands of neglect. / We blew on its fire, well-nigh extinguished, until the tongues of flame shot up in a roaring blaze" (§§28.51–52). It is his firm conviction that enemies are inherited from one generation to the next: "He has long been your grandfather's archenemy, who has swallowed his hatred for you and nurses it" (§29.4).

In Ḥmēdān's view it would be suicide to think otherwise. This Hobbesian view is rooted in the realities of his time. Violent competition among nomadic tribes was exacerbated in a period, roughly the second half of the seventeenth and first half of the eighteenth centuries, that saw an increase in the frequency of severe droughts. New towns in the region, some of them mentioned in Ḥmēdān's poetry, were founded between the fourteenth and the seventeenth centuries, mostly by clans that had been forced to leave their ancestral homes. These lands were not bought but settled by force.[58] When Ḥmēdān warns against putting one's faith in legal documents alone, he is merely stating a fact: "Lands are not given away by a judge's pen, though people pay handsomely for verdicts. / When corpses lie strewn over inherited land, all is decided by the sword, not by right or by wages. / He who argues, 'These are our ancestral lands and are rightfully ours,' is consumed as he speaks" (§§28.16–18).[59]

Ḥmēdān on Power and Wealth in Najdī Society

Just as force might be needed to hold on to possessions, so a chief's position could not be maintained solely by reference to a right of succession. A shaykh must prove that he is worth his salt and deserving of leadership.[60] Ḥmēdān is allergic to the pretense that someone is born to rule: "He said, 'I was a shaykh long before you; my ancestor took possession of it.' / 'Congratulations to your father and grandfather! What a shame they sired a dunce like you'" (§§4.21–22).

Those who have nothing to show for themselves except boasting about their ancestors are to be sneered at. He predicts their extinction, ashes their only trace (§10.10). In another poem, the poet examines the tribal antecedents of an incompetent shaykh who traces his lineage to various prestigious forebears—Wā'il, ʿAmr, and ʿĀmir, the ancestors of ruling clans in Sudayr and elsewhere. He discovers that the shaykh belongs to none of them, but rather hails from a "mongrel race" of outsiders. This *hijā'*, an ad hominem attack in poetry, ends with a blow that finishes the shaykh off: his forefather was a butcher, a trade held in contempt by the Bedouin and, as Ḥmēdān reveals, by the sedentary tribal population of Najd as well (poem 11).

Again, Ḥmēdān balances these views with a recognition of the importance of lineage in tribal society. He acknowledges that those who start out in life as heirs to the achievements of their forefathers are at an advantage. He also states his faith in eugenics (§11.31)[61]—a very common sentiment in Bedouin and other Najdī social groups. But in principle the poet subscribes to an egalitarian ethos, for in certain respects all people are equal: "Chivalry and virtue do not depend on inherited position. / We all descend from Noah, common ancestor: nobles, slaves, and lowly folks without pedigree" (§§12.2–3). And yet, "Though all people stem from a single tree, their characters differ, as ordained by the Lord" (§12.4). Many slaves, for instance, surpass noblemen in virtue (§12.23). He scoffs at the notion that having forefathers who ruled is a precondition for becoming a shaykh: "If your ancestors and father were not rulers, then you cannot be praised? How ridiculous!" (§16.6).

On the other hand, Ḥmēdān cannot escape the belief, prevalent in Najd, that lineage and character are closely intertwined. When it suits him, he even makes use of it for the purpose of ridiculing an opponent, as with the shaykh who is pilloried as descended from a butcher: "A man's roots make for good or bad, as the quality of grain is determined by the seed" (§11.31). This principle that quality is inherited is equally applied to women. His words of advice, "Before taking a wife, check her mother's ancestors," (§30.16) refer to personal conduct but are informed by a value of the importance of parentage: it is generally understood, for instance, that the mother's father exerts the strongest influence on children's characters.

Similarly, in his assessment of wealth the poet vacillates between his egalitarian instincts and social reality. In accordance with the traditional view, the rich merchant is asked what benefit he will derive from his gold when he dies. Heirs, who may come from afar and may even be virtually unknown to him, will reap the fruit of his efforts, while he faces his Lord with empty hands. Money also tends to lift otherwise unworthy men to a high rank, while lack of money robs the virtuous and noble of their dignity. It distorts the natural hierarchy and promotes falsehood at the expense of truth: "Wealth covers your back like a fur coat, and hides sores and blisters from view; / It has the power to make plain women pretty, and make up for some men's defects" (§§4.16–17).

On the other hand, without financial means one cannot hope to live a dignified life, especially when one gets on in years.[62] "His prestige equals his worldly wealth" (§20.37) and "But were he a man of substance, his every word would be obeyed: all are at his beck and call with food and drink. / As soon as a man's wherewithal dries up, he is shunned" (§§30.3–4). Ḥmēdān's attachment to his palm trees is similar to the value a Bedouin places in his herd of camels. In both cases affection springs from an innate beauty, but also from a deep awareness of the insurance it offers for hard times: "You're best served by deep-rooted date palms when years of disaster bear down on you: / In an idyllic palm garden giving restful midday shade, where you can listen to the soothing coo of the doves. / Husband your goods and gladden your children: great will be your gain as harvest comes" (§§26.19–21). Like the merchant, the peasant and the Bedouin will face their Lord alone and naked. But these groves and herds, it is assumed, represent "good" value in and of themselves,[63] unlike the suspect gleam of gold that can be traded for less-respectable ware and used for evil purposes.

Ḥmēdān, in spite of his criticisms, is a spokesman for traditional Najdī values. That may explain his undiminished popularity, together with the appeal of his stylistic innovativeness; the raw directness of everyday language; the theatricality the poet endows his personal and domestic life with; and the narrative quality of his poems that present a harsh—but, in the view of Saudi critics, on the whole not unflattering—image of the political and social realities in Najd of his day. And as today's store of Najdī proverbs and sayings demonstrates, that era remains in many respects the bedrock of current Najdī mentality.

Najdī Proverbs and Sayings in the Poetry of Ḥmēdān

The two major collections of Najdī proverbs and sayings have mined Ḥmēdān's work.[64] The items may consist of an entire verse, a hemistich, or a few words lifted from a verse. More often, items may partly overlap with maxims in his poetry or express the same meaning in somewhat different words. If we were to filter these materials with such a coarse sieve, we would arrive at a total of about 350 items in these collections that can be related to verses by Ḥmēdān. Though the actual number is much lower because many are overlaps, Ḥmēdān's presence in these collections is considerable. Conversely, these elements, derived from habits of thought, from culture, and from the economic and political environment, have been cemented into the structure of Ḥmēdān's oeuvre.

There is hardly a poem by Ḥmēdān without such items. If one takes a wide-angled approach like this, there are thirteen poems with an average of one or more references to proverbs and sayings for every two verses. The highest ratio is attained, as one might expect, in one of the "wisdom poems" in *mutadārik* meter: fifty-one items in as many verses that correspond to items in the collections.[65] These are clustered around popular motifs, such as the difference money makes to the esteem in which an old man is held; the shame of avarice and greed, such as the refusal to feed someone who breaks a self-imposed fast or who refuses to freely contribute some urine as a treatment for wounds; the futility of unrealistic expectations, such as sounding the alarm in a graveyard or the illusion that a hermit in a cave will be left alone;[66] the advantages of a preemptive attack on an enemy; the foolishness of building on the edge of a sandy cliff; the emptiness of boasting, such as the boasts made over the coffee cups by knights who out in the field take fright at the flight of a little bird; and, an especially popular sentiment, that caution is of little avail against the arrows of fate. Similarly, another poem in *mutadārik* features the popular maxim that one should not marry before knowing the mother of the prospective bride.

Much of what otherwise would have remained obscure in Ḥmēdān's poetry is explained by reference to these two collections. They also shed light on some of his choices in making a point. For instance, the "false" prophets Sajāḥ and Musaylimah feature in Najdī proverbs and in other Nabaṭī poetry as examples of a deceptive attraction that leads one astray.[67] This demonstrates that knowledge of this sort does not presuppose literacy on the part of the poet.

From the verses that entered these collections one may gain an impression of elements in the poetry that proved especially attractive to popular attention. On the subject of how the treatment of old men depends on their financial situation, the one that attained proverbial status is: "'At your command,' some say to one man. 'What do you want?' they growl at another" (§5.7).[68] In a verse on the same motif, the second hemistich is identical to the popular saying, while the first hemistich provides the meaning: "But if your pockets are empty you'll suffer humiliation: you will hear, 'Such a demanding old man'" (§16.4).[69] And on the subject of how important it is to have resources: "For broken bones dirhams are the best cure" (§26.29)—a proverb also found in Snouck Hurgronje's collection of Meccan proverbs.[70] Or take the expression of the sentiment that one has had one's fill of something: "I have packed up my equipment at the well: let someone else take my job, if he feels like it" (§5.15).[71] And somewhat related, the advice: "When your children have grown up, it is best to keep to yourself," (§9.8) which also made it into the collections of proverbs.[72]

In another proverb a sarcastic quaintness of expression turns some verses into folksy wisdom: "Like boiling hoes to produce broth, milking billy goats instead of camel udders" (§7.2).[73] The hemistichs, each separate, entered the sphere of popular metaphor to express the utter uselessness of certain actions. For the same reason the following verse achieved proverbial status in its entirety: "If a dumb ox comes asking for your daughter's hand, give him a kick and say, 'Shoo!'" (§23.1).[74]

We can also measure Ḥmēdān's status as a poet of war and peace from the frequency of connections with the proverb collections. At the heart of opinions on the subject of war and peace is the saying: "The power to rule is not acquired through pen and paper," or in the words of Ḥmēdān: "Lands are not given away by a judge's pen" (§28.16).[75] "Do not think that going to war is like eating a lovely dish of buttered paste" is the saying that sums up the dangers of starting war without proper preparation.[76] This sobering lesson is further captured in the saying, "There can be no peace before graves are sprinkled with corpses."[77] Ḥmēdān's practical advice has proved more popular: "Retaliate at once and settle the score" (§16.13).[78]

Significantly, one of Ḥmēdān's most quoted sayings pours scorn on claims to preeminence because of birth (§§4.21–22).[79] The popularity of the notion that rule should be based on merit can be gauged from the many references to the expression "eat and let eat," and its variations, as in the verse: "The ruler eats and provides nourishment, protects his subjects from want and fear" (§27.3).[80] The following expression on the theme of protection turns a positive into its opposite: "A black dog that feeds but does not guard" (§27.5).[81]

Pithy sayings in words that are slightly rough around the edges and that provoke an element of mischievous curiosity are much in vogue. On the subject of power, for instance, take the first hemistich of the verse: "Prosperity sparkles like a heady wine, safe in the hands of a privileged few" (§24.1).[82] Again, the second hemistich, which is not part of the saying, expresses a condition that gives it an elitist interpretation. This is in line with Ḥmēdān's conviction that the opinions of the great majority of people (in his view, the riffraff) are of no account and could even be dangerous to the community and the conduct of its affairs. Though his verses seem to enjoy the favor of this "riffraff," he does not pull his punches when he states whom his advice is meant for: "Don't pin your hopes on the views of the vulgar herd" (§22.41). A ruler who ignores his counsels is denigrated as a "mini-shaykh" and is snubbed in turn: "Giving advice to men like this is like pouring water on barren soil" (§24.7).[83] This advice on how to deal with advice itself achieved proverbial status.

Even in his capacity as a self-avowed scandalmonger, Ḥmēdān's words reverberate through the collections: "Giving judicious counsel, exposing scandals" carries the opposite meaning in the maxim: "If you do not give advice you won't be pelted with mud" (§26.3).[84] If this maxim was current in Ḥmēdān's time, he may have wished to display his audacity by turning it around like this.

In the collections one also finds many examples of two or more nouns in a construct state, or otherwise closely linked, that provide a concise characterization and are used as a figure of speech in conversation. These are sometimes cross-referenced to Ḥmēdān's poetry. Examples are: "They flail as if shaking locusts from a boxthorn" (*daggat ʿōshaz al-jarrādah*, §10.2); "Like sagebrush his roots are easily plucked," i.e., of someone who is of no account (*maglaʿ shīḥtin*, §14.23); "Of no more use than broken handles on a bucket," i.e., ineffectual men who are a burden on others (*kasr al-ʿarāgī*; §12.28); "an ox without a halter," a blunderer who creates havoc if not stopped (§10.3); "the apparition of a specter," i.e., an unwelcome sight, such as the sight of an approaching guest for a miser (*shōf shīfah*; §25.6); "a cat could despoil him of his cavalry coat," i.e., of a swagger that conceals cowardice (§17.4).[85]

Expressions that employ the figure of speech of *itbāʿ*, an intensification achieved by repetition with a change of initial consonant, belong in a category of their own. A number of these in Ḥmēdān's poetry have also been included in the collections of proverbs: *yiḥiṭṭ w-yighiṭṭ* "pay up or shut up"(§1.4); *yʿēzil wi-ybēzil* "to squander someone's goods" (§17.11); *anṭal min ʿAnṭal* "more thievish than ʿAnṭal" (§13.6); *yashkhir w-yankhir* "breathing hard and grunting" (§17.21).[86]

Imprecations, curses, expletives, threats, oaths, prayers, and a wide variety of interjections are integral to the poet's style. They lend it an everyday, conversational color, and enhance its verisimilitude. Some of these are found in the collections of Najdī proverbs and sayings; for instance, the curse "May God prevent that sort from multiplying" is extended by the poet over two hemistichs: "How I wish that her sort were eradicated from decent society, but if not, I wish there were fewer of them" (§19.42).[87]

Nabaṭī Poetry

This poetry used to be, and still is, very much in vogue in the Najd, the central part of the Arabian peninsula. The earliest examples of Nabaṭī poetry may go as far back as the thirteenth century.[88] By the time the Jabrid dynasty of the Banū

Khālid tribe became established in eastern Arabia in the fifteenth and sixteenth centuries, Nabaṭī poetry is already well attested.[89]

In the oral culture of the Arabian interior Nabaṭī poetry maintained its status as the principal medium of artistic exchange among townspeople and peasants, like Ḥmēdān, and the Bedouin, commoners as well as tribal grandees—including poets and aficionados who were literate and familiar with classical Arabic poetry. For this reason, in addition to its artistry as a subject of literary interest, it is an important source for our knowledge and understanding of culture and history in Najd. There are, furthermore, remarkable correspondences between its prosody, images, similes, vocabulary, and phrasing and those of early Arabic poetry that originated in, or was inspired by, the Arabian desert environment.

The language of Nabaṭī poetry is based on the Najdī vernacular, but it has an idiom and repertoire of its own, with many "archaic" features reminiscent of the vocabulary and turns of phrase of early Arabic poetry (§22.34).[90] For instance, the poet's exhortations to his messenger to mount an *ʿēdihiyyah* (classical Arabic *ʿīdiyyah*), a hardy camel mount, would sooner be understood by the great Umayyad poets Jarīr and al-Farazdaq than by today's city dwellers in Riyadh or Cairo.[91] A study of early specimens of Nabaṭī poetry show that it has gone through several stages of development.[92] By the time Ḥmēdān composed his work it was well established as a literary form. There is a substantial enough collection of poems by his immediate predecessors to provide us with a yardstick to measure to what extent Ḥmēdān forged his own distinctive style.[93] Geographical isolation is usually given as an explanation for this thematic, stylistic, and linguistic continuity. The economy, natural conditions, tribal customs, and spirit of the vast Arabian interior (the wellspring of the Arabic language and its earliest poetry) showed little change or development until the end of the nineteenth century. Therefore, in addition to its intrinsic worth, this poetry offers an interesting comparison with early classical poetry that may further our understanding of it, and vice versa.

In more recent times, Nabaṭī poetry has come under incessant fire from those quarters that for religious, political, and educational reasons regard it as a relic from a backward and ignorant past. Though this opinion is alive and well, it has failed to have any appreciable influence on the popularity of this mostly vernacular, freewheeling poetry. Most of these critics are unaware that Nabaṭī poetry has a long and respectable literary pedigree, and that without it society would be immeasurably poorer, cut off from the richest source for knowledge of its history and cultural roots. Perhaps this does not cause them any concern. Fortunately, most people do care. If we are to judge by what is on offer in bookfairs in the region, in the media, and on social media, interest in Nabaṭī poetry has only increased. This is as might have been expected from increased access to what in itself was the true expression of popular culture, and not just for the uneducated but, even more so, for the leading classes of that tribal society to which Ḥmēdān undoubtedly belonged, though he occasionally liked to present himself as a peasant who earned his living by the sweat of his brow and was frequently hard up.

Language, Meter, and Rhyme of This Edition

As in classical Arabic poetry, each Nabaṭī verse consists of two hemistichs. On paper the poem therefore looks like two vertical columns placed side by side. Even before Ḥmēdān came on the scene, poems with a separate rhyme at the ends of each of the two columns appeared. Prior to that, a poem had a single rhyme at the end of each verse, as in classical Arabic poetry. As early as the nineteenth century, this additional rhyme requirement was being generally respected by the poets in the Nabaṭī style. That Ḥmēdān's poems are without exception composed with a single rhyme at the end of each verse confirms the relatively early date of the work—had we not known it already from other sources.

Again as with classical poetry, Ḥmēdān's poems have quantitative meters of a fixed length that in principle is the same in each hemistich. There are patterned variations, however, mostly at the end of the line. A distinctive feature is the absence of a succession of two short syllables, though interestingly it is possible to scan some very early specimens with such a succession.[94] The reason for this is that this possibility is excluded in the vernacular by elision of one of the short vowels. Another distinctive feature is the creation of long syllables of the consonant–short vowel–consonant pattern, often by connecting the last consonant of a word with the first consonant of the next word and, if necessary, a shortening of the long vowel between both consonants. In scansion of Nabaṭī poetry, word borders as they would appear in Arabic orthography or transliteration must be disregarded. This is entirely in keeping with the performance-based, predominantly oral culture of the time, part of the Arabian *majlis* culture (somewhat similar to the style of the French salon, but with observance of the Najdī gender segregation). In these sessions poems would be recited from memory.

Like so much in Ḥmēdān's poetry, his choice of meters is unusual. Out of the thirty-four poems (some of which are more in the nature of short pieces of verse), fifteen are in a meter that does not exist in classical Arabic poetry: a succession of eight long syllables with no short syllables.[95] Thus the meter produces a steady drumbeat that may convey a deadpan quality: like someone who excels at keeping a straight face while telling a joke, Ḥmēdān dishes up outrageous content in a meter that does not bat an eye.

The fifteen poems in this meter ostensibly feature scenes from daily life.[96] Some of it comes close to peasant burlesque. In others the ordinary turns grotesque and humdrum characters go through bizarre metamorphoses. The satire is not targeted at anyone in particular, but rather at the human condition in a Najdī town. In two other poems in this meter we encounter the poet's pleasure-loving son Māniʿ in the company of his gluttonous and sensual belle, Sarāh (derisively called by the diminutive Swērah in the Arabic text).[97] After an introduction that bristles with barbed sarcasm, the poems depict explicit scenes of sexual rough-and-tumble so vociferous and passionate that they wake up the entire town (poems 17 and 18).

In some poems in this long meter the rhyme foot is refined by the introduction of one short syllable in the penultimate position (poems 5, 15, 16, 24, and 27). This produces a recurring snickering sound that reinforces the poem's contemptuous, gleefully malicious thrust. One poem, with the extraordinary rhyme ending on a double *f*, *-aff*, opens with the unsettling line: "If a dumb ox comes asking for your daughter's hand, give him a kick and say, 'Shoo!'" (§23.1). The ox, in the symbolism of the extensive bestiary employed in Ḥmēdān's poetry, stands for an utterly dull fellow who employs violence against anything standing in his way.

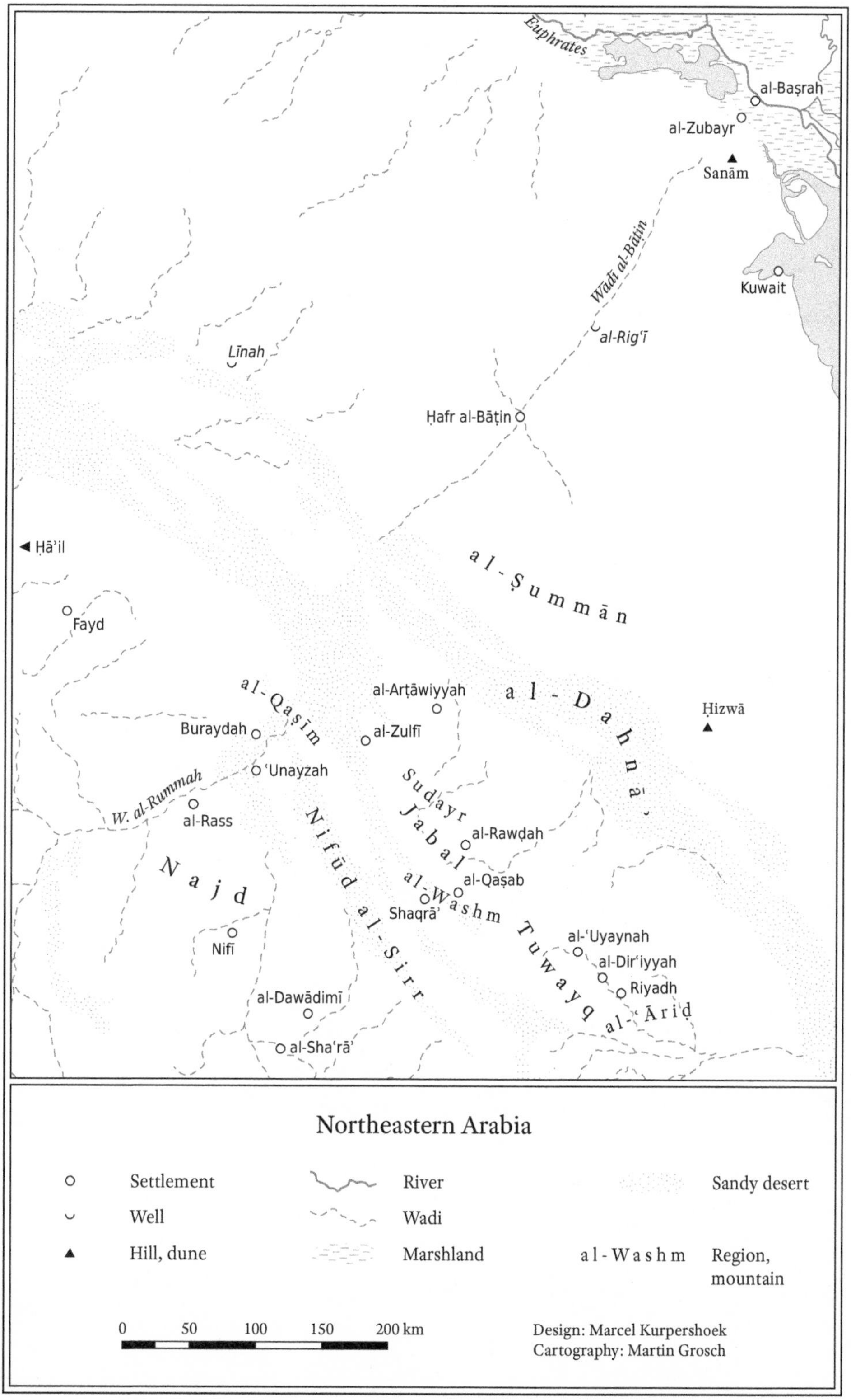

al-Baṣrah

al-Zubayr

▲ Sanām

Kuwait

Euphrates

Wādī al-Bāṭin

al-Rigʿī

Līnah

Ḥafr al-Bāṭin ○

◀ Ḥāʾil

al-Ṣummān

Fayd ○

al-Dahnāʾ

al-Arṭāwiyyah ○

Ḥizwā
▲

al-Qaṣīm

Buraydah ○   al-Zulfī ○

○ ʿUnayzah

Sudayr

W. al-Rummah

al-Rass ○

al-Rawḍah ○

N a j d

Jabal

al-Qaṣab ○

Nifūd al-Sirr

al-Washm

Tuwayq

Shaqrāʾ ○

Nifī ○

al-ʿUyaynah ○

al-Dirʿiyyah ○

Riyadh ○

al-ʿĀriḍ

al-Dawādimī ○

○ al-Shaʿrāʾ

Northeastern Arabia

○	Settlement	︶	River	░	Sandy desert
︶	Well	⌁	Wadi		
▲	Hill, dune	▦	Marshland	a l - W a s h m	Region, mountain

0   50   100   150   200 km

Design: Marcel Kurpershoek
Cartography: Martin Grosch

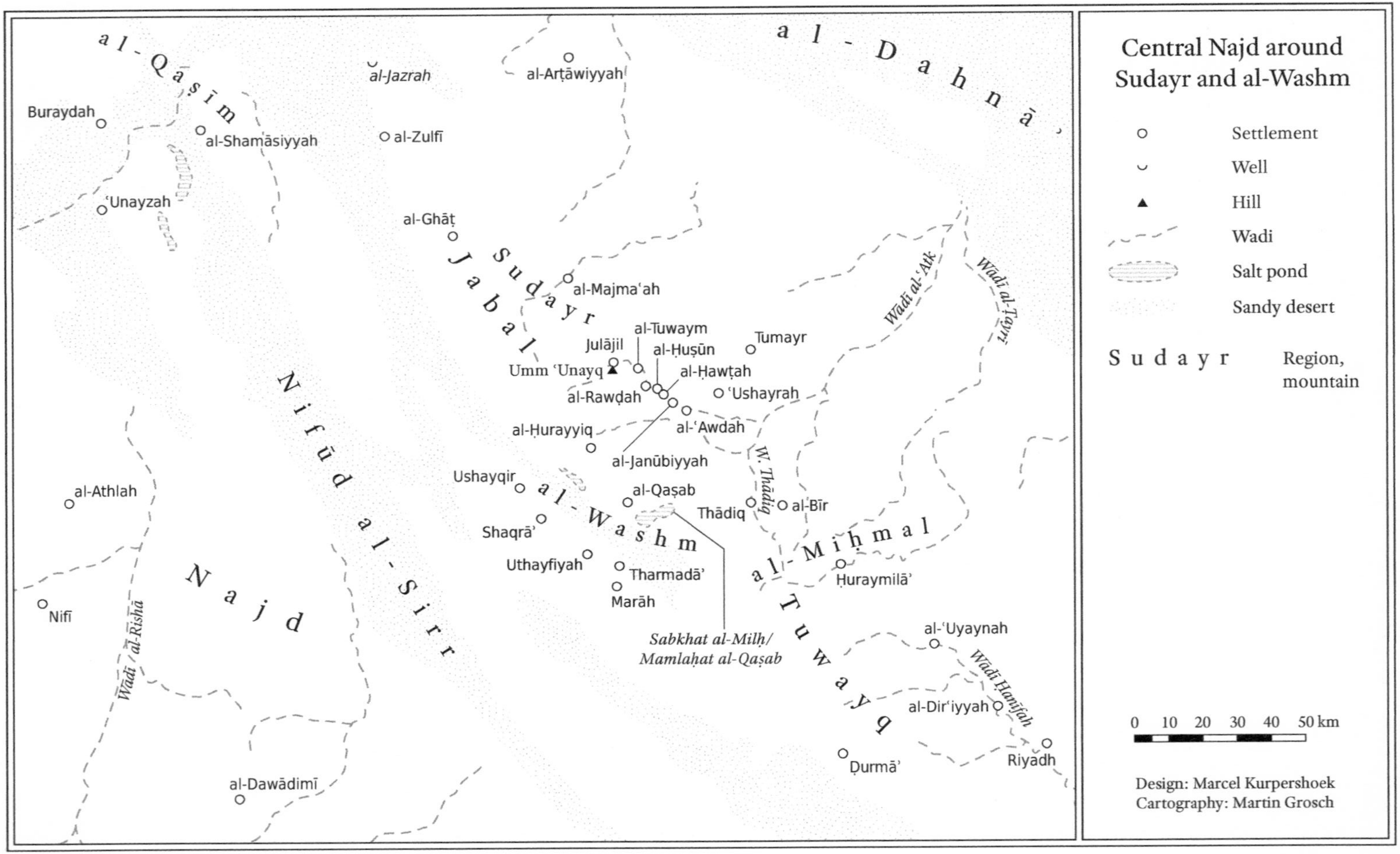
Central Najd around Sudayr and al-Washm
Settlement
Well
Hill
Wadi
Salt pond
Sandy desert
Sudayr
Region, mountain
0 10 20 30 40 50 km
Design: Marcel Kurpershoek
Cartography: Martin Grosch
al-Qaṣīm
al-Dahnā’
Buraydah
al-Shamāsiyyah
‘Unayzah
al-Jazrah
al-Zulfī
al-Arṭāwiyyah
al-Ghāṭ
Sudayr
Jabal
al-Majma‘ah
al-Tuwaym
Julājil
Umm ‘Unayq
al-Ḥuṣūn
al-Ḥawṭah
al-Rawḍah
Tumayr
‘Ushayrah
al-Ḥurayyiq
al-‘Awdah
al-Janūbiyyah
Nifūd al-Sirr
Ushayqir
al-Qaṣab
al-Washm
Shaqrā’
Thādiq
al-Bīr
W. Thādiq
Wādī al-‘Atk
Wādī al-Ṭayrī
al-Miḥmal
Uthayfiyah
Tharmadā’
Marāh
Ḥuraymilā’
al-Athlah
Nifī
Najd
Wādī al-Rishā
Sabkhat al-Milḥ/ Mamlaḥat al-Qaṣab
al-Ṭuwayq
al-‘Uyaynah
Wādī Ḥanīfah
al-Dir‘iyyah
Riyadh
Ḍurmā’
al-Dawādimī

Note on the Text

The text of this edition is based on ten manuscripts and three printed editions.[98] The first edition of Ḥmēdān al-Shwēʿir's poetry is found in the first volume of Khālid al-Faraj's *Dīwān al-Nabaṭ*, published in 1952 in Damascus. It presents the work of four major Najdī poets in the language of Nabaṭī poetry. It opens with the work of Ḥmēdān al-Shwēʿir, followed by that of the poets Mḥammad ibn Liʿbūn, ʿAbdallah ibn Ribīʿah, and ʿAbdallah ibn Sbayyil. The edition by al-Fawzān, who originates from Ḥmēdān's town of al-Qaṣab, is also a critical study of his work. The edition by al-Ḥamdān, who was born in the nearby town of al-Bīr, adds some new fragments of verse, based on oral sources and manuscripts. In all of these editions, and in particular the last one mentioned, lines or words from Ḥmēdān's verses are replaced by ellipses. The reasons given are that they contain sensitive materials: obscenity, or unflattering comments on some towns and clans. The manuscripts do not show such inhibitions.

The greatest number of poems by the earliest known Nabaṭī poet, Abū Ḥamzah al-ʿĀmirī, are found in the manuscript named after its owner, ʿAbd al-Raḥmān ibn ʿAbd al-Muḥsin al-Dhukayr.[99] Many of the pages are ink-blotted; it is said that the manuscript fell in water. The eleven pages devoted to nine poems by Ḥmēdān did not escape this fate, but are in relatively good shape. The date of the manuscript is unknown.[100]

The oldest known manuscripts with Nabaṭī poetry that can be dated with reasonable certainty are the two acquired by the French traveler Charles Huber, who visited the Rashīdī court in the northern Arabian capital Ḥā'il in 1878 and 1883–84. It is not known where and from whom he obtained these manuscripts.[101] But when he purchased them they cannot have been very old. They feature the work of the wealthy and learned poet Muḥammad al-ʿAbd Allāh al-Qāḍī from the town of ʿUnayzah in al-Qaṣīm province, who died in 1868, a little more than ten years before Huber's visit. The poet ʿUbayd ibn Rashīd, nicknamed "the Wolf," who together with his brother ʿAbd Allāh established the Ibn Rashīd dynasty in Ḥā'il that, for much of the nineteenth century, eclipsed the Saʿūd princes in Riyadh, died in 1865. Generally speaking, the great majority of poets in the

Huber manuscripts are well-known names that recur in later published collections of Nabaṭī poetry.

The oldest poems in the Huber manuscripts, such as the verses of Quṭn ibn Quṭn, al-ʿUlaymī, and Barakāt al-Sharīf, date from the seventeenth century.[102] It is highly unlikely that these poems survived over a period of centuries solely through oral transmission. Three of the longer poems by Ḥmēdān are included in the Huber manuscripts.[103]

Most of the Saudi collections of Nabaṭī poetry are based on two voluminous manuscripts. The great majority of Ḥmēdān's poems are among those collected in the MS written by ʿAbd al-Raḥmān ibn Ibrāhīm al-Rabīʿī from ʿUnayzah (d. 1981/2 at the age of ninety-three). The other is Muḥammad ibn ʿAbd al-Raḥmān ibn Yaḥyā from the Sudayr region (d. 1993/4 at the age of ninety). The latter has not included poems by Ḥmēdān. But it is interesting to note that he obtained most of the poems from the poet Ibrāhīm ibn Juʿaythin (1844 or 1845–1943), who was known for his prodigious memory.[104] Al-Rabīʿī used to accompany his blind father, who knew many poems by heart and was the *rāwi*, transmitter, of the work of the poet Muḥammad al-ʿAbd Allāh al-Qāḍī.[105] Al-Rabīʿī and Ibn Yaḥyā were in correspondence and probably shared information on their common passion.

It is clear, therefore, that the written tradition of manuscripts was closely intertwined with the prevalent oral milieu in which Nabaṭī poetry flourished. And it was not a one-way street. Poems that were recorded in manuscripts would return to oral circulation when they were recited and again committed to memory.[106]

This oral culture did not achieve the status of officially sanctioned cultural expression because that would conflict with the religious standard—though this did not stop some men of religion from indulging in it. This all helps to explain the sorry state of many of these manuscripts, the undoubted loss of many more, the uncertainty surrounding their origins, and their relative neglect until recently.[107] It comes, therefore, as no surprise that the quality of the writing of many manuscripts reflects the semi-literacy of the scribes. Mistakes made by earlier copyists were likely to have been uncritically repeated. On the other hand, those who were more familiar with the living culture and formal requirements of meter and rhyme would have been tempted to add "corrections" as they saw fit. The older the poetry, like the work of Ḥmēdān, the greater the likelihood of distortions.[108] Though the writing of many manuscripts leaves much to be desired, the task of establishing the text was facilitated by the occurrence of most poems in more than one manuscript and the existence of the published versions.

While it is quite possible to write Nabaṭī poetry by using essentially the same system of orthography as the one used for classical Arabic, scribes with limited knowledge of literary Arabic often wrote the poems in an improvised, more or less phonetic manner. For instance, *tanwīn* is commonly written by adding a *nūn* to the end of a word. If a word according to the vernacular pronunciation begins with a consonant cluster, due to the elision of the initial short vowel, the vocalic onset is written as a prefixed *alif* instead of *sukūn* on the first consonant, which may lead to misunderstandings.[109]

For example, in one manuscript the first hemistich of a verse is written ونجاك امندنيا طرف, pronounced as *w-in jāk mn ad-dinya ṭaraf*, where the correct form would be وان جاك من الدنيا طَرَف. According to the metrical scheme of long syllables, it is scanned: *win-jā-kim-nad-din-yā-ṭa-raf*. One way to dissolve consonant clusters for metrical purposes is to connect a final consonant with an initial consonant and add a short vowel, which in the above example is the vocalic onset, expressed by the *alif* before the *mīm*.[110]

I have not included all the poems and verses found in these sources. My reasons for this vary from mistakes in attribution to what I perceive to be an incompatibility of language and style with the body of Ḥmēdān's work. Verses that are incomprehensible, because the context is missing or because they have been transposed from another poem in the same meter and rhyme, have also been left out. Some short pieces, mostly based on oral sources, seemed of dubious authenticity and little significance. Yet, despite numerous variant readings in the manuscripts and in the published editions, the overall impression I have of the material is of a surprising degree of conformity among the texts.

When choices had to be made, I considered factors such as what was contained in the other texts, the effect a reading would have on the meaning, and conformity to the meter. There are some differences in the order of sections of verse and individual verses, particularly in two of the long poems in *ṭawīl* meter on the subject of the poet's self-imposed exile from his hometown of al-Qaṣab to Uthayfiyah, and the poem in which he encourages Uthayfiyah to rise up against its overlords in the town of Tharmadā' (poems 22 and 28). The political issues and ruling personalities mentioned in these poems are imperfectly known from the chronicles. It is also quite likely, especially in the case of complex and long poems, that parts of the original may have dropped out in the course of transmission. In the second half of these poems, where the poet switches from advice on how to deal with the vicissitudes of life to the political situation, variations in the order of verses from one source to the next may result in significant discrepancies in meaning. The chosen verse order is the one I deemed most satisfactory in the context of the poem and Ḥmēdān's work as a whole.

Notes to the Introduction

1 In transliteration from classical Arabic his name is written as Ḥumaydān al-Shuway'ir. Because his work is in the idiom of the Najdī vernacular poetry, called Nabaṭī poetry, his name and other names mentioned in this poetry are transliterated in a way that more closely reflects the pronunciation of what is predominantly oral poetry (it is recited on social occasions). This transliteration is the one accepted among specialists in the field of Najdī linguistics and Nabaṭī poetry (see Bibliography). In the introduction, names of towns and other geographical features mentioned in his poetry will be transliterated according to their classical Arabic spelling in order to facilitate identification. Occasionally, where appropriate, names and words that occur in the vernacular text may be given in the introduction and the endnotes (e.g., if they occur in book titles or as official family names) according to the classical Arabic transliteration. For more information see the note on the edition at the end of the introduction. Poems and verses will be referred to by the number given them in this edition. A full transliteration of the poems will appear as part of the web-based materials for this edition on the Library of Arabic Literature's web site at www.libraryofarabicliterature.org. This will allow the reader to get a more precise idea of how this vernacular poetry is pronounced. For instance, it is not possible in a script developed to represent classical Arabic to render features such as changes in diphthongs or the merging of the phonemes *ẓ* and *ḍ*.

2 In the oral tradition of Nabaṭī poetry in Najd, lines of verse are commonly simply referred to as "speech," *gōl* (*qawl* in classical Arabic), also known, from the same verb, as *gīl* or even *jīl* in some places.

3 In his discussion of parallels between Ḥmēdān and the poet al-Ḥuṭay'ah (d. ca. AD 676–77), Saad Sowayan mentions that Ḥmēdān may have followed al-Ḥuṭay'ah in his use of self-mockery. But he argues that Ḥmēdān must be seen in a different light because the general thrust of his sarcasm and invective is concerned with "weighty social and political issues" in which he champions the cause of "the downtrodden, poverty-stricken man who suffers from the despotism of rulers, the greed of traders, and the venality of judges," whereas al-Ḥuṭay'ah's self-derision was merely a device by which "he sought to forestall other poets' vituperations against him," Sowayan, *al-Ṣaḥrā' al-'arabiyyah*, 462–63. While Ḥmēdān's poetry presents a coherent moral universe, unlike the work of

al-Ḥuṭay'ah, there are indeed striking similarities, starting with the diminutive form of their monikers. One may note, for instance, that both poets include in their self-mockery close family members—al-Ḥuṭay'ah expresses his loathing (*baghḍā'*) for his mother, and Ḥmēdān addresses his wife in similar terms: Ibn Qutaybah, *The Excellence of the Arabs*, 34–37; al-Ḥuṭay'ah, *Dīwān al-Ḥuṭay'ah bi-riwāyah wa-sharḥ ibn al-Sikkīt*, 100–1; al-Jundī, *al-Ḥuṭay'ah al-badawī al-muḥtarif*, 72–73; §§1.9–11. Yet both poets are also depicted as hardworking family men and al-Ḥuṭay'ah receives praise for his concern for his daughters: al-Ḥuṭay'ah, *Dīwān*, 84. Al-Ḥuṭay'ah says that he is struck by the ugliness of his face: *Dīwān*, 133; al-Iṣfahānī, *Kitāb al-Aghānī*, 2, 163–64; al-Ḥuṭay'ah, *Dīwān*, 74. In a number of poems Ḥmēdān pictures himself as a stooped, feeble graybeard; and in folktales about him he is described as diminutive in stature. Both men traveled to Iraq to escape the effects of drought in Najd. Perhaps most remarkably, some of their verses show the same deadpan, tongue-in-cheek quality, as in al-Ḥuṭay'ah's verse about an unwelcome guest: "He repeated his greetings and I told him, 'Take it easy! Just greeting me once will do for you,'" and Ḥmēdān's poems 5 and 8. Both poets have in common that their buffoonery in shorter pieces elicited the wonder of collectors and commentators—even more so than the "serious" poetry that makes up the major part of their *dīwān* (as noted by R. Blachère, *Histoire de la littérature arabe*, 2, 328).

4 The scholar who first noted this theatricality is Dr. Saad Sowayan in his pioneering study of the historical roots and development of Najdī poetry, and its relation to classical Arabic poetry, *al-Shi'r al-Nabaṭī, sulṭat al-naṣṣ wa-dhā'iqat al-sha'b* (*Nabaṭī Poetry, The Authority of the Text and Popular Taste*), 487–88. In his discussion of Ḥmēdān's predecessor, the poet Jabr ibn Sayyār, Sowayan notes: "It is like a theatre play in poetry invented by Jabr's imagination, as we previously discussed with regard to his verse on his meeting with the beautiful girls bathing in a pond; a tragedy invented by Jabr in which he himself plays the character of the hero." And: "Verses of wisdom with Jabr, and after him Ḥmēdān, feature standard characters and caricatured scenes taken from the social and political reality of their days."

5 Both sources are of questionable value for biographical purposes. Some of the events alluded to in the poetry can be corroborated from Najdī chronicles, but often a considerable degree of ambiguity remains. For instance, if a ruler is referred to as Muḥammad this may refer to Muḥammad ibn Aḥmad ibn Muḥammad or his grandfather Muḥammad. Similarly, mention of one of the many similar episodes in the perpetual warfare among Najdī towns may involve dates that are many years apart.

6 The chronicles reflect the anti-Bedouin bias of al-Yamāmah's townspeople, and in particular the class of ulema and others with a formal background in religion who wrote these chronicles—a bias fully shared by Ḥmēdān, as in §§30.17–20.

7 Al Juhany, *Najd before the Salafi Movement*, 148–49.

8 It is no coincidence that, for fear of losing their regional preeminence, these towns held out the longest in resisting the Saudi onslaught.

9 Cf. his verse "I hail from a people who trade in fire bush from the desert and digestive salts," §18.2. In Najd salt and al-Qaṣab have become proverbial in the same way as the expression "bringing owls to Athens." Three examples are: "Like presenting the people of al-Qaṣab with a gift of salt," "cheaper than salt in al-Qaṣab," and "no use trying to sell salt to the people of al-Qaṣab," al-Juhaymān, *al-Amthāl al-shaʿbiyyah fī qalb al-jazīrah al-ʿarabiyyah,* 8, 22; 10, 22 and 314.

10 The town is now called Uthaythiyah.

11 Ibn Khamīs, *Al-Muʿjam al-jūghrāfī li-l-bilād al-ʿarabiyyah al-suʿūdiyyah, muʿjam al-Yamāmah*, 204.

12 Al Juhany, *Najd,* 106–7, 150; al-Fākhirī, *al-Akhbār al-Najdiyyah*, 100, "no one, be it in his lifetime or even afterward, came close to his stewardship, the extent of his realm, his might in men and arms, his properties and chattels." Also, al-Bassām, *Tuḥfat al-mushtāq fī akhbār Najd wa-l-Ḥijāz wa-l-ʿIrāq*, 183; Ibn Khamīs, *al-Muʿjam*, 200; and Ibn Bishr, *ʿUnwān al-majd fī taʾrīkh Najd*, 98.

13 If a Hijri year falls predominantly within one year of the Gregorian calendar, then only that year is mentioned. If a considerable number of months of the Hijri year falls within two years of the Gregorian calendar, the two years are mentioned and linked by a dash.

14 Al-Fākhirī, *al-Akhbār al-Najdiyyah*, 100; al-Bassām, *Tuḥfat al-mushtāq*, 184.

15 Al-Faraj, *Dīwān al-Nabaṭ*, 17.

16 Al Juhany, *Najd*, 56–59.

17 Al-Fākhirī, *al-Akhbār al-Najdiyyah*, 90–91, 96; al-Bassām, *Tuḥfat al-mushtāq*, 161, 170.

18 Al-Ḥamdān, *Dīwān Ḥumaydān al-Shuwayʿir*, 26.

19 Introduction of Ibn Khamīs to al-Ḥamdān, *Dīwān Ḥumaydān*, 40.

20 Al-Ḥamdān, *Dīwān Ḥumaydān*, 40. A single member of the family still bears the poet's name: Ibrāhīm al-Shuwayʿir, ibid., 22.

21 Al-Ḥamdān, *Dīwān Ḥumaydān*, 40. Sowayan, *al-Shiʿr al-Nabaṭī*, 450.

22 Sowayan, *al-Shiʿr al-Nabaṭī*, 451.

23 Sowayan, *al-Shiʿr al-Nabaṭī*, 493. Maskūf means "covered", i.e., the narrow market streets of the old town were covered to protect people from the sun.

24 Sowayan, *al-Shiʿr al-Nabaṭī*, 494.

25 Sowayan, *al-Shiʿr al-Nabaṭī*, 568.

26 Sowayan, *al-Shiʿr al-Nabaṭī*, the chapter "Rumayzān wa-Jabr ibn Sayyār," 449–96.

27 Sowayan, *al-Shiʿr al-Nabaṭī*, 403, 450.

28 Al-Fākhirī, *al-Akhbār al-Najdiyyah*, 74; al-Bassām, *Tuḥfat al-Mushtāq*, 130.

29 Al-Ḥamdān, *Dīwān Ḥumaydān*, 23–24.

30 I visited the area in October 2015.

31 Sowayan, *al-Shiʿr al-Nabaṭī*, 450.

32 This is the meter with the highest ratio of long syllables to short ones in this collection. See also introd., n. 41.

33 Jabr ibn Sayyār ridicules a self-important but fatuous chief in terms similar to those Ḥmēdān uses in poem 12.

34 A reference to Moses's unintended killing of an Egyptian: Q Qaṣaṣ 28:15.

35 Sowayan, *Nabaṭī Poetry*, 169–79.

36 Julius Euting describes how in 1883 at the court of Ibn Rashīd in Ḥā'il, al-Qasṭalānī's life of the Prophet, which he had brought from Cairo, was read to the prince by the prayer leader, as well as al-Muʿallaqāt poems: *Tagbuch einer Reise in Inner-Arabien*, 2, 58.

37 The passage in question is Q Ṭā Hā 20:85–95.

38 Sowayan, *Nabaṭī Poetry*, 174, "These literate Nabaṭi poets (. . .) were imitated by illiterate poets and eventually became thoroughly assimilated into the Nabaṭi poetic tradition."

39 It is also used by Jabr ibn Sayyār, whose work generally makes a somewhat more "literate" impression, as in the line, "Greetings, as many as the movements of a pen on paper, a new sheet with a full pot of ink to hand": Sowayan, *al-Shiʿr al-Nabaṭī*, 459. Recent examples of this trope are found in Clive Holes and Abu Athera, *The Nabaṭī Poetry of the United Arab Emirates*, 57, 88.

40 Sowayan, *al-Shiʿr al-Nabaṭī*, 491.

41 This is a meter with a more balanced ratio of long and short syllables (two to one, in the variant used) than *rajaz*.

42 Rushaydān ibn Ghashshām, the brother of Rumayzān, the chief of al-Rawḍah, puts it succinctly in one of his verses: "It is best to begin one's verses with wise counsel, words of advice for friends who need and deserve it"; and take Jabr ibn Sayyār's formulation: "A letter came to me from my friend and advisor": Sowayan, *al-Shiʿr al-Nabaṭī*, 430, 459.

43 Exactly the same elaborate conceit is used by his predecessor Jabr ibn Sayyār who complains of trouble getting to his feet, his need of a walking stick, and the low esteem he is held in in his household, even among his children: "like a shriveled waterskin discarded at a well:" Sowayan, *al-Shiʿr al-Nabaṭī*, 481–82. This scene is a descendant of a motif as old as Arabic literature itself. See, for instance, the comment by Nefeli Papoutsakis,

Desert Travel as a Form of Boasting, 27, about Ru'bah ibn al-ʿAjjāj: "Complaining about his wife's rudeness to him as an old man, he remembers his former constant journeying in quest of sustenance."

44 The attribution of the poem has been the subject of an inconclusive debate, and as the *hamzah* no longer occurs in spoken Najdī, is construed as a possible indication of Ḥmēdān's literacy, see al-Fawzān, *Ra'īs al-taḥrīr Ḥumaydān al-Shuwayʿir*, 210–48.

45 E.g., the poet and chief of al-Rawḍah, Rumayzān ibn Ghashshām, compares the end of his tryst with his beloved, i.e., the time when the world smiled on him, with the advent of "the evil old hag with eyes like red-hot glowing embers," "the devil riding with her on the saddle," determined "to cut the cords binding the lovers with her treachery": Sowayan, *al-Shiʿr al-Nabaṭī*, 461–62.

46 See Ḥmēdān's new twist to the clichéd motif of the *ṭāmiḥ*, a woman who is dissatisfied with her husband, in §1.11. It has the same meaning in classical poetry, e.g., al-Ḥuṭay'ah's verse about a woman who was on the lookout for another man and loathed (*abghaḍat*) her husband so much that she poisoned him (al-Iṣfahānī, *al-Aghānī*, 2, 172). In other Najdī poetry, this is normally used as part of the boast about a man's attractiveness: any woman of social ambition, a *ṭāmiḥ*, dreams of marrying him. But Ḥmēdān does the opposite: if his wife wishes for a better match than him, an old poet of little means, then he is resigned to such a fate.

47 E.g., the section on "women and marriage" in al-ʿUbūdī, *al-Amthāl al-ʿāmmiyyah fī Najd*, 5, 2025–29. This clearly reflected the way in which men talked about their wives at a postmenapausal age and once they had become emotionally disengaged from them, as illustrated for instance by the casual remark of a tribal shaykh in Tabūk reported by Charles Huber: "One of the first things he told me was that he had taken a new wife, a young one, because the old one had become completely useless; he himself was aged somewhere between fifty-five and sixty," *Journal d'un voyage en Arabie, 1883–1884*, 468.

48 Similar in meaning is the maxim "Old women should be hung by a rope from the Pleiades and then let loose and fall down": al-Juhaymān, *al-Amthāl*, 2, 200. It is explained as a warning against danger, such as slander and betrayal of secrets.

49 See also introd., nn. 41 and 65. The Index of Poems gives the meter for each poem immediately after the poem's number and the first line in Arabic.

50 See Sowayan, *al-Shiʿr al-Nabaṭī*, 481, for a poem in the same meter by Jabr ibn Sayyār on the theme of old age with complaints, images, and vocabulary similar to that in the preludes to Ḥmēdān's poems in this meter.

51 Jabr ibn Sayyār used similar hyperbole in describing his halcyon days, as in the line, "Fighting in close combat for my share of booty, or plunging into the sea of passion with my lovemates": Sowayan, *al-Shiʿr al-Nabaṭī*, 490.

52 Ḥmēdān's poem of apologies to Ibn Muʿammar has been compared to the pre-Islamic poet al-Nābighah al-Dhubyānī's poem of excuses to al-Nuʿmān ibn Mundhir, the king of al-Ḥīrah. See n. 91 to §21.52.

53 The abandoned camp scene is as old as Arabic poetry itself. An example is the elaborate version of it in one of the pre-Islamic "Suspended Odes" (*al-Muʿallaqāt*, prize-winning odes that supposedly were hung in Mecca's sanctuary) by the poet Labīd ibn Rabīʿah. Its first line is: "There is almost no trace of those abodes, either halting-places or longer encampments, at Minā, and Ghawl and Rijām have become desolate," Alan Jones, *Early Arabic Poetry, Select Poems*, 455. Its popularity has continued in modern times, as most famously exemplified by the Egyptian singer Umm Kulthūm's rendition of Ibrāhīm Nājī's poem "al-Aṭlāl" ("Traces of an Abandoned Camp").

54 Al-Bassām, *Tuḥfat al-Mushtāq*, 159, without mention of the year in which this happened.

55 When Jabr ibn Sayyār handed over the stewardship of al-Qaṣab's affairs to his relative, Ibrāhīm ibn Rāshid ibn Māniʿ, he composed a poem with advice that reflects this political ethos: "If you send a message to your adversary, use spearheads as your pens; / For ink use shields and thoroughbred horses, with eagle-like knights in the saddle. / Then trick and deceive, even as you give solemn promises, for cunning is the surest way with the enemy," *al-Shiʿr al-Nabaṭī*, 452–53.

56 Again, a trope as old as Arabic literature itself. For instance, al-Aʿshā tries to assuage his daughter's fears for his life because of his fearlessness as a desert traveler, "the inevitability of death being an excuse for plunging into dangers," Papoutaskis, *Desert Travel*, 33. So too, al-Mutanabbī's verse, *wa-muttaqin wa-l-sihāmu mursalatun / yaḥīdu ʿan ḥābiḍin ilā ṣārid*, "Many, while trying to escape from an arrow, run from a failed shot into a hit."

57 Al Juhany, *Najd*, 95.

58 Al Juhany, *Najd*, 71: "The customary means by which the right of priority was determined was force."

59 The saying is "rule does not come by way of ink and paper," al-Juhaymān, *al-Amthāl*, 2, 301. This line occurs in exactly these words in a poem by ʿAbd Allāh ibn Rashīd, a nineteenth-century ruler in the northern city of Ḥāʾil, Musil, *The Manners and Customs of the Rwala Bedouins*, 302–3. The second hemistich is, "but through the sword and not committing sin." But as Ḥmēdān's line shows, the saying as such was current centuries earlier.

60 The poet Rumayzān ibn Ghashshām, himself an eminent political leader, states that one's inheritance and one's personal achievements are intertwined: "Whoever dies without passing on his traits to his offspring, is like a fire starved of fuel": Sowayan, *al-Shiʿr al-Nabaṭī*, 474.

61 Al-Juhaymān, *al-Amthāl*, 6, 233–34, "no head and no roots."

62 Jabr ibn Sayyār expresses the same notion: "a man without wherewithal is not held in respect": Sowayan, *al-Shiʿr al-Nabaṭī*, 466.

63 Cf. §§26.19 and 26.22; also Kurpershoek, *Oral Poetry and Narratives from Central Arabia*, 4, *A Saudi Tribal History*, "Camels & Palm Trees as Symbols of Bedouin Life in the Haḍb and Cultivators in the Wādi," 134 ff., and Sowayan, *al-Ṣaḥrāʾ al-ʿarabiyyah*, p. 373, "Palm garden and camel herd."

64 Al-Juhaymān, *al-Amthāl*, and al-ʿUbūdī, *al-Amthāl*.

65 The exception is poem 26, a short piece in the *al-mumtadd* meter with an average of two items per verse.

66 One of the more common sayings, it also occurs in a poem by Jabr ibn Sayyār, "I shout and cry but don't see any succor, as if I had sounded the alarm in a graveyard": Sowayan, *al-Shiʿr al-Nabaṭī*, 494.

67 See "The deceit of Sajāḥ's prophesying," in a poem by Jabr ibn Sayyār: Sowayan, *al-Shiʿr al-Nabaṭī*, 487.

68 Al-Juhaymān, *al-Amthāl*, 1, 63–64.

69 Al-Juhaymān, *al-Amthāl*, 6, 113–14; 9, 293; 10, 216–17, "an old man is of no use"; al-ʿUbūdī, *al-Amthāl*, 664.

70 Snouck Hurgronje, *Mekkanische Sprichwörter und Redensarten*, 102–3. Al-Juhaymān, *al-Amthāl*, 3, 83; al-ʿUbūdī, *al-Amthāl*, 506.

71 Al-Juhaymān, *al-Amthāl*, 4, 263–64.

72 Al-Juhaymān, *al-Amthāl*, 2, 98–99.

73 Al-Juhaymān, *al-Amthāl*, 1, 220–22; al-ʿUbūdī, *al-Amthāl*, 1476–77.

74 Al-Juhaymān, *al-Amthāl*, 1, 380–81; 6, 227.

75 Al-Juhaymān, *al-Amthāl*, 2, 301.

76 Al-Juhaymān, *al-Amthāl*, 1, 231.

77 Cf. §§24.20 and 29.13. Al-Juhaymān, *al-Amthāl*, 7, 194.

78 Al-Juhaymān, *al-Amthāl*, 1, 391; 5, 295, 322; al-ʿUbūdī, *al-Amthāl*, 200.

79 Al-Juhaymān, *al-Amthāl*, 7, 136; 8, 330; 10, 336; al-ʿUbūdī, *al-Amthāl*, 1518–19.

80 Al-Juhaymān, *al-Amthāl*, 6, 133–34; 8, 138; 6, 52–53, 171–72.

81 Al-Juhaymān, *al-Amthāl*, 3, 256; al-ʿUbūdī, *al-Amthāl*, 632, 751.

82 In one version, "rule" is substituted for "prosperity"; al-Juhaymān, *al-Amthāl*, 2, 301–2; 8, 331–32; 10, 360; al-ʿUbūdī, *al-Amthāl*, 1519–20. Intoxication is often used in this poetry as a metaphor for being lovelorn or frenzied, as in Jabr al-Sayyār's line: "When I finally stole a kiss from her, I felt as if I had been struck down by a strong, old wine (*mudāmāt*)": Sowayan, *al-Shiʿr al-Nabaṭī*, 491.

83 Al-Juhaymān, *al-Amthāl*, 6, 206; 7, 328.

84 Al-Juhaymān, *al-Amthāl*, 3, 49–50.

85 Al-Juhaymān, *al-Amthāl*, 2, 186. Al-ʿUbūdī, *al-Amthāl*, 1379. Al-Juhaymān, *al-Amthāl*, 3, 94; 6, 41; al-ʿUbūdī, *al-Amthāl*, 1015. Al-Juhaymān, *al-Amthāl*, 2, 158; 5, 89–90. Al-Juhaymān, *al-Amthāl*, 4, 76–77; al-ʿUbūdī, *al-Amthāl*, 697. Al-Juhaymān, *al-Amthāl*, 2, 77–78; al-ʿUbūdī, *al-Amthāl*, 1300–1.

86 Al-Juhaymān, *al-Amthāl*, 9, 218; al-ʿUbūdī, *al-Amthāl*, 1693. Al-Juhaymān, *al-Amthāl*, 9, 279; al-ʿUbūdī, *al-Amthāl*, 1754. Al-Juhaymān, *al-Amthāl*, 1, 395. Al-ʿUbūdī, *al-Amthāl*, 1730.

87 Al-Juhaymān, *al-Amthāl*, 5, 81–82.

88 Abū Ḥamzah al-ʿĀmirī, one of the earliest known representatives of the Nabaṭī tradition, eulogizes the sharif of Medina, Kubaysh ibn Manṣūr ibn Jammāz, who was killed in 1327/8, Sowayan, *al-Shiʿr al-Nabaṭī*, 255–83.

89 In the MS written by Sulaymān ibn Ṣāliḥ al-Dakhīl with the title *Kitāb al-Baḥth ʿan aʿrāb Najd wa-ʿammā yataʿallaqu bihum* one finds ten poems by Ibn Zēd, an otherwise unknown poet, in praise of the Jabrid ruler Ajwad ibn Zāmil, who died in 1507: Sowayan, *al-Shiʿr al-Nabaṭī*, 299. It has no poems by Ḥmēdān.

90 Sowayan, *Nabaṭī Poetry*, is an excellent introduction and makes for a delightful read. For the linguistic aspects one should also refer to Clive Holes, "The Language of Nabaṭi Poetry."

91 The same word for a messenger's capable riding beast is used by the poet Jabr ibn Sayyār: Sowayan, *al-Shiʿr al-Nabaṭī*, 480, 489.

92 This development is explored and described in Sowayan's *al-Shiʿr al-Nabaṭī*.

93 Sowayan, *al-Shiʿr al-Nabaṭī*, 567–68.

94 Sowayan, *al-Shiʿr al-Nabaṭī*, 182.

95 Sowayan, *al-Shiʿr al-Nabaṭī*, 173.

96 See the Index of Poems where the meter of these poems is marked as "long."

97 The diminutive Swērah, "little Sārah," occurs in the Najdī expression: "A plate of flour and butter paste prepared by Swērah," i.e., a woman who does not even know how to prepare such a simple dish. The expression refers to a job that should be easy to carry out but is bungled by an incompetent person: al-Juhaymān, *al-Amthāl*, 4, 358. Another Najdī

expression is: "Divorce Swērah and marry her sister," i.e., if you are not satisfied with someone or something, then seek to replace it with a better alternative: al-Juhaymān, *al-Amthāl*, 10, 198.

98 The fourth edition, the one of al-Ḥātam listed at the beginning of the Index of Poems, does not add much value compared to the earlier edition by Khālid al-Faraj, and it lacks explanatory notes.

99 Sowayan, *al-Shiʿr al-Nabaṭī*, 199, 256.

100 In some poems the rhyme consonant is written at some distance from the rest of the second hemistich to form a kind of third column.

101 They are currently in the National and University Library in Strasbourg. See my article "Two manuscripts of Bedouin poetry in Strasbourg National and University Library and the travels of Charles Huber in Arabia" (forthcoming). Part of his journey and sojourn was in the company of the German scholar Julius Euting, with whom he had a famous falling out. Huber was murdered by his Bedouin guides on his second journey. Both their travel diaries were published (see bibliography). There is no mention of these MSS in Huber's *Journal d'un voyage* nor in his article "Voyage dans l'arabie central."

102 For instance, in another manuscript a poem composed in honor of Barakāt al-Sharīf is dated 1674/5. Yet another early poet, Rumaizān ibn Ghashshām, died in 1680. These older poems must have been copied from earlier manuscripts, which remain unknown to us.

103 These poems are included in five to eight of the listed MSS, the highest number (poems numbered 21, 22, and 28 in this edition). In addition, one of the Huber MSS has six pieces attributed to Ḥmēdān. But these are badly mangled versions of poems that in this edition are based on other sources. In the section on manuscripts on the website www.saadsowayan.com they are listed in the index that has been added to the MSS, but they have not been included in the copy of the Huber MSS.

104 In addition, Ibn Yaḥyā made use of the library of the Āl Khalīfah rulers of Bahrain, Sowayan, *al-Shiʿr al-Nabaṭī*, 197.

105 Sowayan, *al-Shiʿr al-Nabaṭī*, 197–98. This is mentioned in a MS by Muḥammad al-ʿAlī al-ʿUbayd, *al-Najm al-lāmiʿ li-l-nawādir jāmiʿ*, 76.

106 This was most likely also the case with the long poems by ʿAbdallah ibn Sbayyil that I recorded from a Bedouin near his hometown of Nifī, as described in my "Praying Mantis in the Desert."

107 Many manuscripts in Arabia were burned at the time of the heightened Wahhābī spirit that accompanied the conquest of most of Arabia by the Ikhwān, the army of settled Bedouin tribes who provided the shock troops of King ʿAbd al-ʿAzīz.

108 With regard to the more recent poets, the situation is somewhat better. In the case of Ibn Sbayyil (d. 1933), for instance, his daughter Sārah, who was still alive when I visited Nifī in 1989, was the certifying authority of the *dīwān* published by his grandson.

109 For other examples of misunderstandings created by this improvised phonetic system of writing, see Sowayan, *al-Shiʿr al-Nabaṭī*, 204.

110 In their compositions in this meter poets frequently had to resort to the introduction of short syllables to complete their line, as in this case the first syllable of *ṭaraf*. These are the initial four lines of this edition's poem number 4 as they are written in the MS of al-ʿAssāf:

النفس ا نجت لا محاسبها   فادين اخيار مك ا سبها

كا نك لا لجنة مشتا ق   تبغي نعيم ابجا نبها

ادنيا روضت نوا ر   صيورا ريح تطيرابها

فنجاك امندنيا طرف   فشكر مولاك الواجبها

In transliteration it would be written thus:

an-nafs in jat li-mḥāsibha / f-ad-dīn xyār mikāsibha
ćānnik l-al-jannah mištāg / tabği an-niʿīm b-jānibha
w-ad-dinya rōḏat nuwwār / ṣayyūr ar-rīḥ tṭīr ibha
w-in jāk mn ad-dinya ṭaraf / f-iškir mawlāk l-mūjibha.

The final word has been adjusted in accordance with al-Dhukayr MS.

Arabian Satire

~ ١ ~

لاح المِشيب وبان في عَرضائي ونعَيت من بعد المِشيب صَبائي
ونعَيت خلٍ كان في ماضٍ مِضى لاحتْ عليه نوازح البَعْداءِ
و مَرْةٍ جَهالتها عليّ كبيره تحَسِبني أخرج من نِقا الدهْناءِ
تقول حِطّ وقِطّ والا ففارِق مالي بشَوف الشَيبة الشَمْطاءِ
قِلت ايّها الشَوق الذي من قَبِل ذا ما هوب شَرْهٍ يوم عَصْر صَبائي
واليوم خالفْت الطبوع وكَثّرني مِنك الكلام وزادت البَغْضاءِ
هوذا فطمعٍ بي فهاك دراهم وان كان بغضٍ ما لِقيت دَوائي
البِغض نفْسٍ ما تِطيب جْروحه وحْشٍ جِفولٍ فاتن الفَرْقاءِ
ذي عادةٍ حِبّ المِحبّ وعاده ما قطّ رافَق صاحب البَغْضاءِ
وان كان تبَغي فيّ هِمّات الصِبا ترَاي عنها قِد طِوَيت رْشائي
وان كان هو بِغضٍ وصَيدك طاح لِخذي ثلاثٍ واضْرِبي البَيداءِ
قَلّتْ دَنانيري وعِذت بهَمّه جَذّتْ حبالي عن جمام الماءِ
العام انا لي كِدّةٍ ماشومه هَبّت عليها الجانح اليَمْناءِ
اسلَفْت فيها يوم ثمّ جَذّت عنها العَصَيرالى انها بيضاءِ
وادلجت راسي مرّتين تِوجّد وِصْفقت بالوُسطا على الطَرفاءِ

~ 1 ~

My temples flecked with gray 1.1
signal old age, a farewell to youth![1]
I mourn my beloved of time past:
she drifted away, a distant memory.
Now a stupid wife crushes me:
she thinks me lord of mountains of gold,
Barking, “Pay up or shut up and get out!
What use do I have for a senile graybeard?”
“You were always my darling,” I said, 1.5
“but youth and its appetites have left us,
We’ve grown apart and I’ve had enough
of your harping, your nasty words.
Are you trying to squeeze money out of me?
But there’s nothing I can do if you hate me;
It’s impossible to appease a soul full of hate,
a monster that forever bucks and bolts.[2]
It’s better to abide by love’s time-honored code:
never get trapped with a partner who loathes you.
If you seek to rouse my youthful drive, 1.10
I have put away my well ropes and retired.
Do you hate me so much that you want a better match?[3]
Then away with you: you’re three times divorced!”
I feel poverty’s pinch—it’s on my mind;
my frayed ropes can’t draw water from the well.
My year of labor at the well met with bad luck
when scalding southern winds came on in a rage.
I gave it my all and then hauled in my ropes,
but have nothing to show for all my toil day and night.
I shook my head in grief, 1.15
snapped thumb and middle finger: All gone!

وارْكَبْت من غالي النِشيد بكاعَب   غَـرّا تشـادى السـابق الخضـراءِ
حَيرانـة الدِمْـلوج ضـامِرَة الحَشـا   مـا مَسّهـا خُـبْثٍ ولا سَـقْواءِ
مَـصْريـة الالوان ناعـمَة الصِـبا   قـامت بـرِدْفٍ كِنّهـا عَجْـزاءِ
هـركولةٍ ياما اتْلفَتْ من جـاهل   حَقّـت علـى ديـرانهـا الانواءِ
سْكَنَتْ قصور الوَشْم شرقي النـقا   مـا لاوذت مـن بارح الجَوزاءِ
وانْذَرْتهـا عن شَيخ قومٍ ناقـص   تِـرْثة حـضورٍ شَـذّ من حَوّاءِ
ما شاخ جَدّه قَبِل ابوه ولا لْهم   حَقٍ ولا عِـدّوا من القِـدْمـاءِ
اَمْسَى يِسيد بْدار حَيٍّ قِد غَدوا   يِشْـبه لثَورٍ خـار في قَصْبـاءِ
يَمّمْتهـا ابن نُحَيط كسّاب الثَنا   وَرْث الشـيوخ من اوّل الدِنْيـاءِ
وِلْد الحـدَيثي الذي من لابـه   تِـرْثة تمـيمٍ وفرعها العَلْيـاءِ
يابن نُحَـيط الله ـلي من عَيـله   خلّيـتهـم بالوَشْـم في رَجْوائي
يَـرْجوني وانا ارْتِجي من خَيّـر   والفَضْـل من نـدوا يِدَيك دْوائي
وصَلّوا على خيـر البرايا مُحَمّـد   مـا ناض بَـرْق بْليـلةٍ ظَلْمـائي

~ 1 ~

Then I sang a song about a comely maid,[4]
a temptress shaped like a dark racehorse,
Plump calves clasped by anklets, wasplike waist,
her charms untouched by ill health or dropsy,[5]
Skin smooth, a creamy Egyptian tinge,[6]
a round behind heavy on her gait,
Stunning looks that spelled ruin for many a youth.
May the lands where she lives be blessed with rains,
In al-Washm's homesteads, east of the sands
that offer shelter from the hot summer winds.
I warned her against a tribal chief of ill repute,
a villager, one of Eve's offspring gone bad,[7]
His father the first shaykh in his line,
not one to be counted among those of ancient rank.
He lorded it over a deserted realm
like a dumb ox mooing in a field of grass.[8]
I gave her as a gift to Ibn Nḥēṭ, a most worthy man,
who boasts a lineage of shaykhs, as old as the world;
He is the son of al-Ḥdēthī, whose clan
stems from Timīm's foremost branch.[9]
O Ibn Nḥēṭ, may God help me provide for a family
left behind in al-Washm. They hope for sustenance,
And look to me, while I look for a benefactor
whose kind hands will be my cure.[10]
Prayers for Muḥammad, the best of creatures,
as frequent as flashes of lightning in a dark night.

يا مجَلِّي تِسَمَّع لعَودٍ فِصيح   فاهمٍ عارفٍ في فنون العرب
اِفْتِهِمِ من عَليمٍ مجَرِّب حكيم   باخصٍ بالذوارب ومَكْوا النِكَب
اَنْذِر اللي تِدانا بِقُرْب العجوز   تَذْبِحه والنِسَم مثل فَوح اللَهَب
من تجَوَّز عَجوزٍ فهو نادمٍ   لو يفرِّش ويَلْحَف ثمين الذهب
ما خَبَرْنا يساهَر ياكود القِريص   جِعْلها الله تساهَر على ادنى سِبَب
بَطْنها مِلْتوي مِثْل بَطْن المِعيد   ما على وَرْكَها ما يرِدّ الحَقَب
لَى مِشَت مثل قَوسٍ حَناه السّتاد   مايلٍ راسها كِن فيها رِقَب
دايمٍ بالدِجى صَدْرها لِه فَحيح   مِثل شَذْب النجاجير صَلْب الخَشَب
المَره لَى عَقَب عِمْرها الاربعين   وراسها عِقْب ذا بالمِشيب اقْتَلَب
حِطّ له حِفْرةٍ بالثَرا عِمْقها   قامةٍ وارْمها واثْن منها الرِكَب
اذْفِنَه دَفْنَة الجيفَة الخايسه   لا تَرَعْرع تَرى ما يجيها طَلَب
ايّ قِرْب العجوز ايّ بِنْتٍ رِهوز   النَواهد ركوزٍ زهنّ المَلَبّ
عَينها عَين ريم جِفَل واستِذار   نافرٍ شاف زيلة ظعون الصَلَب
والرِدايف زِمَن والخَواصر هَفَن   والعجيب العَجَب لَى رِمَيت السَلَب
بين هذي وهذيك فَرْقٍ جِلي   مِثل ما بين صَنْعا وديرة حَلَب

~ 2 ~

Mjalli, listen to me, this eloquent graybeard,
    a sage steeped in savoir faire;
Learn from a man clever, tested, and wise,
    a penetrating mind, prescient about the blows of fate:
Make sure to give a wide berth to older women,
    who breathe and spit deadly, red-hot flames.
Marry an older woman and you will regret it,
    even if you are decked out richly in gold.
Victims are kept awake to treat snakebite:
    I hope she'll never sleep a wink, all night.[11]
Her belly is creased and wrinkled, like a worn-out camel,
    her haunches so skinny her belt keeps slipping off.
When she walks she stoops like a curved, well-crafted bow,
    her head tilted to one side, as if she has a crick in her neck;
At dusk her chests hisses as it heaves,
    like the sound of a carpenter planing hard wood.
Once a woman has passed the mark of forty,
    and her black tresses are streaked with gray,
The moment has come for you to dig a trench
    six feet deep: throw her in with a rope around her knees!
Bury her there as you would a rotting corpse;
    don't be scared: no one will come to seek revenge.[12]
Such a difference between this hag and a buxom girl
    whose breasts swell on her lucent chest,
Who has the startled eyes of a gazelle
    alarmed by the figures of Ṣalab hunters,[13]
Whose bottom is pert and full, waistline toned and slim;
    just imagine the wonders when her clothes are off.
These women are at opposite extremes,
    as far apart as Sanaa and Aleppo.

~ ٣ ~

شِفْت جْمَلينٍ بالعارض   زِبَـدهـا فوق غَوارِبها
حَـطّوا الدِين لْهـم سِـلَّم   ولا ادري وِشّ مْقاصدها
ولا ادري وِش هي تَبْـغي   ولا ادري عن مِـطالبها
كان الباطن مِثل الظاهر   يا وِيلك ياللي تْحارِبها
وان كان مخالف ظاهرها   فكلٍّ يَقْرا عِـقـارِبها

~ 3 ~

I saw two rutting camels in al-ʿĀriḍ,[14] 3.1
    mouth foam on their withers.[15]
For them religion is simply a ladder to climb;
    why, I cannot tell,
Nor what purpose they have,
    or what demands.
If hidden intentions match appearances,
    disaster awaits those who fight them;
If they are the opposite of what we see, 3.5
    Qur'anic verses protect against the scorpion's sting.[16]

النَفْس ان جت لِمْحاسبها   فـالدين خيار مْكاسبها
كـانك للجَنّه مِشْتاق   تَبْغي النِعيم بْجانبها
الدِنْيـا رَوضـة نُوّار   صيوّر الريح تطير بها
وان جاك من الدنيا طرَف   فـاشْكِر مَولاك لمُوجبها
لَيّـاك تْغَيّرها فَسْقِه   تغيّر عَـنْك مْعاذِبها
تَـراها خَلّتْني اجْـرَد   تجَدّد وانا اقالِبها
غَـدَتْ لي في خَـدّجِه   كنّ القِرطـاس تَرايبها
غَـدَتْ يَمٍّ وانا يَمّ   ولا عـاد الله بجايبها
وانا انـذَرْتك عن المِـقْفي   لا تِتْـلِف نَفْسك تِتْعِبها
وانا اخْبِرْك تَـرى المِبْغِـض   ما هوب يوالَف صاحبها
واحْذِرْك مشيرٍ غَشّاش   وِدّه بيـرٍ يِـرْميك ابها
واحْذَر بالاصحاب بْطَيني   وانْظِـر عَينَيه وحاجِبها
واحْذَر عن بِنْت العِشْرين   لَيّـا القـاري يقـاربها
لوكان يـدرّسهـا عـالِم   خَطِرٍ يَشْرَب من شاربها
والفَقِـر عـارٍ بالمَوسـم   لو رَخْصت بِه جَـلايبها

~ 4 ~

When man comes to be judged by his Lord, 4.1
his strongest testimony is observance,
Should he yearn for entry to Paradise,
to enjoy its shade and easy comfort.
This world is like a flowering garden;
it will be blown away by the winds.
If this world smiles on you,
thank your Lord for making you content.
Beware of opening its gate to lustful sin, 4.5
and thereby forfeiting its sweet fruits.
The world stripped me until I stood bare;
fickle, she left me to wonder what to make of her.
She came to me in the form of a plump beauty,
her breasts lustrous as pristine sheets of paper.
Then she went one way and I the other:
I hope to God our paths never cross again!
I warn you, if she gives you the cold shoulder,
do not run after her and exhaust yourself.
You should know about malicious people: 4.10
be careful, don't get close and friendly with them.
I warn you against heeding the advice of impostors:
given a chance they will push you down a well.
Watch out for those who harbor nefarious intent:
examine their eyes and brows for telltale signs.
Pay close attention to a twenty-year-old girl,
otherwise the Qur'an teacher will sidle up to her
And slake his thirst during lessons
with a heady draft from her lips.
In season, when goods are cheaply priced, 4.15
poverty is a shameful thing.

~ ٤ ~

والمال اوْبار يغَطّي دْبَرٍ   ولْهود بجانبها
ويزيّن بِيضٍ قَواصر   ورجالٍ يَرْفا عايبها
وشبّ التِبن قْضا عاجز   اللهٰ يخيّب خايبها
اللهٰ من قومٍ يامانع   اَمْسَى جاهلها شايبها
ان جِيت احاكي واحدهم   عن الدِيره وِنوايبها ٢٠،٤
قال انّي شَيخٍ من قَبلِك   جَدّي عَفّى جوانبها
فنِعْمٍ فِي ابوك وجَدّك   والخَيبه في عَواقبها

Wealth covers your back like a fur coat,
    and hides sores and blisters from view;[17]
It has the power to make plain women pretty,
    and make up for some men's defects.
It's a lousy revenge to set stubble fields on fire:
    may God thwart those losers and their schemes. . . .[18]
I ask you, Māniʿ, what kind of folk are these,
    whose elders are as foolish as their youngsters?
When I questioned one of them 4.20
    on the district and its conditions,
He said, "I was a shaykh long before you;
    my ancestor took possession of it."
"Congratulations to your father and grandfather!
    What a shame they sired a dunce like you."

بالعَون مــنيفٍ قــاله لي   يقول غَلاك يوم انت صِبي
تَـرى الشايب عند عياله   وامّ عــياله مثـل العـَزِبِ
لو يطْلِبــهم رَدّة لِقْــمه   قـالوا مخِلي وِش ذا الصّلبِي
كلوا فَــيده هـم عــادوه   عِقْب التِمسّك بالسْببِ
احْـفَظ مـالك تجي غـالي   حِـتّى يلاقونك بالعِْتبِ
كَذّبْت مــنيفٍ ــفي قَوله   وتبَــيّن لي مــاكان غـَبي
احــدٍ يْقــال له لَبّــيه   واحــدٍ يِقــال له وِشّ تِبي
حَتّى امّ عيالي زَهْدتْ بي   نَسْــيَتْ زِمــاني وِطَرِبي
فِقَدَت مِــنّي شِ ما اطْريه   عــلى بِهْــمي وعـلى رَكبي
يوم فْيَدي مِثْل الشَوحَط   واليوم دَلّى ورا ذْنِبي
لوهو يِشْرَى كان اشْـريه   وارْخِص به مـالي وذْهَـبي
اشوف عْظـامي تُوجِـعْني   وظهَيري من حَـدّ حْقِـبي
وهجُوسي تَسْــري بالليـل   خَوفي من مَوتٍ بطَـلِبي
والدِنْيـا عـامرهـا دامــر   مـا فيـها خَيـرٍ ياعـْرِبي
صَــدّرْت وطَوّيت العِـدّه   وِيْعَقّبْــني من كــان يِبي

~ 5 ~

I swear to God, it was Mnīf who said to me: 5.1
    "You are only appreciated in your prime."
It seems that, to his children
    and their mother, a graybeard is just a hanger-on.
If he asks them for a little bit to eat,
    they say, "Ugh, what a scrounger!"
Yet they have spent all his savings and grown hostile,
    even though he had always provided for them.
Keep a tight grip on your purse and you'll be everyone's darling, 5.5
    a warm welcome on every doorstep.
First I scoffed at these ideas of Mnīf;
    now I must admit that he was no fool.
"At your command," some say to one man.
    "What do you want?" they growl at another.
Even the mother of my children scorns me—
    she's forgotten the fun we had in our good old days.
She misses that of which I should not speak:
    when I am on my hands and my knees.
Today my prick, once as hard as yew,
    dangles listlessly between my legs:
If I could buy one, I would do so right away, 5.10
    gladly spend on it all my wealth and gold.
As it is, my bones are sore all over,
    and my back hurts below my belt.[19]
Anxieties race and keep me awake at night:
    I fear death is in pursuit of me.
In the end all that flourishes comes to naught;
    expect no good from this world, my friend.
I have packed up my equipment at the well: 5.15
    let someone else take my job, if he feels like it.

~ ٦ ~

مَوارِدِ حِيضان الحروب هَماج　　　تزَجّه حِيران الرِبيع زِجاج

باثَرْ فِتنةٍ تاهت قوادى مشيرها　　　سَعَى بْها بَعْض القرود وْماج

الَى فتحوا هل النِقاريس بابها　　　غَدوا لِك عَنْها بالشقوق وْلاج

وخلَّوك فيها مثل راعي حَريقه　　　حَريقة صِريعٍ مِقْتِفيه عَجاج

هم يحْسبون الحَرب رَقْصٍ وعَرْضه　　　ومْطايَزٍ عِنْد مهاة غْناج

الحَرب يبْغي مْصَقَّلات الهَنادي　　　ما هي حْبوبٍ تنَثَّر للدجاج

كما قومٍ اعتاضوا قِذىً في عيونهم　　　غَدَوا لك من عِقْب الاسود نْعاج

وكم نِعْمةٍ زالت من اسباب غَيّهم　　　وعلى اعْراضهم بالذَمّ قيل حْراج

وِاسْتبْدلوا فَقْرٍ وذِلٍّ بْغَيّهم　　　وَسْقتْهم عِقب القَراح هَماج

~ 6 ~

Water from the pools of war is brackish, 6.1
fouled by camel calves in days of spring.
When strife broke out, sound minds were at a loss:
some ill-starred wretches let war loose and it ran free.
Once these sly dogs had pushed its doors wide open,
they scampered through the cracks in the wall,
Leaving it to you to quench the fire
set ablaze with dry twigs, fanned by gusts of wind.
They think that war is all sword dancing and merry songs, 6.5
with shapely, cow-eyed coquettes for company.
War is the clash of sharp-edged Indian swords,
not handfuls of grain strewn as chicken feed.[20]
Men once like lions become meek as lambs
blinded by motes in their eyes,[21]
Great riches were destroyed by their delusion,
their honor and reputation were stained.
Their conceit was rewarded with poverty and shame,
and sweet water replaced by brine.[22]

~ ٧ ~

طالب الفَضل من عند الشحاح   مِثل من اهدَى زِمان الصَرام اللِقاح

او مِثل طابخ له الفاس يَبْغي مَرَق   او حالبٍ له تيوسٍ يَبيهن مناح

الخصَى ما بِهن دَرٍّ يِذكُر يِشاف   غَير بَول يِهلِك شَرابه ملاح

اربَعٍ يَرْفِعِنّ الفِتى بالعيون   الظِفَر والكَرَم والوِفا والصلاح

وارْبَعٍ يِنْزِلِن الفِتى للهَوان   البُخل والجِبن والكِذب والسِفاح

وارْبَعٍ يِنْزِلِن الفِتا للزراج   لَين تَبْرَى جنوبه بِيانٍ صِحاح

رَوشَنٍ عالِي فَوق كلّ المَلا   مِغلَقٍ ما هَوِتْه الوجيه السماح

ومْكاشَخ هدومٍ بغَيرِ القِدا   او ذِليلٍ يزَرّق طوال الرماح

او رباعيةٍ فَخْرها بالحَمام   هي نفاد الدوا ما تْعَرف الصياح

وكلّ من هو تِعِب جَدّه وابوه   اغْتَنَى واهْتَنَى واكتِفَى وِاسْتَراح

وكِلّ من ذَوّق الضِدّ صِحْن الدما   من حدود البُواتر وسُمْر الرماح

خَذ بها مِدّةٍ ما يزوره حَريب   وامّن السِبل عِنْده بداره وساح

وكِلّ مِن هو تِدَيّن لِيُوفي الديون   يَحْسب انّه نِفَه من ديونه وَراح

ما دَرَى انّه يِزيد الديون بديون   وزاد هَمّه همومٍ وهو ما استَراح

ومن بَغى الحُكم وسَيفه بالاغماد   ذاك طَيرٍ تِنَهّض بليّا جَناح

~ 7 ~

To look for kind favors from misers
    is like fertilizing date palms during the harvest
Or like boiling hoes to produce broth,
    milking billy goats instead of camel udders—
Who ever heard of milk from testicles?
    They produce disgusting urine, rank to the taste.
Four virtues redound to a man's reputation:
    courage, generosity, faithfulness, and probity.
Four vices will bring him the utmost contempt:
    avarice, cowardice, deceit, and fornication.
Four things send a man into the wilderness
    until his ribs protrude from his wasted body:
A guest room high above the crowd below,
    with a closed door, unvisited by fine gentlemen;[23]
Gaudy clothes worn by an ostentatious fop;
    long spears brandished with bravura by a sissy;
A flintlock, once a proud pigeon gun,
    emptied of bullets, unable to fire and roar.
If your father and your grandfather have worked hard,
    you will have gained joy, contentment, and comfort.
Be the first to give the enemy a taste of blood
    from sharp-edged swords and tawny lances:
Thereby gain respite from a foe's attack,
    securing the country's roads for easy travel.
Whoever takes a loan to pay off old debts,
    thinking to balance his accounts and relax,
Unaware that he has heaped debt upon debt,
    only adds to his troubles and will not find rest.
He who wishes to rule with his sword in its sheath
    is like a wingless bird trying to fly.[24]

ما يَنال الّا العَذاب او يِسْتِفيد   ما اسْتِفادت من نِبُوّتها سِجاح
يومِ جَت لمسَيلِمْه صارت عَروس   والمَهَر خَلّى لها مِثْل فَرْض الصباح

~ 7 ~

Such men will suffer pain without benefit,
    like Sajāḥ who made no gain from her prophesies:
When she joined Musaylimah as his wife,
    his dowry was to cancel the dawn prayer.

~ ٨ ~

١،٨ اِدعو للخـاطـر يامــانع   بافْـعىً بالدَرْب الَى راحِ
اللهَ لا يَبْـلاك بْسَـيّه   يَبْـلاك بواحد فَـلاّحِ
لَكِنّ الطـايه من عِـقْبه   مْـراح شـياهٍ سِـرّاحِ
يِعْـطى السّحّه نابٍ ذارب   مِـثل المِخْـراز الَى راحِ
٥،٨ اَطْلِب وارْجي وادْعي وامّن   عَسـاه ونَسْـله للمـاحي
وجِلْده يَذْرى مِثل الجَمْشه   مـا يِسـتَلْقيه السَرّاحِ
يِعْـبا له زَرْنيخ ونُوره   ومِكْرادٍ مـا وافَق طـاحِ
اما يِعْـطَب وهو المَطْلب   والا يِطْلَع جِلْدٍ صـاحي

~ 8 ~

Mānī‘, say this prayer for my guest: 8.1
"May a viper bite you on the way!"
If God wishes to afflict you with evil,
He will inflict such a peasant on you.
This guest left my roof terrace covered
in date pits, like the droppings of fat sheep;[25]
With sharp teeth he gobbled up all my dates
as fast as a needle stitching leather.
I ask, hope, pray, and say "amen" 8.5
that he and his offspring be wiped out.
Let his skin be scattered like limestone dust,
if it is of no use for making leather thongs.[26]
Or let his skin be drenched with arsenic and lime,
then smoothed by a sharp-edged plane—
It will either be ruined, and how I wish it would,
or it'll serve as a decent piece of leather.

~ ٩ ~

انا سَـهـرٍ بِمْنَـيحيّـتي   وهو مِجْلنْطٍ بِسَـطوحِـه
انا آكـل من شَين ثْماره   وهو لِه زَيـنـه وِبْلوحِـه
عطـاه الله صَيحـة غفـله   تُودِع نِسْوانـه في نَوحِـه
والّا دَرّاجـه منْفــارق   تِنْشِب لي راسه في صَوحه
ولّا رِصـاصـه من دَرْجِه   تِطْلِع لي طِعْمه مع رُوحـه
لو يَذْكِـر لي وقتٍ راح   وِشْ لِه بالجَـيّه والرَوحـه
ادْخِـل به مع باب الطَلْحـه   يَمْلا ذِرْعـاني بِطَروحِـه
تَـرى العيـلان الى كَبْـروا   واجُود اللي يَكْفي رُوحـه

~ 9 ~

I spend the evening working at the well; 9.1
he spends his stretched out on the roof.[27]
I eat the worst, rotten fruit
while he feasts on the choicest dates.
May God strike him down suddenly
and make his female household wail,
Or let a pulley fly off
and smash his head on the rim of the well,
Or let a bullet fired from a flintlock 9.5
spill his food and his soul.
I wish he'd recall our days of old
and how adorable he was as a toddler
When I carried him at al-Ṭalḥah gate
in my arms, soiled clothes and all.
When your children have grown up,
it is best to keep to yourself.

~ ١٠ ~

لقيت انا بالناس عَيٍ جاهل   ما لحَق والقادي بنُص مراده
يجي امورٍ ما يعَرف قياسَها   ويدَقّ دَقّة عَوشَز الجَرّاده
من لا يصير بْقَدِر نفْسه عارف   هذاك ثَورٍ ما عليه قْلاده
بالناس من هو للرفيق مخادع   يُوهِم صديقه صادقٍ بِوْداده
كِنّه سَرابٍ في نَهارٍ لامع   والغِشّ ما غَيره لِجا بِفْواده
بالناس من يِكْرَم الى جا ضايف   وان ضِيف يَزْحِر كِنّه الوَلّاده
من خَلْقتِه ما ذاق زاده غيره   لو هو ذبابٍ ما وِقَع في زاده
وبالناس ظَفرٍ ما سِمع في هَوشه   ولو هو حَضَرها كان شِيل شْداده
وبالناس من هو يِفْتِخِر في نفسه   من غير فِعْلٍ يفتخر باجْداده
مِثل غَضاةٍ بالضوا مِشْتَبّه   يِصبِح مورِّثْها يصير رْماده
وبالناس من هو يدِّعي بديانه   مِتْمِسِّكٍ بديانِته واوْراده
عند الخَلايق غافلٍ ويحَسِّن   ياخِذ شريطه مِثل جارى العاده
عنده لراعى الصاع مُوسٍ جيّد   واللي بلا صاعٍ له المِكْراده
فاحْذر خداع الخاين المِتْعَبِّد   لو دام ليله والنهار عْباده
كم غَرّ فيها من غَريرٍ جاهل   حَطّه لِمثْله مِثل فَخٍّ صاده

~ 10 ~

Even wise men achieve at best half of their goals. 10.1
other people bumble about, refractory and stupid:
Unable to fathom matters they are confronted with,
they flail as if shaking locusts from a boxthorn.[28]
Someone who doesn't know his true worth
blunders blindly like an ox without a halter.
Some men scheme and deceive their companion,
feigning sincerity and friendly affection—
They are like a mirage on a blistering day, 10.5
and conceal trickery, nothing else, in their hearts.
Others enjoy hospitality when visiting as guests,
but sigh and moan as if in labor when hosts:
It is their nature to keep the food all for themselves,
and they don't even let a fly land on their plate.[29]
Some "brave" men have never entered battle:
as soon as they did, they'd be robbed of their mounts,
Braggarts with nothing to show for themselves
except boasting about the valiant deeds of ancestors;
They burn brightly at night like a shrub thrown on the fire, 10.10
then turn to ash in the morn and vanish without a trace.
There are some among us who make a show of piety,
with strict observance of rites and mumbling of prayers.
Duping those who seek their succor as men of God,
they stipulate a fee: it's business as usual.[30]
For the well-to-do they wield a razor-sharp knife,
and fleece the indigent, scraping them clean.
Beware of these holy quacks and their treachery,
no matter how many days and nights they spend in worship:
Woe betide the ignorant fools who inadvertently 10.15
fall into the traps these impostors have laid for them.

وبالناس من هو لَغْوِيٍ بلْسانه   والا بنانه ما تهِمّ اضداده

يَشْرى اللغا يُوذي القِريب وجاره   مِتْرَدّي حتى بحَبْل جْهاده

وبالناس من ينْقِد على جْهل العَرب   وهو جِهولٍ والجْهَل مِعْتاده

وبالناس من هو للنوايب يِرْتِكي   يبَدّي اضيافه بقُوت اوْلاده

وبالناس من يَجْمع حَلالٍ يَدِفْنِه   بجْمالته وتْجارته وكْداده ٢٠،١٠

ويفوز به غيره وينْقِل ازْرِه   يوم الحساب الى هَلَك ما فاده

Certain men are admired for their eloquence,
 but their deeds fail to impress the enemy:
Relatives and dependents suffer from their blabbering,
 while their own efforts result in nothing.
There are others who accuse their fellows of ignorance
 though they plumb the depths of stupidity!
Some men fend off disasters, like a mighty rampart
 feeding their guests first, even before their own children,
Unlike those who squirrel away what they have amassed 10.20
 from camel transport, trade, or tilling the soil:
Others will benefit from their profits on Judgment Day,
 when they stand naked and their gain turns to loss.

اسباب مـا فـاجى الضِمـير وذار   كَرى العَين وذْموع النَظَير نِثار
شيٍّ فِجَـاني من زِمـاني وراعـني   هواياه في لاجى الضمير كُبـار
الَى شِفْت من يامِر وهودون حِسْبِته   رِديّ المَناسب والجدود هَيار
اميرٍ يسَـمّونه اميرٍ مضَبّب   عـارٍ عـليـه وبالقـيامـه نار
وِطاني رِدي الخال غزّان صِخْره   وانا عَـيلتي مِفْتـاقةٍ وِصْغـار
غَزَينا على قَحْطان لا دَرّ دَرّهـم   هَجَمنـا بليـلٍ والنجوم زْهـار
تِداعوا علينا من بِعيدٍ وجَلبوا   وجَونا كمـا الدَبْوا الى من سـار
تِطارِدَتْ فِرسان رَبْعي وخَيلهم   وِتقـادَحَنّ سيوفهم شَرار
الَى ما هَزَمنا جَمْعهم جا كِمّيهم   يَـزْمي كمـا مَوجٍ زِفَـر بِبحـار
وزادوا علينا واسْتعَزّت قلوبهم   وحَـلّ الفَـنا فينا وِفكْري حـار
وجَت خَيلنا هَلْها تِجرّ رْماحهم   مِنهَـزِمـةٍ تِشْبه حَمامٍ طار
جينا ذِليلينٍ وذْبحت شيوخنا   حَفـايا عَرايا والمقَدّر صار
غَزينا وجِينا وابْرَق الريش ما غَزا   ابا الحاسّ ما ناض الجَناح وطار
لِك الله لو هو حاضرٍ يوم كَوننا   نهـارٍ عَبوسٍ فيـه عَجٍّ ثار
تِبهَبه وثوبه كل سـاعه يِبِلّه   ويَرمي بحَذرِيّه بغير عْيار

~ 11 ~

A sudden shock upset me, deprived me 11.1
of sleep, and made my eyes drip with tears.
This epoch of dread surprises
rips my soul apart with terror:
I fell in with an undeserving leader,
born of base parentage and dodgy lineage,
An inept commander, an "emir fettered in iron,"
a shame that condemns him to the fires of Hell.[31]
I joined his raid, cajoled by the rotten bastard,[32] 11.5
driven by the needs of my family and little ones.
We went to rob Qaḥṭān, may they fall on evil days,
advancing by night as the stars lit our way.
They saw us from afar, raised the alarm, mobilized,
and marched on us like swarms of locusts.
Our horsemen clashed lances with their cavalry
and sparks flew as the sabers clanged.
They feigned retreat, then a hidden reserve surged
and with a howl they rose up like a wave.
They took heart from seeing us overwhelmed, 11.10
massacred our raiders while I stood by, powerless.
Our horsemen fled on foot, dragging their lances,
crestfallen, like scattered pigeons.[33]
Our chiefs were killed; humbled, we returned
barefoot, stripped naked as fate had decreed.
We went on the raid but the coward shirked the task:
he sat with folded wings, like a lice-ridden raptor.[34]
I swear to God, had he been with us in battle
on that grim day when fate lurked in the swirling dust,
He would have wavered and pissed himself, 11.15
and shat copiously in his pants from fear,[35]

ذِليـلٍ فلا يومٍ يشـاهَـد بهَـيّه — وهو بالقَهـاوي فـارسٍ كـرّار
وهو كما المدغوش في سـاقـة الفلا — يَصْهِـل وبالتـالي نِهـيق حْـمار
الَى هَـمْهَم المزغول باوّل صَوتـه — تَـرى تالي صوتـه عليـه عـيار
تَخيّر لجَـدّه بين عَـمْرو ووايـل — بَغى عـامرٍ يِعْـمق عليـه وحـار
الَى عاد مَا انْتِب من تميـمٍ وعـامر — ولا انِتب لعـالين الاصول تْشـار
تِقَهْقَـر ولا تـرقى مَراقي صِعيبْه — عَوّد وهَوّد ياذِليـل الجـار
تِتبَّعْت ديوان المَناسب ولا حَصل — اَلْقَى له اصـلٍ بَيِّن المِعْـبار
واجْهَـدْت بالدُوره وظَـنّي لِقَـيته — جـدوده بيـاسيرٍ ولا له كـار
شِحيح فـلا يَبْـذِل من الخَير حَبّـه — وللشـرّ بـذّارٍ قِصيف اشـبار
الى نَوى للجود او هـمّ بالثَـنا — وِسـاويس نَفْسـه للرِدى تِـنْـدار
اشَحّ من المـفطوم في كَفّـه الغَـذا — الى وافِقـه حَـدّ الفطام غْسـار
واشحّ من البيّوض عن واضح النِـدا — الى ظَهَـر نَجْـم التوِيـع غـار
مَحَا الله من يَـزْرَع عـلى غيرِ عَيلَم — ومن كان يَبْني بالهَيار جْـدار
مِدَحْتِه بجَهْلٍ قَبل عِرِفي فيااسَـف — على مَـدْح مزغولٍ بغـيرٍ اشهـار
فـياليت عِرْفي قَبـل من هَـفَت — عموقه وخـاله مِهْـنِته جَـزّار
تَرى الاصل جَذّابٍ على الطِيب والرِدَى — فـلا شكّ نَقّ الحَبّ يالبَـذّار
اجَل عَنك مَدْحي ضاع في غير خَيِّر — كما ضاع في جَيب العَجوز عْطار

~ 11 ~

A despicable poltroon who shirks battle,
but struts and swaggers among the coffee cups;
He is like a feisty mare amid a group of thoroughbreds,
but his loud neighs are a donkey's bray:
At first the faker cleared his throat for a battle cry,
but in the end he just shrieked and yelled.
He first picked ʿAmr and Wāyil as his ancestors,
then added ʿĀmir to the mix for greater luster.
In truth your lineage is neither Timīm nor ʿĀmir, 11.20
and there is not the slightest trace of high birth.
Sober up and stop your ludicrous pretensions:
beat it and calm down, you useless wimp!
I scrutinized works of genealogy but they yielded
no incontrovertible proof in support of his claims.
Then, after an eager search, I think I found the clue:
I traced him to a mongrel breed with no prestige.
For this miser a single grain is too much generosity,
though the niggard sows evil profligately.
Any munificence and ambition that stir in him 11.25
are spoiled by the whisperings of his soul.
He clutches his food more fiercely than
a toddler with stomach cramps after being weaned,
Or a bird with chicks to feed who must be sparing with dew drops,
when Aldebaran announces the end of moisture.[36]
May God blight those who sow seeds on fields with no water;
it's like building a wall on the edge of a sandy precipice.
Alas, in ignorance I sang his praises before I knew,
wasted my laudations on an undeserving nobody.
If only I had been aware of his base origins 11.30
and his uncle's butcher's shop before he got my praises.
A man's roots make for good or bad,
as the quality of grain is determined by the seed.
My eulogies were wasted on that miscreant,
like perfume sprinkled on the bosom of an old hag.

~ ١٢ ~

ياذا افْتِهمِ مِنّي جُوابٍ يِشْتَرَى   مِثْل اللُّوالو من عقودٍ تِنْثِرا
من جاد سَمْته جاد في هذا وذا   والمَرْجِله ما هي بوَرْثٍ تِجْرا
تِسَلْسَلوا من نُوح جدٍّ واحد   حِرٍّ وعَبْدٍ والرِدي البَيسِرا
تَلْقى الجماعه من شِجِرَةٍ وحدِه   وطْبوعهم مختلفةٍ رَبّي قْدرا
يطْلَع بهم خَطْو الكِذوب الماهر   غَوجٍ ولو جُوِّد عنانه يَطْمِرا
ومن الجماعه شايخٍ مِتْشيِّخ   وكلّ النوايب يتّقي عنها ورا
الى مِشَى بالسوق الاه ملوْذَع   عن خاطرٍ يَقْضِب قطابه ما دَرى
ومن الجماعه حاملٍ مِتْحَمِّل   ما فات يومٍ ما لضيفٍ ما قَرى
ان ما يدُورِ الضَيف دَوّرِ بيته   وهو سواة العِدّ عِدٍ يِذْكَرا
ومنهمِ سواة الديك رَزّة عِنْقه   ما زان له زَولٍ بفِعْلٍ يِخْبَرا
ومن الجماعه كالضَبيب المِنْتِفخ   مِتْبَخْترٍ يَسْحب ثوبه من وَرا
كنّ الضِعيف شايلٍ سَبْع الطَبَق   هو ما درى انه خِفّ ريش الحُمَّرا
ومن الجماعه من يِنِطّ بمَرْتبه   في الدين لو هو ما يخِطّ ولا قَرا
يَدْرِق بدين الله دينٍ غادرِ   والله علّامٍ لما هو اضمَرا
ومنهم ملاّقٍ علومه بَرْقه   سِمَلّقٍ ما له مكانٍ يِخْبَرا

~ 12 ~

Listen to my verses of wise counsel, in such high demand, 12.1
like prized pearls unstrung from a necklace.
Poise in conduct and bearing is what makes for excellence;
chivalry and virtue do not depend on inherited position.
We all descend from Noah, our common ancestor:
nobles, slaves, and lowly folks without pedigree.
Though all people stem from a single tree,
their characters differ, as ordained by the Lord.
One may turn out to be a cunning, inveterate liar, 12.5
who bucks like a stallion against tightly held reins.
The self-important man fancies himself quite a shaykh
until trouble starts; then he makes himself scarce.
For fear of being buttonholed by a would-be guest,
in the alleyways he creeps along the walls and hides.
Strong men shoulder the burden of their kin:
every day they serve supper to a guest;
Visitors do not look around but head straight for his house,
as if to a famous well where the water gushes incessantly.
Some walk like a rooster craning its neck, 12.10
but they're never seen dashing out to do valiant deeds.
Others strut proudly, trailing the hems of their robes,
and remind me of a bloated spiny-tailed lizard:[37]
Puny men think they support the seven spheres,
unaware that they are as light as a sparrow's feather.
One man pretends to be of eminent rank
and religious dignity, though unable to write or read,
Falsely donning the mantle of faith,
though God knows well what he truly harbors.
Others play it safe, toadies of dubious repute, 12.15
fickle and capricious, held in no esteem:

الَى حَـلف والَى يِمـينه قـاطع   ولْسيّنـه باللطْـلطه مـا يَسْـدِرا
ومنـهم هـمَيلينه كبيرٍ حَوضَها   لا هـيب لا تِثْـمِر ولا فيهـا ذَرا
وفـيـهم من كِنّـه دقَـيلة قِنْـعـه   دِبّ الليـالي حَوضَهـا ما يِحْفَـرا
يَـدْعون للكرْمـه ولا يَـدْعونـه   والَى حَصَل شَورٍ فعنْهم يِقْصَرا
وان جا خَسـاره فهْو الاوّل منهـم   غَصْبٍ على ذِقْنه ومـاله يِعْشَـرا
وِيمـدّ الى من احْـرِبوا جمـاعتـه   يَـمّ القِطـيف او الحَسا يِتّيجِـرا
لو لا رجـاله راح مـاله صَـلْحِه   ودَقّوه دَقٍّ مِـثْل دَقّ امّ الجِـرا
وِلقَـيت بالعِبْدان عَبْـدٍ جَيّـد   كِلّ المَراجل في يِمـينه تِـذْكَرا
ولقَـيت بالاحـرار حِـرٍّ باطـل   يِسْوَى نصَيفٍ لو يباع ويِشْـتَرى
وِلقَـيت حَيّ القَـلْب فيه مْـرُوّه   والخِبل ما يِسْقيك من رَطْب الثّرى
لو اتِمَـنّى مـا يموت ثلاثـه   وباقي الجماعـه مَوتِهم حَقٍ تَـرى
الظّـفِـر بفِعْـله والكريـم بمـاله   واللي يخَـلّص مِشْكِلٍ بين الوَرى
وباقي الجمـاعـه هم ضيوف بقَـرْيَه   وِكْسَـر العَـراقي بالجمـاعـه اكْـثَرا

~ 12 ~

If they volunteer an oath, they break their vow
as they jibber-jabber incessantly.
Some men are like an untended palm: its basin is wide,
but it bears no fruit and provides no shade,
Unlike small date palms, easy to tend,
that need no one to hoe their basin at night.
Such men are not invited to a wedding feast,
nor are they summoned when council is held;
Pushovers when it comes to tribal dues, **12.20**
always the first forced to "cough up."
When their people are at war, they leave on business,
toward al-Qaṭīf or al-Aḥsā', to do a little trading:
Without their fellows, they'd give up their all for peace,
and be beaten viciously like a cur.
Among slaves you will find men of accomplishment,
second to none in feats of bravery,
Whereas among the noble born some are devoid of value,
worth only a pittance should they be bought or sold.
Chivalrous virtue is to be found among the sincere of heart: **12.25**
the callous won't even let you squeeze water from moist earth.
If I could make a wish, I'd ask that three types of men never die—
for the rest I do not care; let them die in peace:
The knight of valiant deeds, the generous spender,
the mediator who helps people resolve their disputes.
The rest of the people are idle loiterers:
of no more use than broken handles on a bucket.

~ ١٣ ~

احدٍ مبسوطٍ ومْكَيّف   ياكِل ويِنْعِم في داره
لا جا من السوق مْغَلدِم   يِلْقَى له دِرّة مَحّاره
يلْقى عَذرًا يِسْفِر وَجْهَه   تِجْلي هَمّه هو واكداره
ما يومٍ قالت وِش عِنْدِك   تِرْضَى بايساره وِعْساره
ان جاه شويٍّ قَنْعَت به   وان ما جا شيٍّ عَذّاره
واحِدٍ عنده ضَبْعَة غابه   انْطَل من عَنْطَل جوّاره
يَسْمَع حِسّه من بالمَجلِس   كنّه في راس المِنْطاره
تقلّب عَينه ثم تْحَضْرِم   هَرْجِه نَبْطٍ وبيه جْجاره
الّا ومع ذا قَشْرًا شَينه   اشْيَن من قَبْعَة الغاره
وايا هذي وايا ذيك   يا جارك ربّي بجْواره

~ 13 ~

One man enjoys a life of ease and comfort, 13.1
eating at home to his heart's content.
If he enters his house with a frown,
his eyes are livened by a pearl:
The sight of a young lady's uncovered face,
enough to dispel worries and cares.
She would never ask, "What have you brought with you?"
as serene in affluence as in times of need.
She does not complain if he brings home but little, 13.5
and she excuses him for being empty-handed.[38]
One man has a savage hyena at home,
a brutish thief forever ready to pounce
Whose yelp is heard by the men as they meet in the house,
as loud as a watchman shouting from the tower.
She rolls her eyes in fury and snarls,
and unleashes on him a torrent of abuse.
Her foul temper matches her horrible face,
more ominous than the dust of battle.
Can you imagine two things further apart? 13.10
May our Lord grant you His protection.

~ ١٤ ~

يقول الشاعر الحَبْر الفِهيم   حمَيدان المِتَّهم بالعَياره
جوابٍ يَفْهَمه من هو ذِهين   وشَطْرٍ في صعوده وانْحداره
فِكَرْت وحِرْت بالناس اجْمِعين   ومَيّزْت العَزازِ من الخَباره
اشوف الناس عِدْوان البِخيل   وخِلاّن الصِخي راعي الخَياره
ياليت الرِزْق كلّه للكرام   عزيزين النفوس بكِلّ شاره
وكِمْ شِفْت الفَهَد رِزْقِه يِفوته   وكِمْ ضَبْعٍ وقع رزقه بغاره
ولكن قَسْم ربّي في عباده   إله جَلّ في عِظْم اقتداره
الَى جاك الولد بايديه طين   وله غَرْسٍ يحَفّر في جفاره
تَرى هذاك ما ياخِذ زِمان   الى هو جامعٍ عنده تجاره
ولَى جاك الولد زِمْلوق خَندَق   ومن نَوم الصِفَر غاشٍ صفاره
يبيع وْروث امّه هو وابوه   مجيع ما تعَشّيه الفقاره
فحَذْرا ياديب تحِطّ عنده   لك بنتٍ تموت بوَسْط داره
والى جاك الامير ضرَيس يَسْحَن   يغَفّط ما تِضاعَف في جواره
تَرى هذا يِنفّر ما يولّف   ولا للجار عنه الاّ النياره
والَى جاك الامير به الحَميّه   ويَثْني دون جاره باقتداره

~ 14 ~

These are the words of a learned and discerning poet: 14.1
  Ḥmēdān, who has a reputation for irreverence.[39]
My verse is readily understood by thoughtful minds
  that can navigate the peaks and troughs of meter.
As I ponder, amazed at the human condition,
  I distinguish between honorable and treacherous men.
I see people disgusted by the ways of misers,
  and embracing munificent and charitable men.
If only wealth were the preserve of the generous, 14.5
  upright men who show fortitude at all times!
All too often the leopard fails to find nourishment,
  while the hyena's food is served up in his den.
The Lord decrees what is allotted to man,
  God Almighty, Magnificent in His power.
If your son's hands are daubed with mud
  from digging a trench around his date palms,
Before long, you'll see, your boy
  will start a business and make it thrive.
But if your son is a delicate flower, 14.10
  face pallid from sleeping well into the day,
He will sell both parents' inheritance:
  a camel's hump is not enough to sate his appetite.
A decent man should not marry his daughter to him
  for she will die within the walls of his house.
One kind of ruler only cares about stuffing his mouth,
  a grasping despot who despoils the weak in his care:
Such a chief does not attract affection, but repels it;[40]
  those under his wing have no choice but to escape.
Another kind of ruler is the emir who offers a secure haven, 14.15
  resolutely standing up for neighbors under his protection;

تَرى هذا يولِّف ما ينفِّر　　ويكبر عند كل الناس كاره
وبالحِكّام مِفتخرٍ كبير　　الى من شِفت زوله قِلت قاره
سِمينٍ للصَحن لو هو خَروف　　يدبِّر مَير تدبيره دماره
جِبانٍ ما يصادم له ضِديد　　ولا يومٍ صَخى كفّه بباره
خَفيفٍ عند رَبْعه والجماعه　　يعرفونه اخفّ من النجاره
يفاخر بالمَلابس والمُواكل　　لِمِبخَرته على راسه كَراره
ينام الليل هو والصِبح كِلّه　　وقلبه باردٍ ما به حَراره
تَرى هذاك ما ياخِذ زمان　　كمَقلع شيحةٍ ما له قَراره
وبالحكّام من يحمي الرِعيّه　　بحَدّ السَيف عن سَرقٍ وغاره
يسوس المِلْك في قَلبه وعَينه　　ومَقصوده عَماره من دِماره
سواة اللَيث جَرّاعٍ عَنوف　　يسوس المِلْك ولا يِفتق خداره
يزور الضِدّ بجموعٍ صِباح　　بُواديها ومن يَسكن دياره
للصِدقان الَذّ من الفرات　　وللعِدوان امَرّ من الخضاره
الى من البَدو داسوا كِمامه　　يخلّيهم جِثايا بالمَعاره
وبالتِجّار حَرّازٍ بخيل　　يرابي باغيٍ كِثر التجاره
وهو مِستجهِدٍ يجمع لغيره　　حِرمانٍ ولا هو باختياره
فَنى عِمره وهو ما ذيق زاده　　وماله حازمه جَوّد صراره
يِجيه الوارث اللي من بِعيد　　وهو يَقدِم على الله في وزاره

~ 14 ~

He enjoys his subjects' affection, is shunned by none,
and is held in high esteem by people of all ranks.
Another kind of ruler is puffed up with vanity and pride,
big and fat, like a flat-topped outcrop on the plain;
If he were a sheep he would make a fine, fatty dish.
The stratagems he employs to govern are his undoing.
A true coward, he avoids squaring up to his foes;
so generous that not a single coin escapes his clutches.
He carries no weight with his own circle or kin:
they know he is lighter than a sliver of wood.
He takes pride in fine clothes and choice food,
and loves perfuming his beard with incense.[41]
He lies in bed snoring well into the morning;
cold of heart, he feels no sympathy or warmth.
You can be sure an emir like him will not last:
like sagebrush his roots are easily plucked.
The true ruler provides his subjects with security
by wielding the sword against theft and attack.
Affairs of the realm are dear to his heart:
he strives to create prosperity and keep ruin at bay.
Like a fierce lion he rips the enemy to shreds,
but reigns without violating his subjects' rights.
Fearless, he takes the fight to his adversaries,
raiding both Bedouin and villagers at dawn:
Sweeter than the Euphrates to his friends,
more bitter than colocynth to his foes.
Should the Bedouin dare to break his peace,
he leaves the battlefield littered with their corpses.
Many tradesmen are scrawny hoarders,
usurers who only seek to add to their wealth.
The fruits of their labors are enjoyed by others:
driven by their nature, they hurt themselves.
No one ever gets to taste their stores of food:
their wealth is tied up in bundles.
Then from a far-off place comes the heir,
while they, dressed in loincloths, face God.[42]

وطلاّب النَوال من البخيل   كطلاّب الحَليب من الذكاره
وبالتجّار من يذكر بخَيره   وصبّارٍ على كود الخَساره
ومهّالٍ على المعَسِر ليسْره   وجيرانه وضيفه ولخطاره
ترى هذاك يدعَى له بخَيره   وينجيه الولي من حرّ ناره
لعلّه عند تفريق الحَساني   كتابه في يمينه عن يساره
وبالعِبْدان من هو دون عَمّه   وداشرهم فلا يِسْوَى حماره
يموق الى شِبَع وان جاع يَسْرِق   وكَيفاته الى شَمّ الكتاره
وبالنسوان من هي شِبْه صَفرا   والّا بالشِبه تَعْرف مهاره
وبالنسوان من هي مِثْل باقِر   وَلَدها بَيِّن فيه الثُواره
ولا للبوم يومٍ شِيف صَيد   ولا ذِكرَتْ بْقِرَةٍ بالمعاره
وبالنسوان من جِنْس الفَواسق   ولدها جِرذيٍ من نَسل فاره
وهذا من إله الناس قِسْمه   وطَبْع العبد ما هو باختياره
وصلّى الله على سَيّد قريش   عَدد ما جاوب القِمْري هَذاره

~ 14 ~

But asking for gifts from a miser
    is like trying to milk a ram.
Other merchants gain a good reputation 14.35
    because they bear heavy losses with patience,
Giving credit until circumstances have eased,
    and standing by neighbors, guests, and visitors.
From all quarters people pray for them
    asking the Lord to spare them from Hellfire.
When good deeds are reckoned at the Judgment,
    may the book be in their right, not their left, hands.
Some slaves do not measure up to their owner:
    rascals not even worth their master's donkey.
They swagger if their bellies are full and steal if hungry; 14.40
    the smell of roast meat sends them into ecstasy.
The best kind of woman is a pure white filly:
    as foals resemble a mare, so her son carries her likeness.
But if a woman resembles a cow,
    bovine dullness will be the hallmark of her son.
Just as the owl is never seen hunting noble prey,
    no cow is ever spotted on the field of battle.
Some women play fast and loose with morals:
    like rodents they give birth to rats.
God has ordained for each his destiny: 14.45
    it is not for His servants to choose.
May God bless the lord of Quraysh
    as often as the dove coos on the branch.

~ ١٥ ~

ظَهَرْت من الحَزْم اللي به　　سِيد السادات من العشَره
حـطّيت سَنامٍ باليِمْنى　　وَوْطيت الرِقعي من ظهَره
وِلْقَـيت الجُوع ابو مُوسَى　　بانٍ له بَيتٍ بالجحَـره
عليه قـطَيعة دِسْمال　　وِبْشَـيتٍ مِنبَقـرٍ ظهَـره
وحَـاكاني　وحَـاكَيـته　　وَعْـطاني عِلْمٍ له ثمَـره
ما يَرْخِص عندي مَضْمونِه　　واقول بْعِـلْمـه وَخْبَـره
الزِلْفي فيـه زغَـيوِيّـه　　اويّ ذْحوشٍ بْجـزَره
واهْـل مْغيرًا ما بهم خَيره　　وامَـيِّرهم ذاك القَـذِره
مِن قابَل خَشْم العِـزْنيّه　　فالخاطِر منقولٍ خطَـره
من قال انا مِثْل سْلَيمان　　كَرْم السامع ياكل بْعَـره
والخِيس بْوِيْليدٍ مِسْـقى　　ضَبٍ لاجٍ له بوْعَـره
والفَـيحا ديـرة عِشْمان　　ومـقابِلها ديار الزيَـره
اهْـل جـلاجل نعَـيميّه　　من دون الباب ما من ظهَره
اهـل التوَيـم راس الحَيّه　　من وطّـاها ينْـقِل خْطَره
واهـل الداخلْه النواصر　　خـاطرهم مقْطوعٍ ظهَره

~ 15 ~

Once, I came down from the stony heights, 15.1
where lies the grave of the sayyid, one of the Ten.[43]
I made sure to keep the hill of Sanām on my right
as I walked toward al-Rigiʿi's well, from the high ground behind.
There I met Famine in the form of Abu Mūsa,
who had built himself a shack in al-Ḥjarih.[44]
He was wearing a shirt made of rough cotton
under a tattered cloak full of holes in the back.
He spoke to me, and I spoke to him, 15.5
and I benefited from what he told me.
I set great store by what he confided to me
and I'll repeat his words and the facts he mentioned—
In al-Zulfi you will find some sly tricksters
and in nearby Jzerah the men are boorish louts;
Among folks of Mghēra there is no good,
their emir is the greatest piece of filth;
When you face the buttress of al-ʿIrniyyah,
you will have left the danger zone.
Anyone who claims, "I am like Slēmān of al-Ghāṭ," 15.10
pardon the expression, can go eat shit.
Al-Khīs has the strength of tempered steel,
its people holed up like lizards, protected by crags.
Fragrant al-Majmaʿah is the home of ʿUthmān,
opposite where al-Zyerah have settled.
The people of Jlājil, soft and smooth,
stay indoors and don't venture out.
The men of al-Twēm are a snake's head:
step on it and your life is at risk.
In al-Dākhlah live al-Nuwāṣir: 15.15
their visitors leave with broken backs.

~ ١٥ ~

وابن ماضي راعى الرَوضـه   ياخِـذ منـهـم رِبْع الثْـمَره
وابن نحَيطٍ راعى الحصون   الداشـر رَضّـاع البْقَـره
واهـل الحَوطه وقْصَراهـم   نِصْفٍ خَنِيث ونصفٍ مَره
واهـل العَطّار عْـرَينات   الله يَقْـطَع ذيك الشْجَـره
واهـل العَوده عند النَذْوِه   عِدّ وخـيّك وعِدّ عْشَـره ٢٠،١٥
واهل عْشَيره سَيف ومَنْسَف   وَيّ رْجالِ بْذيك الظْهَـره
واهْـل الحريّق جِحْرٍ ضَيّق   مـا ياخِـذ الّا اللي حـفَـره
واهـل تمْـير قـرَيـرِيشـيّه   ما شال العَير شال ظْهَـره

Ibn Māḍi, emir of al-Rōḍah, takes a levy
of one quarter of the harvest from the town.
The emir in charge of al-Ḥṣūn is Ibn Nḥēṭ:
that scoundrel secretly sucks milk from his cow.
Half the denizens of al-Ḥōṭah and their neighbors
love getting buggered; the rest are pansies.
The tribal group in al-ʿAṭṭār is al-ʿRēnāt;
may God eradicate their lineage.
If you invite folks of al-ʿŌdah for a meal, **15.20**
and say, "Bring your friend," you'd better prepare for ten of them.
ʿShērih folks wield the sword and serve a lavish roast:[45]
what excellent men in those rugged desert tracts!
The people of al-Ḥrayyig hide in a burrow tight:
the only way to ferret them out is by digging.[46]
In Tmēr they cut grass for a living
and carry a donkey's load on their backs.

~ ١٦ ~

قال عَودٍ زَلَف له سنينٍ مِضَت   زلّ عَصْر الصِبا والمِشيب حْضَره
حاضِرهِ بالمجالس يتالى العَصا   زِهِد فيه الوَلد والوَغد والمَره
من بِقَى معه مالٍ فهو غالي   يكْنِسون الحَصى بالعَصا عن ثِره
وِان بِقي ما معه شٍ فهو خايبٍ   قيل عَودٍ كِبيرٍ وفيه الشَره
يامجلّي تِسَمَّع نِبا والدٍ   قاصرٍ بالعَضا وافيٍ باصغَره
كلّ من لا بَعَد ساد جَدّه وابوه   لا تِردّ الثَنا فيه يالمسْخَره
وكِلّ من يبْذِر الجود في جَلْعدٍ   مِثْل من بَرْقَع الباشَق وصَقَّره
بَرْقَعه يحْسِبه فَرْخ شيهانةٍ   والخَنا باطلٍ عاطلٍ ماكَره
مِثْل بانٍ بَنَى فوق تَلّ الرمال   ما لِه اصلٍ سلوب الثَرى تقعَره
والذي يِرْتجي الفَضل عند اللِئام   مِثْل مِسْتَفْزِعٍ صاح في مَقْبَره
بارةٍ في ضَحى اليوم عن باكرٍ   عند راعى العَقِل خَير من جوهَره
وكلّ من زاره الضِدّ ولا زاوَره   ما تمَلّل حَريبه ولا ذيَّره
ثم رِدّ القَضا بالقَضا بادِره   غارةٍ بالضحى مَرّةٍ تَبهَره
وان بَغى ينْتشِر وانْت ما تِنْتِشِر   فاصْحِبه لا يبَرْقِعك يا الدوكَره
لو تِجي عابدٍ لابدٍ له بغار   ما يِحبّ القِشَر جاه من نَخْشَره

~ 16 ~

These are the words of an old man who watched the years roll by, 16.1
youth a distant memory, his hair streaked with gray.
He uses a stick to attend the assemblies,
and is held in scorn by his son, young children, and wife.
As a man of means, you remain dear to them,
and they'll brush the stones from your path,[47]
But if your pockets are empty you'll suffer humiliation:
you will hear, "Such a demanding old man."
Listen carefully, Mjalli, to the counsel of your father, 16.5
weak of limb, but a master of speech and thought.[48]
If your ancestors and father were not rulers,
then you cannot be praised? How ridiculous!
To pour buckets of munificence on bare rock
is like hooding a sparrowhawk, training it like a falcon,
In the belief that the hood is worn by a juvenile peregrine,
while the wretched bird is of worthless stock.
This is like building a house on a dune:
when the sands shift it will collapse.
Pinning your hopes of favor on ignoble misers 16.10
is like running to a graveyard shouting for succor.
For a prudent man a penny earned by a morning's honest work
is worth more than a precious stone.[49]
If the enemy strikes and you fail to repay in kind,
your foe does not get stung and feels no fear.
So retaliate at once and settle the score:
a surprise attack in the morning will confound him.
But if he is about to march and you'd rather stay at home,
why not befriend him? But don't be fooled, dimwit!
Even the monk who hides away in a cave, 16.15
hoping for a life of peace, will be disturbed.

لا توَلّى البطَيني على غِرّتِك   والصِديق اعْرِفه لِلمِضيق اذْخَره
فان بالناس نَجْسٍ وذا طاهرٍ   وآخَرٍ مِثْل طِيبٍ وذا عَرْعَره
وآخَرٍ قال احِبّك وهوكاذبٍ   طَهّر الهَرْج والقلب ما طَهَّره
وآخَرٍ من صباخ الثَرى مَنبتِه   لو بِذَرْت النِدى في يِدَيه انكَره
وآخَرٍ عند قومٍ وانا خابِرِه   لو يمالَى على بابهم سَوجِره
يا حَكايا جَرت ياعيال الحَلال   امْرها مِشْتِبِه والاديب نْشِره
من حصانٍ بِلودٍ جِذَثْ به يِدَيه   اذْبَرٍ غارِبه خارب السِكَّره
ياشوَيخ نِشا من طيورِ العشا   ضاريٍ بالحَساسات والقَرْقَره
فارسٍ بالقَهاوي وانا خابره   بالخَلا تاخذه فَرّة الحُمَّره
تاجرٍ فاجرٍ ما يزَكّي الحَلال   لو يجي صايم العَشْر ما فَطّره
عاطلٍ باطلٍ فيه من كِلّ عَيب   لو تَبي منْه بولٍ فلا يِظْهِره
لو تِجي خالتِه تَطلِبه كَفّ مِلح   مِخْطِرٍ ضِلْعَها بالعَصا يَكْسِره
ماتت امّه وهي ضِلْعَها عايبٍ   كِلّما جَتْ تِزيد العَشا كَسَّره
فيه رِبْعٍ ذِليلٍ ورِبْعٍ بخيل   وفيه رِبْعٍ خنَيثٍ ورِبْعٍ مَره
ياضِيَيب الصِفا ما تِجي الّا قِفا   ما تجي الّا مع النَخْش والنَجْحَره
مِثْل راعي جْلاجل مع ابن نحَيط   اذرِكه من زِمانٍ وهو يَسْحَره
يَسْحَرِه مِثْل ضَبٍّ هوى صِلّتِه   والمَلا لو تجي الجحر ما تَقْدَره
قال ياضَبّ هذا جَرادٍ ضِفَى   والسِبايا ثقالٍ تَبي جَرْجَره

~ 16 ~

Do not be beguiled into companionship with a sneak;
seek a true friend and cherish him for your day of need.
Some men are foul and mean, others pure;
some are like a fragrant scent, others barren as juniper trees.
Some may say, "You are so dear to me!"—a blatant lie:
they keep their tongues clean but their hearts stay soiled.
Others hail from brackish salt flats:
you can lade them with gifts but they'll stay indifferent.
If an outsider attaches himself to the group, watch out: 16.20
he may conspire with the enemy to break the lock of the castle gate.
There are tales galore about events, my friends;
fishy affairs brought to light through my intellect.
I single out a worn-out horse with crippled knees
and ulcers on his withers, about as much use as a broken lock.
I mean you, little shaykh from a flock of nocturnal birds,
fond of malicious gossip and empty chatter,
A shining knight over the coffee cups. I know him only too well:
in the desert he faints at the whir of birds in flight,[50]
A rogue trader who pays no alms tax on his wealth, 16.25
who will never offer supper to someone breaking his fast,
A despicable good-for-nothing who boasts all the vices:
he would not even give you his urine.[51]
Should his aunt ask him for a handful of salt,
she risks having her ribs broken by his cudgel.
His mother's ribs were always sore:
he'd hit her like a fiend if she didn't skimp on dinner.
A quarter of these misfits are weaklings, a quarter misers,
a quarter are buggers, a quarter sissies.
The lizard of the rocks crawls out backward 16.30
when prodded with a stick and pulled.
This is the tale of Ibn Nḥēṭ and the emir of Jlājil,
who trained his eye on him and put him under a spell.[52]
He bewitched him like a lizard hidden in his hole,
where ordinary men will struggle to coax him out.
He heard the words, "Hey lizard, there are locusts everywhere out here;
so much booty that you'll need all your strength to gather it in."

فاظْهَرِه للفِضا من كِنين الذَرا   ثم جوَّد عَنِه ساكِف المَجْحَره
ثم قال احْمِلوا ياعياله عليه   واحدٍ بَلِمِه وآخَرٍ عَقَّره
ما يِرِدّ الحَذَر عن سهومِ القِدَر   والشوَيعِر حمَيدان ياما انْذَره
بالِتحِفّظ عن الباب والطالِعي   وِاثَر القومِ مِكْتَنَّةٍ بالذَره
ياعيال النِدَم يارِضاع الخَدَم   ياغَذايا الغَلاوين والبَرْبَره
قِلْت هذا وانا في زِماني بِصير   كِلّما زان صَرْف الدَهَر كدَّره
فأيها المِرْتِحِل من بلاد الدَعَم   فوق مَنْجوبَةٍ كِنَّها الجَوذَره
رَوهِجَتْ بالعَراقيب رِبْد الضَحَى   شان رَكّابها زايلٍ ذَيَّره
لابن ماضي محمّد رِفيع الثَنا   من بَنَى بيت عَمْر النِدا مَفْخَره
ان دَعَيتِه على قالةٍ بَتّها   وان نَخَيته على واردٍ صَدَّره
ياابن ماضي جِميع القرى خلَّها   وَانْت فان طِعْتِني فاهْدِمِ المَجْحَره
فانّ اهلْها تمالي عليك العدَا   وِانها هَرْمِةٍ مِثْل خَطْو المَره
وِانّ سِكّانَها ما يِفكّونَها   مِن عدَاهم وهُم بَينهم مَنْدَره
لِقَمَة الحَتْف بانْذِرْك عن بَلْعَها   فانّها لازمٍ تَقْضِب الخَنْجَره
مِقْحِمٍ وان غَزا جَرّها من بِعيد   وابن شَكِر ان غَزَى باقِرٍ وَدَّره
ايّ طَيرٍ الى طار عَشّى الفِريق   وايّ طَير العشا ذاك ابا الصَرصَره
ماكَره كِلّ يومٍ بعَرْض الجِدار   وِكلّ ساسٍ الى اضْحَى الضَحَى نَغْبَره
بين هذا وذالك فَرْقٍ بِعيد   مِثْل ما بَين صَنْعا الى سِنْجَره

~ 16 ~

Thus he was enticed from the safety of his den,
and once out, they blocked the entrance to his tunnel.
Then came the call: "Run and catch hold of him, boys!"
one tied his jaws tight shut, the other cut his hamstrings.
Caution cannot save you from the arrows of fate,[53]
as al-Shwēʿir Ḥmēdān has warned you so often:
Keep a watch on the door and all who pass through—
your enemy is within, hidden in the granary.
Ah, these accursed children, suckled by servants,
inveterate puffers of the pipe and hubble-bubble:
My insight into this epoch gives me understanding:
if fate smiles on you, your luck will soon be roiled.
Rider, you who are about to set out from the land of al-Daʿm
on a purebred camel swift as an oryx,[54]
Hooves as rapid as a fleeing ostrich,
that in the morning bolts from her rider's shadow,
To Ibn Māḍi, Mḥammad, held in highest esteem,
born to the House of ʿAmr, famed for generosity.
When I call on him to help with a weighty matter he fixes it,
and if I utter his battle cry he sets matters straight.
O Ibn Māḍi, do not bother with the other villages:
if you take my counsel, you should destroy them in their lair.[55]
They bear you a grudge and conspire against you,
but their treachery is feeble, like that of women.
The inhabitants cannot secure their town
against the enemy because of their internal strife.
Do not swallow the fatal morsel, I warn you:
its grip is deadly: it will lodge in your throat.
Mighim covers great distances on his raids,
while Ibn Shakir on the prowl is sent packing by a cow.[56]
How can one compare a falcon that feeds an entire tribe
with a chirruping bird that flits around at night?[57]
Its nest is built right there, in the wall, plain for all to see:
you'll see it pecking the ground in the morning.
There's as great a distance between these two species
as there is between Sanaa and Sinjār.

~ ١٧ ~

مانع خَيّالٍ في الدَّكّه   ظَفرٍ في راس المَقْصوره
وان صاح صَيّاحٍ من برّا   وايَق هو وايّا الغَندوره
اليِمْنى فيها الفِنْجال   واليِسْرى فيها البَزْبوره
والى ظَهَر يَمّ السِكّه   تاخِذ جَوخَتْه السَنّوره
تِلْقاه من الخَوف يِرْهَبْن   كِنّه حَداةٍ مَمْطوره
لو تَفْتِش ثَوبه تِلْقاه   نَجْسٍ ثوبه من هِرْهوره
يَنْخى بِلْسانه ويشاني   والذَلّه سَدّت حَنْجوره
عِنْدِه عَذْرا مِثْل الحُورا   نورَه يقادى البَنّوره
كَتْف و رِدْف ونَهْدٍ زامي   وشاخه في شِبْرٍ مَشْبوره
تِلْقاها مِن طِيب المِعْلف   مِثْل الحَمْنانه مَزْكوره
تعَيزل وتبَيزل في ماله   ما قال الجِصّه مَنْخوره
تعَبَى المَثْلوث من الجِهْمه   من ليلٍ يَرْعِد تَنّوره
وتِجِّ الكِحْله من بِكْرَه   تبي به حَكّ الحَتّوره
من عَصْرٍ تَقْعِد بِفْراشِه   تبي به عَكْرٍ وعَكّوره
والزِبْدِه تجْرَعها عَذْله   تبي به ضِيقٍ وِخْروره

~ 17 ~

Mānīʿ sits on his rooftop and plays horseman, 17.1
  a hero doing battle from the safety of his parapet.[58]
At the sound of alarm outside,
  he and his belle sit up and take a peek:
Coffee cup in his right hand,
  hubble-bubble in his left.
Should he venture forth into the street,
  a cat could despoil him of his cavalry coat.
He huddles like a timid monk, 17.5
  or a miserable kite in the dripping rain.
Take a closer look at his long white shirt:
  you'll see its hems are smeared with his shit.
He goes to raise a war cry but his tongue is tied:
  he trembles with fear, and his throat tightens up.[59]
He keeps a heavenly young angel at home,
  a beauty brighter than a glass lamp,
With round shoulders, buttocks, and breasts,
  plump ankles that fill your hand,
Well fed on excellent fare, 17.10
  like a leech swollen with blood.
In her insolence she squanders his money:
  if she raids the store of dates, he doesn't blink an eye.
She gets up before dawn and stuffs herself with pastry,
  having kept the oven roaring all night long.
In the morning light she lines her eyes with black,
  longing for his hard dick to rub her pussy.
In late afternoon she sits curled up in bed,
  hankering to have the itch inside scratched.
She gorges on butter, a saddlebag full, 17.15
  to make her cunt tight and sizzling hot.

وعِنْدَه رَجْلٍ ثورٍ جَيِّد   اجمٍّ يـرْعى ـفي هَوره
اقْصى ما يِبْعِد للطايِه   والمُوقِد وِرْده وِصْدوره
لا قالت عَجِّل جا يِرْكِض   دايم ما يِظْهَر من شَوره
تِـريدِه يِبْـرِد ما فيها   لا حَلّ القارِص بِشْفورَه
حَناها وادْعَى رِجْليها   ما بين الكَتْف وصَرْصوره
ثُمٍّ تِنْخِر وهو يِشْخِر   الى ادْخَل فيها الطَنْفوره
والَى شِبَّك هـذا في ذا   ما هي حالَتْهُم مَسْتوره
تَسْمَع بالسوق مطاقَعْهُم   الى دَلّى يَكْرِب كُوره
ما هيب حريمَة قَرّاش   يِجيها يِقْطِر نَخْروره
بالليل يلقّيها صِرْمه   وَيْدَلّي يِذرا صِنْبوره

~ 17 ~

Her man passes for an excellent little bull:
    hornless, he pastures in his grassy plot.
He gets no farther than the roof of his house:
    shuttling back and forth to the kitchen.
"Hurry up!" she says, and he comes at a trot—
    he would never venture an opinion.
She lusts for him to treat and soothe
    the burning itch that stings her labia.
He puts her on her back, and folds her legs
    between earlobe and shoulder,
Then he breathes hard, she grunts,
    his glans penetrates her with force.
When their limbs are intertwined,
    this bedroom affair is not discreet:
Their shrieks and howls fill the street
    when he ties the saddle tightly on her.
She is not the wench of a poor farmhand,
    nose dripping with snot,
Who turns his back on her at night
    and lets rip without inhibition.

~ ١٨ ~

يقول حمَيدان الشاعر   ايْضـا ويْجَوِّر تَجويـره
انا من ناسٍ تَجْـرَتهـم   ارْطا الضاحي وذْوا الغِيره
والّا فـالتَـمْر محـاربهـم   حَرْبٍ ما لهـم عَنْها خِيره
ولا يطِبّ بنواجِـذْهـم   لا بالبَـرّ ولا بالدِيـره
دايـم شِهْبٍ مَلاغِمهـم   واحِدْهم يَشْرَب ما بيـره
موت المَـيّت مـا ذاقـه   ولا شـاله باظـافيـره
مـا فيهـم رَجّالٍ طيّب   الّا العِتْوي رَجْل سْوَيره
نِعْـمٍ بكْراعـه وِذْراعـه   عـند النَدْوه وعند النِيره
وسـلاح الليـل الى سَـلّه   دلّت تَضْـرِب مِـزامـيره
ـالى سَـلّه ثـمّ بَلّه   قـامت تَقْطِر مِصاهيره
ولَى مِنّه حَـضّب منهـا   واقفى واقْبَل فيهـا عَيـره
والَى مـنه تَوضّـمهـا   دَلّت تَصْفِـر مِصافيـره
دَلّى يَشْخِـر وهي تنْخِـر   ما تَفْـرِق هـذا من غَيـره
لو تَسْـمَـع حِسّ مطاقْعهـم   يَسْـمَعه النـايـم بِعْشَيره
وهو يهَـمْهِم وهي تِزْهِـم   مـا يَكْفي هـذا عن غَـيره

~ 18 ~

These are the words of Ḥmēdān the poet, 18.1
who delights in bursting vain pretensions.[60]
I hail from a people who trade in
fire bush from the desert and digestive salts,[61]
Locked in a never-ending battle with the date palms,
not a battle of their own choosing.
They never sink their teeth into this dainty dish,
not even a bite, be it in the desert or at home.
Their mouths are crusted and caked: 18.5
just one of them could drink a well dry.[62]
They live and die without ever tasting a date;
they don't even touch it with their fingers.[63]
The only one of them to enjoy any of life's comforts
is this wild tomcat, little Sārah's man.
How well honed are his fleshy arms and legs
when he digs for food or runs to escape.
When he unsheathes and wields his night sword,
his flutes strike up a tune to a beat gone wild.
Once it is drawn and gets moist 18.10
it begins to leak and drip with fluid.
He embraces her and presses her tight,
his penis moving smoothly to and fro, in and out;
Then he clasps her violently and draws her close.
you hear the slosh and squelch of their parts;
He snorts, she groans with abandon,
their pants and grunts merge into one,
In farts as loud as thunderclaps,
loud enough to make sleeping lovers sit up.
Spiritedly she neighs and he whinnies, 18.15
reaching fever pitch at the same time.

واخَذْ هذا يَضغَط هذا   ويكَوِّد تالي تَنْجيره
يِسْمَع من شِدَّة ما فيهم   كلٍّ ثَوَّر لِه تَثْويره
انا وِيّاك يابنتي   خَرّبنا نِصف هالدِيرِه
هيّا وِيّاك للصانِع   نشِير الله ثم نشيره
ياخِذ من فَيدي بالمِبْرَد   وانْتي يَنْفَخ بك مِن كِيرِه ٢٠،١٨

~ 18 ~

When they start to press as hard as they can,
    and he ties the saddle tightly on her back,
They toil away and reach climax,
    accompanied by a salvo of farts.
My daughter, you and me both,
    have brought ruin upon almost all of this town.[64]
Now let us repair to the blacksmith
    for his counsel, but first ask God's guidance.
He will restore my dick to shape, **18.20**
    and fill you with hot blasts from his bellows.[65]

~ ١٩ ~

يومٍ دَلّوا زَرارِيعنا للحَريث   رَوّحَتْ بِه سوَيره عن العَيثَرِ
العرب يِظْهِرون النَخَل والعيال   وهو يَشْري لها المِسْك والعَنبَرِ
حاطّ له حُرْمتين جِعْل ما هوب زَين   جِعْل هو عِقْب هذا يهَبْد الشَري
يومٍ جا ما عَطاني لبَيبِيْدِةٍ   اتَدَفّا بها يوم ظَهْري عَري
يومٍ جَتْنا سوَيره من العارِضِ   كِنّها ضَبْعِةٍ حَلّ فيها سْعَري
لَيت مانع الى قِلْت لِه طاعني   يوم تَوّه بمَطْلوبِه مشَبْهَرِ
قَبل تاخِذ بقَلْبِه زهَرْة الرِبيع   في ذَرى الغار غَرّه بها المَنْظَرِ
ويِتشَرْبَك بحَبْل الشَرْك بالشِبَك   ثم يِصبِح على راسه مْكَنْعَرِ
اِحترِزْ من سهوم الدَهَر بالحَذَر   وأَنْت ما لك عن اللي لك مْقَدّرِ
يومٍ قامت وشاف اللذي تَلّها   من وَراها زِمَى رِدْفٍ مْزَبّرِ
ما دَرى ان اِلنثايِل وِكثْر التراب   من وِسيع الدواخِل وهو ما دِري
ياصِبِيّ اِسْتِمع من عوَيدٍ قِضَى   الدَهَر مَدّبِه لَين ما قَصّرِ
ما بَقِي مِنه غير العَصَب والعظام   مِثل عُودٍ على الدرب ومْقَشّرِ
كِلّ مِن كان قَبلك بيومٍ وليل   شاوِرِه والخَبَر عنه لا تَقْصِرِ
حِطّ بالك لما كان اوصّيك به   فان هذي وصاةٍ على خاطِري

~ 19 ~

Our plowmen labored in the fields 19.1
while he was distracted by little Sārah.
Our folks struggle to tend palms and raise children
while he busily buys musk and ambergris.[66]
The benighted wretch fancies he should have two wives:
I hope he starves on a diet of bitter apples.
He would not even spare me a wool vest
to cover my bare back against the winter cold,
When sweet Sārah came to us from al-ʿĀriḍ 19.5
wild-eyed like a hyena struck by rabies.
How I wish Māniʿ had heeded my advice
as he embarked on life's endeavors,
Before this spring flower captured his heart,
dazzled him with her good looks in a shaded bower,
And ensnared him in her nets,
making him fall head over heels in love.
Guard against the arrows of fate,
though we must submit to what is ordained.
When she stood up and he saw her ample behind, 19.10
swelling like a massive sand dune,
The dimwit did not realize that such mounds
point to a slit as wide and cold as a trench.[67]
Now, boy, listen to an old man who has spent
his life being punished by fate
Until, frail with age, he has become a bag of bones
like dry twigs lying on the road, broken and bare.
Turn to those who have lived a life,
benefit from their counsel and instruction.
Pay attention and heed the advice 19.15
I wish to impress on your mind.

لا تِضِمّ التي ما تعرْف السوى   تجْعَل الزَين شَينٍ ولا تَسْتِرِ
يِذّن العَصْر والعَيش فوق الرَحى   والقِدِر مُوصِخٍ واللِبَن مخوِرِ
ولا تضمّ التي تِشْتِري للّغا   دايمٍ هَرجَها بالكلام الزِري
لى نِشَدها بَعلها بهَرجٍ لِطيف   طَوّحَتْ حِسَّها ما ادري ما ادْرِي
إنذفه في ثلاثٍ تِبَعها ثلاث   لاجْل تاكِل طَعامِك هَنِي مَرِي
لا تضمّ الّذي يِطّوّح طَيّها   الضحى وانْت بالمَقْبِره تِقْبَرِ
لا تِضِمّ التي قد حَكي بامّها   تحْسِب العَيب باري وهو ما بِري
ولا تِضِمّ الذي ما تخلّي العَباه   دايمٍ كِنّها تَلْعَب العَيفَري
من جَهَلْها تخلّي وَلَدها يِصيح   ما تِسَنَّع لها مَورِد ومَصْدَرِ
يوم تَظْهَر من البيت وِشْ هي تَبي   تَبي عند غَيرك طَعامٍ طِري
اِتْرَكه ياالخِبل يانكيث الحَبِل   لا تِجَزَّع ولو قيل ياالمِتْفَرِ
طَلّق العاهر وخَلّها تِنطِلِق   من حبالِك عَسَى بطْنَها للفِري
لا تضمّ الذي عينها واذْنَها   بالمزاغيل والصاير المِسْفَرِ
وِدّها كل من مَرّ مع سوقَها   من شِريف وطِريفٍ يقول اظْهَري
لا تِضِمّ الذي ما تربّى الحلال   اغْبرٍ طَبْعَها والزمان اَغْبَرِ
لا تضمّ الذي ما تِملّ الرِديف   تَسْري الليل للي لها يِحْتَري
ولا تضمّ الذي ما تخلّي الرِفيق   حينما غاب رَجْلَه فهو يِحْضَرِ
الوَعد مِثل من قال كِخّي واِكّ   في قيام العَشر وان ظَهرْت إظْهَري

~ 19 ~

Do not marry a lazy slut
    who shamelessly turns good into bad:
At the end of the day the grain is still in the quern,
    the pots have not been scrubbed, the milk has gone off.
Do not marry a gossipy chatterbox
    who can't keep her foul tongue in check.
If her husband politely asks her for something,
    she bawls, "I don't know, I don't know how!"
Repudiate her thrice and thrice again;
    that way you may enjoy your food in peace.
Don't marry a woman whose well shaft has collapsed,[68]
    who, as soon as you are buried, can't wait to have sex.
Nor a woman born to a mother of ill repute:
    don't be fooled, shame is bred in the bone!
Nor a woman who's always getting dressed to go out,[69]
    footloose and fancy-free, an irrepressible dancer
Who leaves her baby boy behind in tears:
    the slovenly scatterbrain has no sense!
What do you think she is looking for?
    Tired of you, she is on the track of a new taste.
Give her the boot, idiot, you worn-out piece of rope!
    Don't worry if you're called a donkey driver.[70]
Repudiate the floozy and set her loose,
    untie her bonds, let her belly be slashed!
Do not marry a woman who is all eyes and ears
    at doors that are ajar and cracks in the walls:
She is dying for any old passerby,
    high-born or low, to say to her, "Come!"
Nor one who doesn't attend to your goods,
    a good-for-nothing in an age of good-for-nothings.
Do not marry a wife who still clings to her co-rider,[71]
    and night after night rushes into his arms.
Nor the woman who is in thrall to a former lover:
    he is always there when her husband is away.
Their tryst starts at the late prayer during Ramadan
    with "Cough, cough," meaning: "Let's slip out;

واقْعِدي عندنا لَين ما يَظْهَرون   واظْهَري والمطوّع بهم يُوتِرِ
لا تضمّ الذي يِنْخَزن دونها   دوم نجّارها بامْرها ينْجِرِ
لو تقول ارْفِقي يامَره بالحلال   دبّري مَرْزِقك ذا السنه واصْبِرِ
بان منها من العَيب ما تكْرَهه   وباشَرت في حلالك لِه تبْذِّرِ
ولو يخطِره شرِيفٍ فلا سرّها   وِدّها انه يخطّر ولا يِخْطِرِ
وان دَخَل باشَرتْه بخبيث الكلام   وان ظهر واندِبت له يقول أبْشِري
صلّط الله عليها قبِلها تِزوم   والضعيّف بمَرضاتها مصخّرِ
مصخّرٍ مَيرٍ ما وِفّق ابن الحلال   غِبْشِته في الزّنا له يخرْخرِ
ياعَسى جِنْسها دايمٍ ما يعيش   عِنْد الاجواد وان عاش ما يكْثِرِ
من جهلها ومن سُوّ تدْبيرها   ما عليها من اللّبس ما يَسْترِ
لا تضمّ الذي ما يحجّب الحجا   دون حِجّانها كنّها تنْظِرِ
يامطوّل حْجيّه عن اللي تويق   يحسب انه الى ناظرت يسترِ
يوم تسْمع صِحِيّبٍ لها له تِويق   لو تحطّه عن الخمْس ما يقْصِرِ
هي على طبْعها عاصيٍ عُودها   ما يعدّل سِوى انه يبي يكْسِرِ
لا تضمّ الذي طِلّقت مرّتين   يوم يطري لها طاريٍ تنْكِرِ
كل يومٍ لها عند اهلْها نِسيب   واحدٍ داخلٍ وآخرٍ يظْهَرِ
شاربٍ مخّهم وآكلٍ مخّهم   غاديٍ عندهم كنّه العسْكري
لا تضمّ الذي ما لها مِن تهاب   خبْلةٍ هبْلةٍ ما لها ماكرِ

~ 19 ~

Stay with me until they file out of the mosque,
then leave as the imam mutters the last prayers!"[72]
Nor a woman who must be kept out of the food store,
but has the carpenter make her a copy of the key.[73]
If you say, "Woman, go easy on the supplies.
this year make do with little, grin and bear it,"
Her vicious temper shows its most repulsive side
as she takes charge and squanders your possessions.
When her husband receives a guest, she gets annoyed
and tells him to go out and visit, not to receive guests.
When a guest runs away from her rude tongue-lashing,
and she sends him a message, he pretends it's fine.[74]
God strike down the brazen bitch,
to whom the weakling is beholden!
Henpecked, the poor fellow is down on his luck:
nose dripping, he labors through the cold of night at the well.
How I wish that her sort were eradicated
from decent society, but if not, I wish there were fewer of them.
She is such an ignorant and clumsy housewife
that she can't even cover herself properly.
Do not marry a woman who shows herself on the roof,
and spies over the parapet shamelessly;
You can build it higher to prevent her peeping,
and conceal her when she takes a look.
But when she hears the voice of her lover down below,
raising it by five arm's lengths will hardly do.
She is so wayward and disobedient by nature,
you will have to break her in order to straighten her.
Do not think about marrying a woman twice divorced,
uninhibited in thought and action;
Husbands come and go at her parents' house:
as soon as one moves out, the next one turns up,
And this new consort feasts on their soups and meat,
taking liberties with them like a quartered soldier.
Do not marry a woman without shame or fear.
Dumb and empty-headed, she's not from a good nest.

يوم تِصْبِح تِدُوج بوسْط البَلَد   كل دارٍ تبايع به وتِشْترِي
كلٍ من كان يَرْضى بدَوج المَرَه   وِذّك انّه بنَعْلَينها يِصْطَرِ
المَرَه كِنّها الشاه بين البيوت   يَطْمَع بفَرْسَها الكلب لو هو جَرِيّ
لا تضمّ الذي راضِعة روحها   دايمٍ خالي شِقّها الايسَرِ
لا تضمّ الذي عِمْرها مِنتِهي   كان تَرجي عيالٍ بهم تِذْكَرِ
هي سِفينَتَك لكن غدا الله عليك   ما دَرَيت انها ذَبَّتْ الانْجَرِ
لا تضمّ اللذي تِلْتِفِت بالطريق   حِطّ بالك لها في قِفا العايِرِ
قِل وِش اللي مريبك على الالتفات   ياضراب الخَنا بالثلاث اظْهَرِي
يوم قَلّ الحَيا عندها واتّسَع   وَجْهَها حَلّ في عَينَها الانْكَرِ
ما دَرَتْ بالتّلِفّت سهومٍ تِصيب   بالضِمايِر بِها الكَسْر ما يِجْبَرِ
فيها بَعْض المَرَض جِعْلَها ما تِطيب   من ذنوبٍ مِضَت جِعْل ما تِغْفَرِ
وِشْ تدوّر وَراها وذا طَبْعها   كِنّ ما غَيرها في البَلَد يِذْكَرِ
لو ابوها يِهِدّ الجموع بعَصاه   او بشَلْفا على الكَبْد تَفْرِى فَرِي
او اخوها يخَلّي قِرينه يخور   مثلما خار عِجْلٍ مع السامِري
لا تضمّ الذي باردٍ جَمّها   كِلّ شٍ يابس وسَكْفَها يمْطِرِ
ما تذوق اللذاذه وعِمْرك يِروح   في قِصَى لو حَلالك من الاحْمَرِ
لا تضمّ الذي رَزْنةٍ بالمكان   صَخْرةٍ ما تقَلّل بهيب بْشَرِي
ما تِكَلّم ولا عندها لك جواب   وبِسكاته يِزيد المَرَض باكْبَرِ

~ 19 ~

She paces the streets in the center of town,
stopping for gossip at every door.
A man who allows his wife to walk the streets
deserves to be thrashed with her sandals,
For a woman about town is like a fat sheep
eyed lecherously by hungry dogs, even by the puppies.
Do not marry a woman who feeds on her own teat, 19.55
whose left breast is always sucked dry of milk,
Nor an old hag whose youth has shriveled up,
if you want offspring, bearing your name;
She may be your ship but God has put her out to sea:
weren't you aware that she had raised anchor?
Nor one whose gaze is always fixed on the street:
take up post in a corner and watch her closely!
Confront her: "What are you looking at?
Out, you lecherous hellcat! Here is your divorce thrice."
She took liberties, modesty beat a hasty retreat, 19.60
and her face assumed a saucy expression;
She did not know that glances are as lethal as arrows,
and that inner wounds do not heal.
She is unhinged—because of past sins
let her stay like that, let her be damned!
Why trouble yourself with such a character?
She's not the only eligible lady in town.
Let her father menace and wave his cudgel about,
and slice through livers with his lance;
Let her brother smite his foe until he lows 19.65
like the calf brought by the Sāmirī.[75]
Do not marry a woman whose well has dried up;
she is arid, yet unchaste; her roof still leaks.[76]
You will never taste joy but waste your life away
in dire straits, even if you have gold to spend.
Stay away from stolid women who do not stir;
you couldn't move rocks like these with a crowbar.
She never utters a peep, even in reply,
until everyone goes bilious at her stony silence.

~ ١٩ ~

لا حَديثٍ يسَلّي ولا من فراق   قَلب لا يَحْزَن وعين لا تِنْظِر ٧٠،١٩
ذا هو اللي يسِرَّه الى فارِقَتْ   لَين تاخِذ سِواها ولو تَخْسِر
لا تضمّ الذي قاضبٍ خَلْفَها   من ضَنا غيرك لْخَلْفها يَمْتِر
ما دَرى انه عليها سواة الرديف   قاضبٍ في يِدِه تَكّة المَيزِر
ومْحَشومٍ على كل حالٍ يِصير   مِخْصِبٍ وَقْتِك او مِقْصِفٍ مِذْهِر

No pleasant conversation, no separation: 19.70
a heart without feeling, an eye without vision.
It's such a relief when she makes herself scarce.
Get fresh blood to take her place, no matter the price.
Beware of a wife with children by a former husband
who tug at her skirts and are still breastfed.
The cuckold is then saddled with a fellow rider
secretly pulling at the strings of her pants.[77]
Make sure you are respected at all times,
be you affluent or scorched by drought.

~ ٢٠ ~

نِشا من غَرامِ القيل بالقلب هاجس   بـدُولاب فِكرٍ للقُوافي مـعايِس
غَـرايب بيوتٍ مِضَمِناتٍ نِفيسـه   من انواع دِرٍّ غـاليـاتٍ نِفـايِس
فيـاكاتبي قِـم هـات مَصـقولةٍ بها   تـَرْقِص لِفكري زاهيات العَرايِس
قَـرايـض نظـامٍ ناشـياتٍ لَكِنّها   فواوير موجات البحورِ الخَرامِس
فـانا الماهرِ البيطـارِ والشاعرِ الذي   تِطيـع القوافي له بليّـا تَلامِس
اصَفّي حَليّات القوافي من النِـبا   بشِبرٍ طويـلٍ للتِـفـانين لامِس
صِفى لي بها عِرفٍ مكَنّى بنِطْـقها   مهَذَّب لسانٍ فاصِحٍ غيرِ خارِس
افكّـر بمعنـاهـا بِعـيدٍ مَرامَهـا   وعـصرٍ بها لي من جديدٍ ودارِس
ولا نيب اردّ الراس الّا لِمن غـدا   يجيبه على ما هوب للفهم طامِس
فـما كل من يَنْفَخ عـلى الكِيـر صانع   ولا كل من يَرْكَب على الخَيل فارِس
وحِلْو النبا يِسْقي ظما القلب مثلما   بالامواه يِسْقي نابت الزَرْع رايِس
الى عـاد مـا للقـلب يومٍ منـادم   فله في غريب القيل خِلٍّ موانِس
ان كان قَبل اليوم لي راحـةٍ بهـا   احـاد بْسِفَـر ناهيـات الانافِس
حَريـصٍ على مَـرْقَى صِعيبات العلَى   بِهـمّة شِجّاعٍ للملاقا معـانِس
تـرى ما بعَيـني عن مَرام العلى عَمى   الَى قَلّ عنها شَوف من لا يمارِس

~ 20 ~

The urge to speak in verse burst forth 20.1
    from inside, shaping my rhymes: [78]
Exquisite lines studded with precious content,
    strings of pearls from the choicest shells.
My scribe, bring a pristine sheet of paper,
    and let primped damsels dance to my tune—
Melodic verses that swell and roll
    like roaring waves on a pitch-black sea.
I am the expert craftsman who forges verses, 20.5
    working the meter effortlessly.
I pick intricate rhymes from memory's store,
    with a hand that reaches into the inner recesses of art.
The poetic skills I have mastered let me speak
    with polish and eloquence, so unlike a mute.
I ponder poetry's wide range of meanings,
    the new ones of our time and the remnants of old.
I pay no attention to any comment
    unless it shows a correct grasp of meaning.
To be a blacksmith you don't just fan the bellows; 20.10
    riding a horse does not make you a knight.
Useful and pleasant words slake a heart's thirst
    as irrigation quenches dry crops;
When spirits sag for lack of company,
    solace lies in befriending my peerless verse.
If in olden days I enjoyed some leisure,
    now I travel far and wide without respite.
I am bent on scaling the dizzying heights,
    with the zeal of a warrior ready for combat.
My eyes are drawn to the far horizon, 20.15
    unlike those blind to its attractions.

لي هِـمّةٍ تقْوى على قاسي الصِفا   اكَلّف بها عَزمي لِهيب المجانِس
لهـا مَـنْزلٍ فوق السـماكين نايف   وثانٍ لها في حـايرِ الفِكرْ حـابِس
الَى مـا توكّدت الجفـا من رِفاقـتي   ودَبّت من الداني علـيّ النوامِس
تَخيّرت لي عنهـم بالاوطان مَنْزل   وارْخَصْت غـاليهم ببَيع الدنافِس
وسَلّيت نفسي عن هَواهـم وقرْبهُم   بقـرْبي كرامٍ ما تعرْف الدِسـايِس
جِفَوني وعـافوني ونِسـيوا جِمايلي   من القِلّ واوْروني وجيهٍ عَوابِس
ياما سَهَرْت اللَيـل الاحـظ قُوامِهُم   لَى صار كلٍ في كَرى النَوم غاطِس
ياما وَثّقت النَـفْس بحْبال وِدّهـم   واقْنَعْـتَها من زادهـا بالبِسـابِس
امَضّي بهم سَهْلٍ ولا بي جِفـاسـه   وباللين ما لي من اخواني مجانِس
الى الله مـا جَورِ الليـالي ومَكْرَهـا   ومن لا يجِنّه مِدْهِشات الغَوامِس
احَسْب انّني دِرْعٍ حَصينٍ لحيّهـم   وزَبْنٍ لِهم عن ضَيم سُود النواحِس
فلمّا عرفْت اني على الذِلّ عندهـم   وبي طاوعوا حَكْي الوشات المناجِس
بوَجْه الرِضى صَدّيت عنهم ولا لهم   من الوِدّ عِندي وَزْن بعض النوامِس
فلا اظِنّ من يَصْبِر على الهُون والرِدَى   ذِهـينٍ ولو زَوله للالباس تارِس
ومن بالغَبن يـرْضَى فهو صار كالذي   لسُمّ الافاعي بالتِجاريب لاحِس
ومن لا يصون النَفس عمّا يدَنّسَه   ويازي لثوب مْشَرّف العِزّ لابِس
تهـاوَن بقَـدْره كِلّ هَـيسٍ من المَـلا   جَهـارٍ وكلٍ له بالاقدام دايِس
الى عـاد طَير الحِرّ في مَنْزل الحدا   وطَير العقاب امْسَى له الرَخم فارِس

~ 20 ~

My ambition is harder than the hardest rock,
and fires my determination with passionate zeal:
It has shot my fame beyond Arcturus—
and it is also firmly locked in my thoughts.[79]
If my fellows treat me without due respect,
and my kinsmen begin to nettle me,
Then I choose a homeland far away,
leaving loved ones behind, because of these dolts.
I console myself for the loss of warmth and love
with the society of frank and honest noblemen.
My folks had forgotten my bounty in hard times,
as, cold and hostile, they met me with a scowl.
For many nights I watched the stars rise,
the only one awake, not deep in sleep:
I had put my trust in the strength of our bonds
and made do with scraps of food.
I was always easygoing, never rude;
peerless is my kindness to my kin.
O God! The tyranny of Time, its tricks and snares:
none is spared its shocking outrages.
I protected them like a coat of mail,
I was their refuge from calamitous harm.
When I felt that they held me in contempt,
and that they favored my filthy detractors,
I was content to turn my back on them:
my feelings for them are as good as dead.
To stay on in disgrace and ignominy is, I think,
unwise, no matter the finery I may wear.
If you choose to lie back and resign yourself,
that's like licking venom just to see what happens.
If your soul is not kept unsoiled and pure,
its honor protected, swaddled in pride,
Your esteem will be spat on by any lowlife
in public, and trampled upon by all.
True, noble falcons will be valued as low as kites,
eagles ranked below vultures,

~ ٢٠ ~

وصار الرِدي يازي علـى كِلّ خـيِّر   وجارت على صِفْر السموم الخَنافِس

اجَل عَنك ذي دِنيا غَرورٍ بِحِل بَها   على حـالها ذي كِل نَبْـهٍ و رايِس

فـلا يِرتِجي فيها المشَـقّى مـرونه   الَى عاد كَفّه من ثَرى المال يابِس

وعِزّ الفِتى فيـما حَوى من حطامَها   يِمينه لوهو من قطاطٍ حساحِس

ودنيـاك هـذي لو لِحِيٍّ تِـزَخـرَف   ولو فَـرِّشَت ديباجها والسَـنادِس

لي هِـمَّةٍ من فَـضْل رَبّي تِصِـدّني   عن الزَيغ فيها وارْتِكاب المِـدانِس

وقَلْبي على الهِجْران اقْسَى من الصِفـا   الَى اوْحَيت قَول الضِيق من كِلّ حافِس

هــذا نِبـا مِن هو مِن الله يِـرتِجي   جِميـلٍ وهو من رَحْمِته غَير آيِس

وصـلّوا عـلى خَير البَـرايا محـمَّد   عَدَد ما لَعَى القِمْري بِجِذب الغَرايِس

Scoundrels will find welcome with the generous,
beetles seek refuge with deadly scorpions.
This fickle world beguiles and perplexes[80] 20.35
even the shrewd and the savvy.
She shows no mercy to anyone in dire straits,
even if, dirt poor, he has no penny left.
A man may come from a litter of scrawny cats,
but his prestige equals his worldly wealth.
The world entices you with luxury,
parading in brocade and gold-threaded silk;[81]
Thanks to our Lord my aspirations stop me
from going astray and falling into evil ways.
My heart is hard as rock, determined to leave, 20.40
when oafs call me names that unsettle my mind.
In presenting these views I put my hope in God;
I do not despair of His kind compassion.
Now say prayers for Muḥammad, the most excellent of men,
as often as the doves coo on the curved branches of the palm trees.

~ ٢١ ~

الاموال تـرْفع من ذَراريه خـانسِه   والقِـلّ يهفي ما رفَـع من مَغـارْسِـه
الا ياوْلدي صِـفْـر الدَنانيـر عـندنا   تـرفَـع رْجـالٍ بالمُوازين باخْسِـه
وكِم تـرْفَـع الامْوال من فَـرْخ باشَق   تعَـلّى عـلى حِـرٍّ بكفّيـه فـارْسِـه
بـذا الوقت ذا كَثْرَتْ وشاةٍ وصَوّروا   تِصاوير ما لا صار بالزُور طامْسِـه
يقولون ما لا صـار منّي ولا جَـرى   شـَيـاطين ما يُومَنْ بها من وِساوْسِـه
اهـل بْـدَعٍ كِم فَسّـدوا من عَشـيره   وخـلّوا مَـنازِلهم من العِلْم دارْسِـه
قـلّوا هـل الفِعْل الذي يِقْـتِدَى بْهم   وكَثْـروا مُواليـد النجوس المِطـافْسـه
الى مات من نسْل الحَساسيد واحـد   ولا ظـاهرٍ تِسْعـين مِـمّا يجانسِـه
شـاهدْت بالحادي شَياطين مَذْهَب   مَحـاريث سُوٍّ بـل نجوسٍ مناجْسِـه
تعِـدّ الرِدَى عـنّي ولا تَنْقِـل الثَـنا   كِتـاتيب سُوٍّ عن شِـمالي مْراوْسِـه
الى زَلّ مـنّي كِلْمـةٍ مـا عَقـلْتـها   الى حـاضـرٍ هـذا لهـذا ينـادِسِـه
بَنوا فوقها اصحاب الوِشايات واصْبَحت   لهـا وَشْـمةٍ زَرْقـا وبالخَـدّ لاعْسِـه
وبالنـاس من يُورِيك رُويا صِـداقِه   وهو سـارقٍ سَدّك وما قِلْت بالْسِـه
انا شَـيّلوني نَقْـلةٍ مـا حَـمَلْتـها   ولا حاطَها فِكْري ولا اخْتَلّ هاجْسِـه
وقـالوا هل الفَضْـل الذي تاجد الثّنا   تَرَى القَول فيك اليوم كَثْرت نِقارْسِـه

~ 21 ~

Wealth elevates the children of the vulgar herd 21.1
as penury fells the lofty, crashing down like tall trees.
The gleam of gold dinars, my boy, is all it takes
to raise men of otherwise trifling weight.
Money sends many a lowly sparrowhawk soaring
high over peregrines with sharp talons.[82]
In these times of ours, backbiters thrive and spread their lurid tales,
figments of their imagination clothed in perjury.
Theirs is a smear campaign, far from the truth, 21.5
the whispering of devils who skulk about and lie in ambush,
Heretics who scheme to corrupt the society of men
and banish decency and truth from their homes.
Paragons of virtue have become few and far between,
and a wave of newborn filth has taken their place.
For every malevolent envier who dies,
ninety spring up to take his place.
In this twelfth century I observed the evil ways of devils
hard at work planting the seeds of hate—defilers![83]
They tarnish my name and never speak well of me: 21.10
like evil guardian angels, they give currency to calumny.
If, inadvertently, I utter an indiscretion,
they nudge each other and exchange malicious looks.
Slanderers have taken their cue from them to daub me
with a large dark tattoo, tracing it on my cheek.
Some folks make a show of friendship toward you,
learning your secret thoughts in order to inform on you.
They saddled me with a load of calumnies—
things I had never considered, that had not even crossed my mind.
Honorable men, known to all for their virtue, 21.15
told me, "They are out in their masses to hound you,"

يِقولون لي شَيخ الحَنيفي هَجيتِه   حاشا مَعاذ الله ما نِيب دانْسِه
والله مع البَطحا مع البَيت والصِفا   وما شَرَّف المَسْعى إلهي بدانْسِه
فلا قِلْت ما قالوا ولا اقول بالذي   جَيبِه نِقيّ العِرْض بيضٍ مَلابْسِه
عن اتْيان صَرْف الشَين والحَسْد والرِدى   بْعيدٍ وذاك الوَجْه ما نِيب ضارْسِه
فلا اذِمّ شيخٍ يَقْصِر الحَكي دونه   ولا اذِمّ قومٍ تِرْتِكي في مِجالْسِه
على داركم كَم صبّحوا من قِبيله   وكم لايعوا من دار قومٍ فوارْسِه
في عن جميع اللي يدنّس مجنّب   حاشا فلا قِلْت الذي انت هاجْسه
ولا ناب مَجْنونٍ ولا ناب خامِل   ولا شاربٍ خَمْرٍ عَتيقٍ مهاوْسِه
ولا ناب سَكْرانٍ ولا فيّ صَرْعَه   بَلَى الله من هو قِد بلاني بتاعْسِه
فقِلْت لعِثْمان الكريم بْن مانِع   وكِلّ فِتَى ياوي الى من يوانْسِه
هو مارثٍ للجُود والدين والهدا   بعيدٍ عن افعال الرِدى او مدانْسِه
رِموقٍ لعَين الراي ما هو مْغفّل   الَى صار في بعض المَعاني مسايْسِه
فهَل تِرْتِجي لي يابن سَيّار جانب   من العِذر والهَجْس الذي انت هاجْسِه
قولك فلا يصْفي الَى طاح طايح   وعَينِه لمِثْلك بالملاقاة عابْسِه
فقِلْت لعِيسَى دنّ لي عَيدِهيّه   لها قَبْل هذا العام عامَين جالْسِه
رَعَتْ مَرْبَع الغِيطان للرِجْم والشفا   الى الحَرّة العِلْيا سِقاها بطامْسِه
سَرَتْ من تْوال الليل تُوحي دِنينَها   كما اطْواب حَرْبٍ ليلة الزَحْف راجْسِه
كِنّ اشْتعال البَرْق بِرْكون مِزْنَها   سَنا رَوشَنٍ عالٍ تَلامَع مِقابْسِه

~ 21 ~

Explaining: "You lampooned Wādi Ḥanīfah's shaykh." [84]
    God forgive me! I would never stoop to sullying his name.
By God, by the valley of Mecca, by the Kaaba and al-Ṣafā
    and the holy men who walked there:
They lie! I could not say a word against someone
    as pure and radiant as he, his honor unblemished.
I keep clear of vile speech, envy, and mean behavior,
    for I am anxious not to disgrace him.
I will not blame a chief beyond reproach, **21.20**
    nor will I blame the men who attend him at his assembly.
Throughout the land they surprised many enemies in their homes
    and crushed the pick of their cavalry.
It is my nature to stay away from filth:
    how could I say the things you think I do?
I am neither raving mad nor a fool,
    I do not sip well-aged, heady wines,
I am not a drunk or given to bouts of epilepsy.[85]
    May God send these curses on my tormentors.
I spoke my mind to my kinsman ʿUthmān ibn Māniʿ, **21.25**
    for it is natural to seek out likeminded company.
Endowed with munificence, piety, and good sense,
    he is eager not to soil himself with vile acts.
No dimwit, he grasps the heart of the matter,
    clear-sighted and tactful in dealing with thorny issues.
So, Ibn Sayyār, may I harbor any hope at all
    for pardon, considering the premonitions you have had? [86]
You said, "Bended knees will not appease him:
    in battle his frown terrifies men like you."
I ordered ʿĪsā to bring me a riding camel, **21.30**
    one in excellent shape after two years of rest.[87]
It roamed the spring pastures toward al-Rijm and the uplands,
    as far as the high lava fields drenched by the rains
That arrive toward the end of night with a mighty din,
    like the thunder of cannons fired in a night attack,
From clouds ablaze with flashes of lightning around their edges,
    like torchlight flickering on the top floor of a reception room.[88]

سَرَتْ بحَرْف الكاف والنون ساقَها غَرْبيّةٍ تَحَدّى الصِبا من نسانْسِه
تِجِرّ هَشيمِ العام من كِل تَلْعَه وكم عِشّ طَيرٍ في ذَرَى الطَلْح داعْسِه
تقَلّب مجْارٍ حْزومها من محَلّها جميع البِطاحي يِرْتوي منه غارْسَه
ليا ما تَراكَب نَيّها فوق وَسْقَها زَهَت دَلّها ما له جِنيسٍ يجانْسَه
سَرَتْ من رُبى دار ابن سَيّار كِنّها سِبِرْتات حزمٍ صارخاتٍ هجارْسِه
الى الجِبَل الرَعْن الذي ياجِد الذَرى لمِن خاف من امْرٍ للاذهان عامْسِه
تِطامَس بلال القَيظ شَرْوى سِفينه عن الغَرْب يِقْعِدها صِبا عن نسانْسِه
مع الصِبْح يُوضي بَرْقها مِسْتِخيله غَرايس نخيلٍ في ذَرَى العِزّ طامْسِه
تفَيّض على دارٍ وكارٍ ومَوكِب وحُكْم نِظيفٍ ما يصافي مناجْسَه
رِفيع الثَنا عبد الله ابن معَمّر إله المَلا عن صاحب العَين حارْسِه
هِزَبْر التَلاقي واحش الطَرْف والحِمى وراعي جْفانٍ تِجْري القاع دانْسِه
وان قَنّصَتْ شِيخانَها في حْصونَها فهو فيه هِمّاتٍ تُواما عَرامْسِه
بِعيدٍ مجال الراي ما يَسْمع الهذا ولو جاه من اصْغَى جِليسٍ ملابْسِه
ذِكَر فيه فارس خِصْلِتَينٍ من الثَنا وزِدْت بْثلاثٍ واربعٍ ثمّ خامْسِه
كِريمٍ على الاقْفا وسَمْتٍ وهَيبَه وثَوب الثَنا عن جِمْلة الناس لابْسِه
وان دَلّبحن رِكّاب خيله عن القَنا وراحَنّ طِفْحٍ في حَنايا كرابْسِه
له سابْقٍ لا شافت الخَيل مِدبَحِه فهي فيه عَرْجا للمَلابيس دايْسِه
صِفيٍ نِقيٍ ما يرافق بخِذْعه الى من كِلٍ خَشّها في مَلابْسِه

~ 21 ~

The downpours are created by divine command,[89]
driven by a gale from the west that routs the eastern breeze.
The dead wood of the last year is swept along by the deluge,
along with birds' nests once hidden in acacia trees.
The torrent churns up stones from rugged hills,
and floods palm gardens in the valleys downstream.
Grazing has piled layers of fat on my camel's back,
and produced a mount of outstanding beauty.
She sped away from the rolling lands of Ibn Sayyār,
like a flock of birds speeding over hillsides where foxes bark,
Toward the shelter of a mountain cliff
where refugees are safe from terrors that daze the mind.
In the shimmering air of midsummer, my beast surges like a ship
struggling against a western gale that routs the eastern breezes.
At dawn, a vision like the promise of distant lightning:
proud palm gardens planted in a safe stronghold—
You, my messenger, have reached a sanctuary of repute and glory,
known for the fairness of its rule, untainted by corruption.
ʿAbd Allāh ibn Muʿammar deserves the highest respect,
may the Lord of humankind guard him from the evil eye!
A lion feared in battle, its gaze fierce, its temper raging;
a host whose platters spill fat on the ground.
Other shaykhs hunt close to their castle walls:
his zeal makes hardy camels sway from fatigue.
He is farsighted and is not moved by idle talk,
even if it comes from his closest companions.
The poet Fāris attributed two noble traits to him,[90]
but I will add a third, a fourth, and then a fifth:
Generous in his gifts, exquisite in poise and dignity,
he wears the robes of praise most graciously.
When cavalrymen cower from the flying spears,
and the speed of their charge lifts them from the saddlebows,
His racer, seeing the other warhorses bolt away,
prances and curvets, trampling on fallen knights.
Truehearted and pure, he has no truck with treachery,
even if others have concealed it in their clothes.

وضَيف العشا يَلْقى العَشا حَول بيته   ونَسْر الضَحى يَلْقى الغَدا في مِداوْسِه
خَذى العَدل من كِسْرى ومن حاتِم الصَخا   ومن احْنَف حِلْمه ومن عَمرِ هاجْسِه
وهو مِثْل شَطّ النيل ما هوب نِقْعه   الَى بال فيها واحدٍ قيل ناجْسِه
لَك الله ما قَولي بْباغٍ وفاده   عندك ولا كَفّيك منها بيابْسِه
ولكن عِذْرٍ من حَكايا مناجِس   رِماني بها سَلْبٍ تَعاقَب رِسايْسِه
وانا طايحٍ طَيحة جدارٍ متِسانِد   رفيع البنا ما تُوحِي الّا تقايْسِه
وانا زابنٍ زَبْنَة دريكٍ من الظِما   يُوقِف على الرِقعي شِفاياه يابْسه
وانا طايحٍ طَيحة هَزيلٍ مقَصِّر   عَدَتْه الرَعايا خايفٍ من فَوارْسِه
الَى طاحوا ابنا وايلٍ طِحت مِثْلهم   الى حاكمٍ عادل وللمِلْك رايْسه
وانا والذي نَزّل تبارك وهَل اتى   وطه وياسينٍ والاعراف خامْسِه
فلا قِلْت ما قالوا ولا اقول بالذي   جَيبه نقِيّ العِرْض بِيضٍ مَلابْسِه
ولا فاه من فاهي على الغَير كِلْمه   حذا حِبّ من احْيا مِن الدِين دارْسِه
انا اقول ما يِقْفي الى طاح طايح   ولا قويٍ بالمِشاحا يعاكْسِه
وانا كِنْت للدين الحَنيفي تابع   قَولي لفِعْلي فيه والحَقّ آنسه
ياشَيخ اقْبَل عِذر مِن جاك طايح   الى الله ثُمّ اليك والكَفّ يابْسِه
ان قِبَل عِذري قَبْله الله في اللقا   وان وَفْرِه ما قاس الاجيال قايْسَه
تموت الافاعي سُمّها في نْحورها   وكم من قِريصٍ مات ما شاف قارْصِه
وصلّوا على خَير البَرايا محمّد   ما غَرْهَد القِمْري بخافي غرايْسِه

~ 21 ~

In the evening, guests are fed supper in his house,
while vultures dine on his battlefields.[91]
His models are Chosroes for justice, Ḥātim for generosity,
Aḥnaf for forbearance, and ʿAmr for cunning.[92]
He is like the mighty Nile, not a shallow pond
sullied when someone pees in it.[93]
My praise is truly for your sake, not for any reward; 21.55
to you, though your liberal hands never run dry,
I offer my apology for the foul aspersions
cast on me by riffraff—inveterate liars.
I fall on my knees and collapse like the wall
of a tall building crashing loudly to the ground.[94]
I seek your help, for I feel that I am dying from thirst,
lips parched, at the lip of al-Rigʿi's well.
I kneel before you like a feeble camel, worn thin,
left behind by the herd, fearful of predators.
Just as your Wāyil kinsmen kneel before you, so do I kneel 21.60
before a just ruler and skillful leader.
By Him who sent down Tabāraka and Hal Atā,[95]
Ṭā Hā, Yā Sīn, and al-Aʿrāf, five chapters from the Qur'an:
I swear I did not say what they said I did, nor would I speak against one
as pure and radiant as you, a man of honor unblemished.
Not a single word of disparagement was heard on my lips,
only love for the man who has resuscitated our moribund religion.
Surely a man such as he will not dismiss a supplicant,
because no one can face up to him in battle.[96]
I profess myself a follower of the pure religion, 21.65
always, as proven by my deeds, faithful to the truth.
My shaykh, accept the excuses of a supplicant
who implores God, then you, for I am completely without means.
If he accepts my apology, may God welcome him on Judgment Day;
if he rejects it, the course of my life cannot be determined.[97]
Some vipers die from the venom in their throat,
some men die from a bite without seeing the snake.[98]
Now say prayers for Muḥammad, the best of men,
as often as the doves coo in the trees.

~ ٢٢ ~

الايامِ مـا يِـرْجَى لِهن رْجوع   غَـدَتْ بخِـلّانٍ لنـا ورْبوع
مَـرَقت من الدِنْيـا بيَومٍ ولَيـله   واعِـدّ سبوعٍ من وَراه اسْبوع
الايامِ لو تِخْلِف بيومٍ عَذَرْتَها   لِهن بالقـرون المـاضيات وْقوع
وسُود اللّيالي ما دِري عن بطونِهن   تِمْسي عشارٍ وِيصْبِحِنّ وْضوع
انا مِسْتِجيرٍ بالوِلِي عن شرورِهن   علومِ الرِدَى يِلْفِي لِهن رْموع
وانا ادْري بعِلْمِ اليوم وامْسٍ وما مِضَى   وباكِـر فغَـيبٍ والامورِ تْبوع
ومن عاشَر اصحاب التِهامي ولو نِجا   من رَبْع يِنْشي فـي رباه طْبوع
وانا احِبّ يومٍ ما اجي فيه مِذْنِب   ولا نيب مِـفْراحٍ ولا بجْزوع
واحِبّ صياح القَيظ وِرْدٍ وصادر   وصياح غـارات الرِبيع تْروع
وانا احِبّ جلوسي عند حيٍّ يِفيدني   ولا مَـيّتٍ مـا مِن وَراه نْفوع
وانا احِبّ قعودي عند قَومٍ تعِـزّني   لوكان فيهم من صـلَيب طْبوع
وانا احِبّ نَومي بين غِيدٍ دواِلح   الَى مـا يِجي غَيـظٍ بِهن وِهْزوع
ولا دَين ديّانٍ ولا ظُلْمِ حاكِم   يِجُورِ ولا يِعْذَل عـليه خْدوع
فيامانع اِشْرِف لي على راس مَرْقَب   الَى بان من شَمْس النَهـار طْلوع
لَعـلّ على الطَيري شَـلايا ظَعـاين   تِقـافَن مع وادي الخَـليف رْبوع

~ 22 ~

No use praying for the return of the days
    that snatched away our friends and kin.
A day and a night, and then our time in the world is up,
    while I counted off the weeks, one by one.[99]
But we can excuse Time if it misses a day or two,
    busy as it was creating havoc in the past.
What the dark nights carry in their bellies is unknown,
    inseminated at dusk, giving birth at dawn.
I seek refuge from their evils with the Lord,
    in revulsion at the world's odious ways.
The affairs of today, of yesterday, and earlier, these I can fathom;
    but we don't know what lies in store tomorrow.
Even if you escape safely from the company of a backbiter,
    you still face the risk of being infected by his traits.
My favorite day is one passed without sin,
    a day with neither merriment nor anxiety.
I like the noise of herds at the well in midsummer,
    I fear the yells of attacking raiders in the spring.[100]
I enjoy an edifying chat with a lively wit,
    not the company of a dull and useless boor.
I am gracious when people treat me with respect,
    even if they have some pariah traits.[101]
I am fond of sleeping in lush palm gardens
    unless I must pay the price of rage and shame.
I do not relish a usurer's debt or the tyranny of a ruler
    whose oppression and deceit are beyond censure.
Now Māniʿ, climb yonder lookout for me,
    at the first rays of the rising sun,
And see if you can spot a caravan's tail at al-Ṭēri,
    carrying our folks away down Wādi Khlayyif,—

~ ٢٢ ~

رَبوعٍ لِنـا يوم اللَيـالي مـرِيفـه   واليوم مـا عـادوا لنـا بِـرَبوع

ان كان بايام الرَخـا لي مَعـارِف   غَدَوا مِثل بَرّاق السَراب لَموع

فلَى يانَخَلاتٍ لي على جال عَيلَم   حَدايقِ غِلْبٍ شَوفِهِن يَروع

اخَذت بِهن عامَين حِيلٍ زوافِر   من القَيـظ ما خلّنّ في ضَلوع

فلَى يانَخَلات الصَدْر جِضّنّ بالبِكا   وهِلّنّ ياحِذب الجِريد دْموع

حلفت يالما ما تِذوقِنّ بِـرْدِه   مِنّي ولا يِسْقى لِكِنّ جذوع

غَلاكِنّ عِندي قَبل هـذا وانكِرِن   عَليكِن مَيلات الزِمان تْصوع

الَى اذَنْنّي من ضَيم الاصحاب عِفتِهن   ولو هِنّ على شَطّ الفرات شْروع

انا بالسِما رِزْقي ووَعْدي ومَطْلبي   ما هوب في صَبْخا مَراغَة جُوع

تِقَـلّلت من دارٍ وايّا مَنـازِل   وقَبلتها حَـثوَة تـراب كسوع

ياعـاير القَـصب الجنوبي لَعَلّني   اشوفَك من تَحْت السَراب لَموع

نَخيتْ قَـرْمٍ من عَيالي مصَـلّط   الَى نـزِر ما ذاق الطَعام اسْبوع

تَرى ياوِلدي من ثَمَّن الخوف ما سِطا   والانجاس ما خلّوا سِبيلك طَوع

لك عِدّةٍ واعْدادها ما تِـزيدها   والاجـال مـا تَقْوى لِهِنّ دْفوع

فـلا يَلزِم القـالات من لا يِشيلَها   ولا تَلزِم رِقـاب الحَريـم ذْروع

تَـرى المِقـابر نِصفَها من حَريمها   لوكان في وَسْط البيوت مْنوع

وانا ياوِلدي ما انا الذي قَطّر الدما   وجـا الشَيخ يِبْكي عَـبرةٍ وِدْموع

ولا شَكّ فالهِندي قضاكِل عاجز   وشَـراب من دَمّ الخَصـيم كُموع

~ 22 ~

Kinsmen who in earlier times brought me joy and delight
but now are my close fellows no more;
They were friendly with me in days of plenty and ease,
but then flickered and became a shimmering mirage.
My beloved palm trees at the well's edge,
you lovely garden of royal trunks crowned in green;
For two miserable years I toiled there fruitlessly,
as blistering midsummer blasted my frame:
You gorgeous row of palms in the front, shudder and sob,
shed tears, you branches heavy with ripe fruit![102]
Then I swore that I would not let you taste cool water
from my hands, that I would leave your trunks to desiccate—
You were my proudest possession until I was betrayed
by Time and battered by its wicked blows.
Even palm trees on the banks of the Euphrates would be loathsome
if for their sake I put up with unjust treatment.
All I require and desire, all that is promised, is in heaven,
not in a salt flat where hunger stirs up the dust.
I departed, and though it was such a marvelous abode,
I bade it farewell by kicking up dust in its face.
Ah, southern corner of al-Qaṣab, I long so much
to catch a glimpse of you beneath a mirage!
I appealed to the honor of my courageous son
who abstains from food for a week if rebuked.[103]
My boy, if guided by fear, you will not sally forth:
villains will not willingly make way for you.
Take only what you need and travel lightly:
one cannot ward off what destiny has in store.
Arduous tasks are for the strong to carry out,
women do not clothe their torsos in chain mail.[104]
As you know, graveyards receive their share of women,
though they spend all their lives safely at home.
By nature, my son, I am not one to shed blood,
to inflict losses that make old men weep and sob.
The sword's blade is the last resort:
thirstily it gulps down the enemy's blood.

فيَاناق مِن جبّانـة الوَشْم ثوّري   بـرَدّ الخَبَـر والعـالَمـين هَجوع
تبُوج الفيـافي عَن مَرامي خشومِهـا   والصِبحْ زمّـات الهضـاب تْـروع
أبي نَجْـعـةٍ لمحـمّدٍ ابن معـمَّر   والارْياف انا مـاني لَهـا ِبنْجوع
ياما مَـلَتْ يمْنـاه من بَطْن جايع   لمـا غَـدَتْ بنت الحصـان تبوع
يِسْراه ما تَبْـذِر من الشَرّ حَبّه   وِيمْـناه تَبْـذِر بالجـميل زْروع
خذا السّمت والمَعْروف والصِدْق والنِقا   وَحِـيدٍ ولا يومٍ يِقـال خَـدوع
ولا ذار خَيـل الجـار في كِلّ مَنْزِل   وخَـيل العـدَى ياما لِهِنّ يْروع
تبَـدّلْت بـه جـزْوٍ رجـالٍ تنَكَّروا   ولا يـرْتِجَى لارْيا العَوامّ نْفوع
الَى زَعَل هذا اوْ رِضَى ذا وقوطَرَت   طَـرايد جفـالٍ صَكّهِنّ فْـزوع
فانا مِثْل عَودٍ كِبْر في دار عَيِله   وخَـلّوه سـفي تال الزمـان يْسوع
يالَيتني بِشْراك حِزْوَى على الرَخا   ولا البَصْـرَة الفَيحا وَراي طْموع
امّـا ِبني زَيـدٍ فـاوَيّا قِبِيله   لولا انّ فيهُـم مِن صـلَيب طْبوع
ولِقَيتْ بالمِحمَل فِداديم قَـرْيه   رخَـمَةٍ قَشْـرًا كنـاسَـةْ قُوع
لَى شـافوا الخِطّـار عَنهم تَلاوذوا   تَلاوِذ وِبـْرانٍ لِجَتْ بِصـْدوع
وامّـا هَـل وشَـيقر قِبابين صَحصَح   الَى قِـضَبْت هـذا فـذاك نِسوع
تِـزَيَّنْت لاولاد العَـزاعِيز دِيـره   لهُـم في ربا عـالي تميم فْـروع
مِجّـين مَطْـرودٍ مـهينين طـارد   محَـاميـل قـالاتٍ رجـال نْفوع
وحِطّ الجَدي بالظَلْفِتَين وِخلافِك   سهَـيل اليَـماني من وَراك لِموع

~ 22 ~

Camel mount, set out from al-Washm's plains
with my reply, while people still sleep.
Cross the empty wastes, away from the rocky spurs. 22.35
Do not be startled by the sight of buildings in the morning light.[105]
For pasture I would migrate to Muḥammad ibn Muʿammar
and not bother to go in search of grassy plains.[106]
His generosity has sated so many hungry bellies,
when lesser men are forced to sell their fillies.[107]
His left hand has never sown a grain of evil,
while his right hand has sown many fields of charity.
Exquisite poise, virtue, candor, and honesty
are his. He has never indulged in trickery.
The horses of neighbors under his protection are safe, 22.40
but he scares enemy cavalry to death.
Sadly, I was saddled with a bunch of ingrates:
don't pin your hopes on the views of the vulgar herd.
In anger or despair, in a crisis they run in panic,
like herds caught between robbers and their owners in pursuit.
I am like an old man who resides with his family,
lonely, left to fend for himself in his last days.
I prefer to stay on the meager pastures at Ḥizwa's dunes:
I do not pine for Basra's fragrant attractions.[108]
Bini Zēd is a tribe that would deserve our esteem, 22.45
but for some pariah traits in their character.[109]
I found al-Miḥmal's folks to be clodhoppers,
wretched vultures that scavenge on refuse.[110]
They scram at the arrival of guests in search of a host,
like rock badgers ducking into crevices.
The people of Ushaygir scurry in all directions
like desert beetles:[111] catch one, the other bolts.
I found refuge with the sons of al-ʿAzāʿīz,
whose branch stems from noblest Timīm.
They shield the hunted, humiliate their hunters, 22.50
brave men of action, a community's finest.
Set your saddle facing the lodestar,
leave Canopus's flicker behind you, to the south![112]

~ ٢٢ ~

يَاطارشي قِل لابْن مـاضي محَمَّد   تـرَى الشَوىر عِقْبِه قِد بِدَا بِرْجوع
قِـدْ تِهْت انا وَيّاه في ماضيٍ مضَى   ضَـرَبْنا تلاعٍ مـا لِهِنّ فْـروع
هو راح يصـافي بُومةٍ في خَرابـه   جِـنْحْ الدِجَى مـا يِهْتِـني بْهجُوع
يَبي مِنْه ناطورٍ الَى بات خـايف   وهو ضِـريعٍ مـا تِسِـدّ الجُوع ٥٥،٢٢
فان طِعْت شَوري صاف راعي جلاجل   ولا في مصـافاتِه عـليك هْـزوع
فديـرَتْك فيها يابْن ماضي مِطامِع   وديـرَتْـه ما مِنها تِدُوىر طْموع
وان زَلَّتْ امّ عنَيق باق ابن عـامر   وانا ـفي شوَيٍّ من نِبـاه قِـنوع
تَرَى انّ باب سْدَير راعي جلاجل   وغَيـره بيبـانٍ بِغَيـر صْـروع

Convey my message to Ibn Māḍi, Muḥammad:
since we last met, things have gone out of kilter.
In bygone days we two strayed apart
as we blundered our way through gloomy gullies.
He chose to befriend a creepy owl of a man,
who in the darkness would haunt old ruins, awake.[113]
To be under his watch at night was like 22.55
satisfying the pangs of hunger with the dry thorns of Hell.[114]
If you heed my counsel, turn to the emir of Jlājil:
befriending him will not reflect badly on you.
Greedy eyes are trained on your lands, Ibn Māḍi,
but unlike yours his district is not coveted.
Sooner would Mount Umm ʿNēg fly away than Ibn ʿĀmir would cheat;
just a little of their fame would make me proud.[115]
Jlājil's prince commands the gate of Sudayr;
other gates are like doors off their hinges.[116]

لا جا ثوَرٍ يَخَطِب بِنْتِك　　فاضْرِب رِجْلِه قِلْ له قَفّـــــ
والله مـا يِسْوَى مِـلْكَتها　　ولا يِسْوَى قَـرْع الدَفّـــــ
والله مـا يِسْوَى ضِـيفَـتْها　　ولا يِسْوَى ظِلْف وخُفّـــــ
يَظْـهَر في بِنْتِك من بَيـتِك　　وِيْـذَوِّقهـا جُوع وحِفّـــــ
ان سَـلْمت من ضَرْبه بِيـدِه　　ما سَـلْمت من بُفّ وتُفّـــــ
يِـروِحن حِيـلٍ وِمْـلاط　　وِيِجن لِقّحٍ وِمْـرَدَّفـــــ

~ 23 ~

If a dumb ox comes asking for your daughter's hand, 23.1
    give him a kick and say, "Shoo!"
By God, he does not deserve to marry her,
    or the wedding celebrations with tambourines playing.
By God, he is not worthy of her cooking,
    not even a dish of cows' and camels' hooves.
He takes your girl away from your house,
    then exposes her to hunger and poverty.
Even if he does not slap her in the face, 23.5
    she is still at risk of being spat in the eye.
Girls leave home unencumbered and unsaddled,
    only to return pregnant, burdened with a family of their own.[117]

~ ٢٤ ~

النِعْمـه خـَمْرٍ جَيّـاش   مـا يَمْـلِكْهـا كُود الوَثْقِـه
والجُوع خـَدَيديـم اجواد   وِدِّلْــك ياطا كِلّ زَنِقِـه
لَيت ان الفَقْر يشاوِرني   كان ادْهَك بِه كِلّ فُسقِـه
كان ادْهَك به عَيرٍ ينْكِرِ   عِقْب الصَمْعَـا فيه نَهَقِـه
نِصَحْت شُوَيخ بِالمـاضي   ابيـه يبَـرِّق بـزَفِـقِـه
ولا مَقْــصودي يامـانع   الّا محـامـاةٍ وِشَفِـقِـه
نِصْحي في هــذا وامْثاله   ضَـيعَة غَـديرٍ بِبَـلِقـه
يَحَسب الحَرْب الى شَبّت   اَكْل لُحَيم وشِرْب مَرِقِـه
او نَومٍ مـع خَودٍ ناعِـم   زمّ نُهوده مِثل الحَقِـقِـه
رِدْفٍ وافي ووَسْطٍ هافي   وِلْهـا شَيٍّ مِـثل الدَرِقِـه
الحَـرْب يوَقِّـد بِرجـال   وِجْيـادٍ تِـرْبَـط وِنْفِـقِـه
يِشِبّ الفِـتْنه مقـرود   نَزْغَـة شَيطـانٍ وِحْلِقِـه
فـالَى اشْتَدّتْ مَعـالِبها   قَفّـى نايِر مثل السَلِقِـه
كْسَروا عَظْمه وخذوا ماله   خَـلّوا عيـالِه لهم لَعَقِـه
ويخَلّى مَقْضـاة ابْن دِرِمه   مِخْتَـلِطٍ دَمّـه بِعَـرِقِـه

~ 24 ~

Prosperity sparkles like a heady wine, 24.1
safe in the hands of a privileged few.
Hunger, handmaiden of the generous,
ought to trample all misers underfoot.[118]
If poverty were to ask my opinion,
I'd have it crush every godless bastard.
We'd smash each and every brash donkey
that brags and brays with a full belly.
I used to counsel a so-called shaykh 24.5
on how to handle his clan's affairs,[119]
With no other object in mind, Māniʿ,
than solicitude and cameraderie.
But giving advice to men like this
is like pouring water on barren soil.
To his mind, igniting the fires of war
meant supping on meat and broth,
Or sleeping with delicious damsels,
their breasts firm and pert like cups,
Their buttocks round, with wasp waists, 24.10
and plump pussies, as round as shields.
War burns on a fuel of men,
outlay, precious steeds, and money.
Strife is kindled by rotten wretches,
Satan's offspring, ill-starred fiends:
You can count on them, when battle is joined,
to scurry and sprint away as fast as a greyhound.
Break his bones and seize his wealth,
and let his children weep and wail.
Let him suffer the ordeal of Ibn Dirmah, 24.15
whose blood mixed with the sweat of pain:[120]

هـذا جِـزا مِن لا يَتْبَعَ   شَرْعِ اللهِ في كِلّ طْرِقِه
والخاين لا بِدِّه خـاين   تَذْهَب عِيدانـه ووْرِقِه
غَـرَّوه بْنَـقْش السِـروال   وطَقّ الدَمّام وَسْط السْوِقِه
لَيّـاك تْصالِح جِهّـال   قَبْل الحَرْب تْثُور تْفِقِـه
وِيـرَشّ قبورٍ برجـال   وِيَنْعَى الناعي مِمّا طْرِقِه ٢٠،٢٤
ثمّ اِعْذِل فيهم ياعـاذل   تخَلّى لِك لارقاب صْدِقِه
ما عاد تحاذِر من ضِدِّك   كِنّك عُودٍ ساق ووْرِقِه

A punishment for those who refuse
    to abide by divine law in all things.[121]
A traitor will always commit treachery.
    may he be extirpated, root and branch.
His head is easily turned by the sight of patterned breeches
    and the beating of drums in the streets.
Beware of befriending rash fools
    before the guns of war start crackling,
Graves are crammed with fresh corpses, **24.20**
    and the laments of the bereaved ring loud and long.
Then you should start your blame, you who love to find fault,
    and let the dead be your share of alms.[122]
Free of the need to heed your enemy's wiles,
    you will sprout fresh shoots and leaves.[123]

~ ٢٥ ~

امْس بالبِير يَنْشِدْني خَليفه   يِقول وَين انْت بِه مِن ذا النّخيل
قِلْت انا عند من يفْرِش لضَيفه   كِلّ خِشْيٍ وِفا كِبْر الزِبيل
مِقْرِنٍ يوم حطّ الي الدوِيفه   تَسْمَع الما بوَسْطِه لِه صِليل
لو حَضَرْت التَعَذّر وِتْحَليفِه   يوم جاب العَصيده بالطِسيل
ما دَرَيت ان الدوِيفه طِريفه   يِكود بالبير جِعْله ما يسِيل
شَوفهم للضيوف بْشَوف شِيفه   واقفٍ مثل ثَورٍ مِسْتِحيل
ما بهم غَير ذِرّيّة لِطيفه   للمسَيِّر وعَبّار السِبيل

~ 25 ~

Yesterday at the well Khalīfah accosted me: 25.1
  "Where among these palm gardens do you stay?"
I said, "With Migrin who spreads for his guest
  a carpet of cow dung poured from a heavily laden basket:
When he serves up a dish of wheat gruel
  you can hear the water slosh about in it.[124]
You should have heard how he pleaded and swore
  as he served a plate of flour and butter paste.
I was unaware that ground wheat was considered a delicacy 25.5
  until I came to al-Bīr—may the rains pass it by.[125]
For him the sight of a guest is the apparition of a specter:
  so, like an ox, he crouches and refuses to budge.
Laṭīfah's children are the only people
  for visitors and wayfarers to choose."

ياصِبيّ اِفْتِهِم من عْوَيدٍ فِهيم   وفي كلّ غِبّـه من الفِكْر عـايـم
آعَسْف القُوافي بسَبْك المَعاني   واصْخَر صَعَبها بلَيّا شِكايم
اقول النِصايح واعِدّ الفِضايح   عن اللي فَعَلْها ولا اخاف لايم
واعْرِف دروسٍ وكلّ الرموس   وادِلّ الموارِد بليّا عَلايم
واعْرِف الهوى والغوى من زمان   قِطَفنا زَهرها لَيالٍ قِدايم
سِبَحْنا بِبَحْرٍ به الغيّ مِتْرَع   سَهَرنا بلَيلٍ به الواش نايم
ضَرَبْنا تلاعٍ وفيهن ضباع   ضَرَبْنا حزومٍ و فيهِن وَهايم
تَرى بالعَذارى سواة المَهارى   جنانٍ تِجارى على الشَوق دايم
وفيهن مَلايح وفيهن كَلايح   نِسَمهن بوَجْهك يقادى السِمايم
وانا حِرْت يابوك بَين العَذارى   وغَدَيت من بينهن مِثِل بايع وسايم
ذي ما تبيني وذي ما ابيها   وذي ما توافِق وذي ما تلايم
الَى صار ذي حالتي يامجلّي   فخِذ عِلْم عودٍ لما قال عالم
ايا عاشقٍ كلّ عَذْرا مِليحه   هَنوفٍ غَنوجٍ بخَدّه رِقايم
نِظَرها كِحيلٍ وقَرْنٍ طِويل   وخِصرٍ نِحيلٍ له الرِدْف قايم
ومَزّيت رِيقه عَسى ما تِفيد   واغْضَبت ربّك بهتك المَحارم

~ 26 ~

Listen carefully, my boy, to this wise old man,
    for I have swum in the deep waters of thought.
I tame rhymes with sound meanings,
    subduing refractory ones without use of reins.
I give judicious counsel, expose scandals,
    and apportion blame with no fear of censure.
I can read hidden traces and sand-covered trails,
    find wells without help of landmarks.
I am no stranger to passion and love's temptations;
    in my halcyon days I plucked their flowers at night:
We swam in a sea surging with sinful rapture,
    enjoying our nights while the guards slept;
We struggled through gullies surrounded by hyenas,
    clambered on rocky hills haunted by demons.[126]
So let me say: some girls are purebred fillies,
    gardens ever flowering with heavenly bliss.
But not all girls are pretty: some are hideous,
    and breathe winds of poison that scorch your face.
I myself, son, am perplexed by maidens;
    I ended up going from one to the other:
This one doesn't want me, that one I don't want—
    either we can't agree or she is not right for me.
Such is my experience, dear Mjalli,
    so take this advice from an old man who knows.
O lover in the thrall of lovely ladies of style,
    gorgeous coquettes with tattooed cheeks,
Kohl-lined eyes, black tresses tumbling down,
    wasp-like waistlines, bulging behinds,
May you get no reward for drinking their saliva:[127]
    the violation of taboos provokes your Lord's ire.

تفوت اللِذاذه وتَبـْـقى النـِدامـه   سـِرِيعٍ تِكَشَّـف امورٍ عَظـايـم
ولا تَحْسِب الخَيرِ دَرْب الفِسـاد   ووِلْف البَواغي ورَكْب الجَـرايـم
ونِظّـف المَـلابس وِلبْس المَحـابس   وكَبّ العَصـايب وكَسْـع المَحارِم
تَـرى الخَير في راسيات الجذوع   ـالى دَلْبحَنّ السِـنين الحَطـايـم
غِـينٍ ظِـليله يطَـرِّب مِـقيـله   وسَـمْعِك تِمَتَّع بصَوت الحَمـايـم
توَفِّـر حَـلالك وتِفْـرِح عـيالِك   ويَكْـثِر نَوالِك بيَوم الصَـرايـم
وجَنّـاي الارْطا يقَـلِّب يِـدَيـنِه   ـالى شاف وِرْدٍ على الجوّحـايـم
بهـذا الزمـان يبيـن الصِـديق   ـالى بار فـيها رِدِي العَـزايـم
وانا اذْخـر رِفـيقي لهـذا ومِـثْله   ـالى جا نهارٍ يِشيب اللِمايـم
صِـديقي عَـرَفْتِه الى ما لَحَظْتِه   وامَـيِّز عَـدُوّي وفيهم وِسـايـم
حَجـاجـه وعَـينـه لِمَـثْـلي دِلـيل   وغَـبِي المَعَـرْفه فلا هوب فاهـم
ومن لا يمَـيِّز صِـديقـه وضِـدّه   فـهو ثَور هَورٍ يبي له رِدايـم
ولا فاتني كـلّ امـرٍ بَغَـيته   ومَحَـلّي تَعَـلّى مـتون النَعَـايـم
لِقيت الاصول وجَـبْر الكسور   ايجـاد المَـراهِم تَـراها الدَراهِـم

Sensual pleasures pass; remorse remains.
Grave implications quickly come to mind.
Do not think the wrong way is for the best:
consorting with whores and committing crimes,
Strutting flamboyantly in fine apparel,
rings on the fingers, headdress at a rakish angle.
You're best served by deep-rooted date palms
when years of disaster bear down on you:
In an idyllic palm garden giving restful midday shade, 26.20
where you can listen to the soothing coo of the doves.
Husband your goods and gladden your children:
great will be your gain as harvest comes.
The laborer who collects firewood from the desert stands in awe
at the sight of great herds pressing at the well.[128]
At such times you will be able to tell a true friend
from deceivers who have no moral fiber.
I cherish my friends for my hour of need,
for a day that turns your sidelocks gray.
I can tell a true friend with one glance: 26.25
my enemy bears telltale marks that I perceive:
For me, the eyes and brows speak volumes,
while those devoid of understanding flounder.
One who cannot distinguish between friend and foe
is as dumb as an ox that should be locked up in a pen.
In truth, I obtained all I wished for,
my renown shot higher than Sagitta.
I uncovered the root causes of things and found ways to heal:
for broken bones dirhams are the best cure.[129]

~ ٢٧ ~

والله دينٍ باشَر دِينٍ   من باب الغاط الى ضَرما
ان الحاكم يَنْشر منْشار   والعالِم من ليلٍ جْهَما
الحاكم ياكِل ويوكّل   ويفكّ الدار من العَدِما
ولا ضَرّه ما ينفِد كفّه   في بَيته نِعْمه ونِعَما
والعالِم يِدْخِل ما يطْلِع   سْحَمًا تاكِل ولا تْحَما
يحبّ الكامد والجامد   من مال الغير الى وِلما
والّا من ماله محروم   ربّي رزّاقٍ للحْرِما
وانا امْدح في العالِم شاره   ياجُوده في فزع الدّهَما
ولقيت الظالم يامانع   من عامٍ لَموه العلما
واحدهم في كِبْر اللِحْيه   حبّالٍ حطّ به طْعَما
الى جِتْك الطَلْبه في حقّك   وتقابَلْت انت ويّا الخِصما
دلّى يَسمع نبط الخِصمه   تحقّتك الشكّه والتّهما
فالفِز في كفّه دينار   ليّاه يضرّبك اليِهما

~ 27 ~

I swear by God and by all that is holy, 27.1
from the gate of al-Ghāṭ to Ḍruma:
The ruler ventures forth in broad daylight;
the man of religion prefers the cover of darkness.
The ruler eats and provides nourishment,
protects his subjects from want and fear:
No matter how liberally he spends,
prosperity and serenity reign in his house.
A religious scholar takes but never gives:[130] 27.5
he is a black dog that feeds but does not guard.
He gobbles up all he finds, moist or dry,
as long as someone else is paying.
And if that other person has spent all he has, he cries:
"My Lord provides for the down and out."
We must hand it to the cleric:
no one digs deeper into the cooking pot;
Holding forth on oppression and injustice—
the man of religion has appropriated it all.
He grows his beard long and bushy, 27.10
and uses it as bait for those he ensnares.
If you are in court with the claimants
and what is yours is contested in a dispute,
If their loud arguments attract attention,
and they fire accusations and aspersions at you,
Then slip a dinar into the cadi's hand
before false charges bring harm down on you.[131]

~ ٢٨ ~

الايام حُبلى والامورعَوان   فهَل يا تَرى ما لا يِكون وكان
الاعمار فيهن من طِويلٍ وقاصر   وكلٍّ سِوى رَبّ الخَلايق فان
لا تامِن الدِنيا ولو زان وَجْهها   تَرى رَمْيها للعالَمين خْفان
كم غَيَّرت من مِلْك ناسٍ وبَدَّلت   مِكانٍ لناسٍ صار غير مكان
انا ياوْلِدي جَرَّبْت الايام كِلّها   ما كِبْر من عِظْم الامور وهان
حبال الرَخا تُوردك برّيت بالضحَى   وبالضِيق ما تِرْد الخدود قْران
والاوْباش ياما حَدّروا في هَبيّه   طِويلة مَلْقَى جاذبٍ وِشْطان
وعانك من لا تِرْتِجي منه عَونه   ولَى رُبّ راعٍ في جَنابك خان
الى زِواك الحَرْب يومٍ تَناسَعوا   تحَسْبه امْرٍ ما يكون وكان
فصادِم لصَعْبات المَعاني على القِدَى   راع القِدَى بالمُوجِبات مْعان
فلا مَطْلَب العِلْيا بيِدْني مِنيِّه   ولا زادَن ايام الرَخا بِهدان
تَخَيَّرت نَومي فوق صَوّانة الصِفا   ولا جودري في بلاد هَوان
ولو صار شِرْبي مًا هَماجٍ مخالِطه   حَنْظَل وانا لي بالمَعَزّه شان
احبّ عَلِيّ من مِلْك بَغداد وارْضِه   الى البصْرة الفَيحا ودار عْمان
أعلّم صِبيان القَرايا هَل الذَرى   من الناس والّا فالذّهان ذْهان

~ 28 ~

Time is pregnant, events are its midwife.[132] 28.1
Are there things that cannot be, yet are?
While man's life may be long or short,
all but the face of the Lord will disappear.
Do not trust the world, even if it should smile on you:
for humans, it always packs a huge punch.
It takes away possessions, it changes ownership:
status enjoyed one day is gone the next.
In life, my boy, I have experienced all vicissitudes, 28.5
the greatest and the gravest, even in minor things.
When you're rich, drawing water from a deep well is easy;
the hard up can't even fetch it from an open stream.[133]
Scoundrels like to push you over the edge of the pit
from where you cannot be rescued, not even with long ropes.
But you get succor from unexpected quarters
when you are forsaken by your dependents
Who embroil you in war and then abscond:
you think that's something that can never be, but is.
Tackle hard tasks head on but be wary: 28.10
in crises fortune favors the deliberate man.
High aspirations do not hasten one's fate,
and comfort does not lengthen a truant's days.
I'd rather have a slab of rock for a pillow
than sleep on a soft carpet in a land of ignominy.
Even if I have to drink brackish water mixed
with bitter apple, I value self-respect more:
More than owning Baghdad and its territories,
sweet-scented Basra, and the shores of Oman.[134]
Let me give sheltered village lads 28.15
advice not required by judicious minds.

الاوطان ما يَغْدِي بها خَطّ عالِمٍ ولو غَلّتِه يِشْرَى بكل زْمانِ
الَى غَبّت الطَرحَا بدارٍ وِرِثْها بالسيف لا حَقٍ ولا جِعْلانِ
لو قِلْت ذا مِلْكٍ لابوي وجَدّي على الحَقّ مَنْصوبٍ كَلوه بَيانِ
ياراعي القَصْر الذي في قراره ضِعيف القوى ما يِرْتِجي لاعْوانِ
الاوطان ان جا هَوش لا تَرْفَع البنا والابطال للضِدّ القِديم عْرانِ
مْعَفّتةٍ شَبّانها في اكْفانها عراهِنّ من وَبْل الوِطيس دْهانِ
فلو كِنْت في قَصْرٍ حَصينٍ مشَيّد فِضَوه من عِدْم الرجال وهانِ
ولو كِنْت تِعْطي كِلّ يومٍ اخاوَه تَبى العافيه قالوا ذا جَنابه لانِ
من يامِن الرَقْطا على الساق نادِمٍ ومن يامِن الضِدّ القِديم يْهانِ
عَدُوّك لو خَلّاك يَومٍ مِذلّه فهو مِسْرِجٍ للمُولمات حْصانِ
فلا تِغْذ سِرْحانٍ ولا تِدِن مِبْغِض وايّاك والطِمَع الزِهيد تْدانِ
ولا تِحْتِقِر في الدار راعي خيانه كَم شالت اولاد الحرام هْدانِ
فكم عَيلةٍ يَعْقِب لها كَشْف هيبه ولا حِكْمٍ الّا ان يِكون يْعانِ
الَى صِرْت راعي قالةٍ تِتّقي بها عن الواش ما تَدْبيرها باعْلانِ
فشاوِر مِرْجامٍ صِبورٍ صْمَيدِع يعِينك بالنَخْوَى رياه مْتانِ
واتْرِك زاروبٍ خَفيفٍ سِمَلّق رِدي اللقا في المِعْضِلات لْيانِ
واتْرِك باب الذِلّ عَنّي ولا تَكُن الى رَيت راسٍ من عَدُوّك بانِ
فِصِكّه بالهِنْدي على البوق والنِقا وما كِبْر من عِظْم المصيبه هانِ

~ 28 ~

Lands are not given away by a judge's pen,
though people pay handsomely for verdicts.[135]
When corpses lie strewn over inherited land,
all is decided by the sword, not by right or by wages.
He who argues, "These are our ancestral lands
and are rightfully ours," is consumed as he speaks.[136]
Listen, if you are weak and have no hope of help from allies,
your fortress will not protect you.
If your land is attacked, do not raise the walls higher:
only valiant fighters bring old enemies to heel,
Youngsters ready to die dressed in shrouds,
their bare backs sweaty as they do battle.
The thick walls of a fortress won't keep you safe.
without defenders it is easily stormed.
If you pay protection money every day
to keep them at bay, they say, "A soft target."
He who lets a viper wrap its coils round his leg will regret it,
and he who trusts a sworn enemy will be abused.
For now he may prefer to leave you in peace,
but he is already saddling his horses for grim days ahead.
Do not feed a wolf or favor an ill-wisher;
have no patience with greedy, selfish men.
Do not ignore traitors inside your house:
villains have finished off many a coward.
Many acts of aggression end in loss of face:
no ruler can dispense with help from others.
Hide your intention to strike out boldly
before you are ready—hide it well!
Confide in tough-minded men as hard as rocks
who rally to the cry and are undaunted.
Snub the harebrained whining pest,
a flop in battle and a pushover in a fix.
It is an abomination to cower and acquiesce
at the first sight of the enemy.
Hit him with steel, by hook or by crook.
Thus are grave affairs settled with ease.

دَعْ ذا وياغادي على عَيدِهيّه ... ضراب هِجْنٍ من بَنات عُمان
على مِثل رَبْدا مع سَنا الصِبحْ ساقها ... سَنا حاكمٍ طَق النِفير واكان
الى اَقْفَتْ مع حَزْمٍ تُوامَا سبوقها ... كِما بارِقٍ هَبّت عليه يمان
والّا فدانِق في هَوى مِدلِهِمّه ... تِزجّه النَكبا والدبور شْحان
الَى جِيت عنّا للعزاعِيز دِيره ... من الوَشْم تِعزى للعناقِر كان
سَلِّمْ عليهم حينما الْفَيت كِلّهم ... من كان قاصي بالبلاد وْدان
قِل ياهَل الفِعْل الذي يُوجِب الثنا ... تَراكُم حذا الباب الجِديد يمان
قِل اليوم فِكّوها على واضِح النِقا ... عرافةٍ مِنهُم طِريده هان
صُوعوهم بالحَرْب الذي في جَنابكم ... عن الصِلْح ما دام الزِمان زِمان
عِتِقْتوا عن الشَرّ الذي يُوجِب القضا ... ولا ياسع اجداث القبور مْصان
الا يارجالٍ من تميمٍ تِفَقّهوا ... وِصيّة من هو بالصداقِه بان
تَرى عِندكم ضِدٍ بالاوطان مِكْنِع ... احْرَص من اللي يَرْقِبون جْفان
حَسبْت لهم سِتّين سيفٍ معلّق ... والابطال عند الحادثات سْنان
قالوا لنا مَهلا الَى حين نِلْتِقي ... عن نِصْفنا راحوا شِريد بَيان
لنا ديرةٍ عَنها الطَعاميس مِجْنِبه ... بَيان صَفقٍ للحَريب عْيان
اخَذْنا بها الاثمان بادٍ وحاضِر ... جِماجِمٍ تِرْمَى بضَرْب ايمان
قَتَلْنا بها اصحاب الوِشايا جميعهم ... وعانَنا من لا يعان بْشان
حَفَرنا بها بير القضا عِقْب ما غدا ... على ما مِضَى طول الزمان دفان

~ 28 ~

Enough of this, you rider of the sturdy she-camel,
    progeny of racers of Omani stock!
With the speed of an ostrich she starts at dawn,
    like a ruler who sounds the bugle and attacks.
She scorches stony hills, ribbons aflutter,
    like thunderclouds whipped by a southern gale,
Or like a wooden boat in a pitch-black sea,
    tossed by a storm from the northwest, about to be wrecked.
Upon arrival in the land of the men of al-ʿAzāʿīz
    in al-Washm, tributary to al-ʿAnāgir,
Greet them all for they are your destination,
    distant relatives and close kin alike.
Tell them, "Your brave feats deserve praise,
    those of you to the right of the New Gate."[137]
Then say, "Now reclaim your rights by force—
    a camel plundered from you should be easy to retrieve![138]
Unleash a devastating assault,
    seize the opportunity, do not seek peace.
May you be freed from this insufferable evil!
    the grave awaits you at your appointed time.
Men of Timīm, use your good sense and take
    the counsel of one who is a proven friend.
Your adversary crouches ready to pounce,
    as eager as a starving man staring at plates full of food."
I counted sixty swords hanging on their walls;
    but a warrior's pluck is worth more than blades.[139]
They said, "Easy, let's wait for combat;
    half our number will make them run for their lives."
The great dunes lie to the south of our homeland,
    conspicuous, in full view of any marauders.[140]
We exacted a price from Bedouin and townsmen
    in its defense: heads sent rolling by clash of arms.
There we made short work of all our detractors,
    killing them with the help of Him who needs no help.
We dug up the well of revenge when it had over time
    become filled with the drifting sands of neglect.

~ ٢٨ ~

نَفَخْنا بها النارِ الذي قِد طِفَت بِه   وغَدا لِها عِقْب الخمود لْسانِ

فلا يكافي مـالنـا عن رقـابنـا   تَوَلّاه كِفَّـر مـا سَواه فْـلانِ

قِل بيّـض الله وَجْـه جيران دارنا   الَى ما نْشِدوا عن ويش كان وكانِ

حَضْرَتْ لهـم في عَفْجَة القُور وَقْعَه   بها الطَّرَحا شَرْوَى الهَـشيم تَوانّ   ٥٥،٢٨

وقَـفَوّا وقَفَّـينا معِـيفين بَينـنا   وراحت تنـاعي لَيعَـةٍ واحْزانِ

مْهيِّضِـتْه رَبْط الكِريـم بن زامـل   سَـنا الوَشْم راعي دَثْرةٍ وِجْفانِ

We blew on its fire, well-nigh extinguished,
until the tongues of flame shot up in a roaring blaze.
We will not save our necks by paying up:
our enemies are fiends, not the common sort.
Tell them, "May God brighten the faces of those neighbors
who do not forget to ask after our well-being."[141]
They took part in a battle at ʿAjfat al-Gūr[142] 28.55
where bodies lay scattered like dead wood.
Disgusted with the fighting, all returned home
to the shrieks and laments of women mourning.
We were roused to battle by the capture of Ibn Zāmil,
that luminary of al-Washm famed for his great feasts of roast meats.[143]

~ ٢٩ ~

يابن نحَيط اِفْهَم جواب مُهَذَّب   جا من صِديقٍ واضحٍ عِنوانَها
مِن حارَب آباكْ القدام وقال لِك   بالصِلْح انا وَايَّاك من صِدْقانَها
تَراه عابي لِك قِليبٍ مِهْلك   حَذراك لا يِرْمِيك في كِيحانَها
عَدُوّ جَدّك من قِديمٍ دارِس   مِتْجَرِّعٍ بَغْضاك طُول ازمانَها
لو ناش دِقّ الصَيد مِنك حَبايِله   ما ذارَها مِسْتارِدٍ لسمانَها
وان مال الَيه من الرفاقِه واحد   خَرَّب خَفيف الرَوز من ذِلّانَها
نَعْجة كَباشٍ عِند ذيبٍ مِجْلِد   تَراه صِفْرا العَين من صِدْقانَها
لو يُوتليها ساعَةٍ مِتفَرِّغ   عِقْب الصِداقه قَطّ عَظْم جْرانَها
والقِرْب من نار الصِديق غَنيمه   والضِدّ حَذْرا من نِعيم جْنانَها
الله يِجِيرك من طبوعٍ قِبيله   خِرْبَت بفِعْل المِتْرِفين اوطانَها
ولا يدارِج راسها من ساسها   وَكْلَت بها هِيسانها جِيرانَها
هذي عقوبات الزِمان فكَم تَرى   من قَومٍ اخْلى مَكْرَها بِلْدانَها
ولا صِلْحَ الّا عِقب جَرّ جَنايِز   وجماجِمٍ تِهْفَى وعَقْد ايمانَها
فالَى حصل هذا فواسِل بَينهم   حَتّى تِطيع احلامها هِيمانَها
والضِدّ ما خَلّى البلاد بْمَلْقِه   عَيَّنت رِيعٍ طاح مِن رِيعانَها

~ 29 ~

Ibn Nḥēṭ, listen carefully to these polished verses, 29.1
a message from a friend of established repute.
If a scion of your ancestors' foes says to you,
"Let's make our peace and henceforth be friends,"
Know that he is digging a pit for your downfall.
Beware lest he pushes you into its cavernous depths.
He has long been your grandfather's archenemy,
who has swallowed his hatred for you and nurses it.[144]
If his traps snare some of your small game, 29.5
he leaves it alone and waits for bigger prey.
If one of your gang drifts away from you and sucks up to him,
your cowardly lightweight falls apart
Like a yellow-eyed ewe in the company of a wolf,
thinking she's cuddling up to a friend:
For a while she walks in his steps without a care
until, friendship over, he tears her throat to shreds.
It is a fine thing to warm oneself at a friendly fire,
but beware of heavenly bliss offered to you by a foe.
May God protect you from the proclivities of tribesmen 29.10
whose pampered weaklings brought ruin to their land.
Their affairs went askew and turned awry:
good-for-nothings riding roughshod over their neighbors.
These are the harsh punishments inflicted by Time—
many a land was laid waste by the perfidy of its folks.
No truce lasts unless it is preceded by funerals,
with heads rolling and hands tied behind backs.
That is the moment to start your mediation,
when hotheads make room for calmer men.
Flattery alone will not make a foe withdraw: 29.15
did you ever see a mountain cliff split off and go away?

ياقَوم مُوسَى كان في ماضٍ مِضَى   قاتِل وحِنّا قاضبين مِكانَها
عِندي على هذا الحَديث جِماعه   بَدْوٍ وحَضَرٍ حاضِرين ازمانَها

~ 29 ~

Listen, once upon a time Moses was
a murderer. We have followed suit, no different.[145]
This I know from a tradition on which all agree—
Bedouin and settled folks my witness, both.[146]

~ ٣٠ ~

قال عَودٍ كِبِر واعِتِلاه المشيب | وانْحَنَى مِثل قَوسٍ يتالي عَصاه
طاح قَدْرِه وحاله ولا بِه مِزيد | وان وُمَر من عياله صِغيرٍ عَصاه
يومِ عنده حَلالٍ وقَوله مطاع | يَركَض الكلّ مِنهم بزاده وماه
الرَجِل كِلّ ما قَلّ ماله يعاف | وان عَمَى بالكِبَر عَمّس رايه وباه
انكَروا ما مِضَى واجْحَدوه الجِميل | يوم حَقّه وِرِد واكْمَل اللي وَراه
يا مجَلّيِّ تِسَمَّع نِبًا مِن فِهيمِ | وافِي باصْغَرِه قاصِراتٍ عَضاه
عارِفٍ باخِصٍ في جِميع الامورِ | ان غَدَى الراي عن دايرينه لِقاه
لا تناسب بِخيلٍ كِثيرِ الحَلال | مِهَنِته كِلّ يومٍ يقَيِّس عَشاه
ناسِب اللي يرَحّب الَى جوا جياع | والتِبِسِّم بسِنّه من اوّل قْراه
ولا تلَيِّن جَنابك لمن هو ضِديد | او عَدُوٍّ يداهِن بقَلْبه بَلاه
والحَرِيب انْحَرِه قَبْل يِقْبِل عليك | وان تَنَيتِه يِزورِك بدارك تَراه
مِعْلِقٍ مِخْلِبه والطِمَع بك يِصيرِ | اِضْرِبه غارةٍ لَين تَقْلِع مِداه
مِن جِبَن عن عَدُوّه يصَلَّط عَليه | البِخْل والجِبِن للمعادي مناه
كل من داس ضِدِّه وغورَب عليه | خَذ بِها مِدّةٍ ما تِمَشْنَى حماه
والصِديق اِعْرِفه واِذْخَرِه للمِضيق | ذِبّ عَنّه بوَجْهه وِتحَمَى قِفاه

~ 30 ~

These are the words of an old graybeard, 30.1
bent and crooked, who supports himself on a stick.
He is held in no esteem—if in this wretched state
he tells even a child what to do, he is paid no heed.
But were he a man of substance, his every word would be obeyed:
all are at his beck and call with food and drink.
As soon as a man's wherewithal dries up, he is shunned.
if his eyesight fails and he grows confused and lost,
His past is forgotten and the good he did disavowed, 30.5
just when it is his right to receive what he is due.
Mjalli, listen to advice proffered by a clever sage
endowed with a strong mind, though weak of limb,
Who knows all things and has plumbed their depths:
when others are lost, he finds the way forward.
Don't acquire an in-law who is rich but stingy,
whose daily routine is to calculate his dinner's cost.
Acquire one who welcomes hungry visitors with open arms
and a broad smile as he hands them the first morsel of food.
Do not display a sign of softness to an adversary 30.10
or to an enemy plotting your doom.
March on your foe before he pays you a visit:
if you hesitate you'll find him smashing down your door
To sink his claws in you and satisfy his greed:
smite him in a raid that sends him flying.
A display of cowardice puts you at an enemy's mercy:
avarice and gutlessness play into his hands.
Trample your foe in numerous attacks,
and you'll have no encroachment on your sanctuary.
Know who your friends are, save them for a dire day: 30.15
defend them from the front and protect their back.

والمَرَه ضِمَّها لا عَرِفْت امّها   ثمّ صِنْ عِرِضْها لا يِغَرّ بحَياه
والبدوي ان عَطَيته تِصلَّط عليك   قال ذا خايفٍ مَير بالِك عَطاه
ان وَلى ظالمٍ مِفسِدٍ للكِرام   وان ظلم زان طَبْعه وساق الزِكاه
مِثل كَلْب ان رِمَيتُه بفِهْرٍ يروح   وان رِمي له بعَظْمٍ تِبَع من رِماه
حاكمٍ ياكِلونه ومِنهم يَخاف   من رَخامِيّته ماهِنين ثواه
وحاكمٍ هو دَواهم بفِعْلٍ يِشاف   كِلّ ما خالَفوا الحَق فيهم مناه
كِلّ يومٍ عليهم صِباحٍ شرير   غير ذَبْح اللحى عَزْل بَوْشٍ وشاه
مِثل جِنْس الحبارى يعَرْف الطيور   يوم جا حاذقٍ مُوثِبٍ من سِماه
نادر الحِرّ يِدْعي عَضاها لهوم   والتِبِع تِطْرِده مَرْشَةٍ من خَراه
هيه ياراكبٍ من فَوق حمرا رِدوم   مِن خيار النِضا طَبْعَها ما حَلاه
عَيبَها زَورها ما يِنوش العضود   خِفّها سالمٍ ما رِقِع من حَفاه
يانِديبي على كُورها تِستِريح   فِرْجِتك ساعتَينٍ بحِفْظ الإله
من بلاد القِصَب سِر وتِلفي شرَيق   دِيرةٍ بالوَشِم قاصَرتها مَراه
ديرةٍ للعَزاعيز سِقْم الحَريب   عَلّها الله بوَسْمٍ وصَيفٍ قِفاه
عِمّهم ياندِيب بسلامٍ جميع   عِدّ ما هَلّ وَبْلٍ وهَبّت هَواه
قِل لهم شَوري اللي مِضى من قِديم   بالهُم يِخْلِفونه يِجيهم قضاه
اِحْرِبوا واِضرِبوا دون حِذْب الجِريد   واِذكِروا قَول حاتم ولاشٍ سِواه
مَوتِكم بالبواتِر لكم كِبْر كار   ومَوتكم بالتَواجِع عليكم زَراه

Before taking a wife, check her mother's ancestors,
  safeguard her honor, let no one get close to her.
Being kind to a Bedouin allows him to take liberties:
  he says, "This man is scared," so do not give him an inch.
When in power he is a tyrant who corrupts the realm,
  but when oppressed, he behaves and pays the tithe,
A dog that scampers when you throw a stone at it,
  but if you throw a bone it will follow you forever.[147]
If a ruler trembles before the people, they will eat him alive;
  because he is so feeble, they will ravage his realm.
Another ruler may govern them with an iron fist:
  whenever they are unruly, he brings them to heel—
Each day he reaps a crop of vicious morning raids,
  massacres and booty of camels and sheep.
Thus, the bustard lives in fear of the falcon
  that pounces on him like a bolt from the blue:
The peregrine will tear the bustard to pieces,
  while a drop of bustard shit will scare off a lesser falcon.
Ho, rider on the well-fed, light-brown she-camel,
  sweet-tempered, born from the hardiest of mounts;
Perfect, with a breastbone that does not chafe against the muscles,
  and foot pads that have never needed treatment for bleeding.[148]
My messenger, sit comfortably in the saddle:
  your desert crossing will be short, in God's keeping.
Set out from the land of al-Qaṣab and head east
  to a district in al-Washm that lies next to Marāh:[149]
The homeland of al-ʿAzāʾīz, scourge of the enemy—
  may God bless it with rains in winter and late spring.
Greet them, my messenger, with a collective salute
  like a heavy downpour driven by a stiff breeze.
Tell them, "Heed the advice I gave you long ago.
  If you disregard it, you will be made to pay the price.
Fight hard for your curved palm fronds;
  remember the verse of Ḥātim, nothing else.[150]
To die on the tips of sharp blades brings renown;
  to succumb to the pain of infirmity brings disgrace.[151]

من ذِبِح دون مـاله وحـاله شِهيـد   وان حَيـا بالسَعـادِه ولِه كِبِر جـاه
لا تَحَسبون مِن ذَلّ عِمْرِه يِطول   فـانّ ذا المَوت لا بِـدّكِم من لقـاه ٣٥،٣٠
جَدّكم رَخْـمِةٍ مـاكِرٍ للطـيور   لَهّس العِنقـري كل حَـلاوي نِمـاه
واظْهَر الله عيـاله وسَبَّب لهـم   شَوِر عَودٍ فِـهيمٍ قِليـلٍ خَـطاه
اِفْطِموا مِن فِطَم دَيـد مِن قَبـلكم   فَطْمَة الوِزع عن دَيده اللي غَذاه

To die defending goods and chattels is a martyr's death:
survival means a life of felicity and high repute.
Reckon not that docility adds to your span of life: 30.35
man can never evade his appointment with death.
Your grandfather, a scavenger born of falcons,
whetted the appetite of al-ʿIngirī with his tribute of dates.[152]
Fortunately, his sons turned out to be real men,
and they were lucky to have this old sage's counsel.
Wean him who took pleasure in weaning others before you,
as a toddler is weaned from the breast that feeds him."[153]

~ ٣١ ~

ابا اوَصّيكم ياالذّهنا　عَن نَطْحَة قومٍ بتْحِيّه
اِخْفِرْهم ثُمّين اِنْهَرْهم　قَبْل يفاجونك بالهَيّه
اَنْشِدْكم عَن خَمْسه مَدّوا　اَمْسِ مَدّوا بالمارِيّه
لو تِنْظِرْهِم عِند المَدّه　واحِدهم يَنْطَح لُه مِيّه
كِلٍ يَنْصِب يُورِي طِيبه　عِند المَزْيونه سَرْدِيّه
ساعَة جِينا عِند القارِه　جانا رَجْلَينِ حَرْبِيّه
ما مَعهم تَفّاقٍ يَرْمي　راعي مِشْعابٍ وِقْنِيّه
مْطَوّعهم شَدّ الباقِر　يقول ما لي عَنها نِيّه
اهْوَى به راعى المِجْحان　بِشْتِه مَصبوغٍ بِدْمِيّه
و راعى المَقْرون عبيد الله　والله ما يِسْوَى شاهِيّه
وحْوَيدِر قَفّى مِنْحاش　يَدْلونه دَلْي الجِلْدِيّه
وِوْهَيّب قَفّى من شَرْق　يِشْبه لَرْبَدا مَرْمِيّه
والخامِس رَجْلٍ ما اعرِفه　اقْفى يَرْمي مع حَدْرِيّه

~ 31 ~

Smart fellows, heed this piece of advice: 31.1
do not greet any strangers you bump into.
Watch them carefully, then say, "Scram!"
before all of a sudden they turn violent.
Ask them: Did you hear about the five fellows who set out?
Yesterday they marched beyond the road mark:
If you had seen them striding forth with such panache,
you'd say each could take on a hundred men,
As they vied in swagger and displays of mettle 31.5
to impress the maiden of al-Sardiyyah.[154]
On reaching the flat-topped outcrop
two warlike men came toward them,
Not the sort to carry loaded guns:
just camel prods and heavy canes.
Our pious mate who had a cow in tow
said, "No way will I let go of her."
He was attacked by the man with the stick,
his cloak spattered with his blood.
'Ubaidallah, the man in the fancy dress, 31.10
by God, is not even worth a penny.[155]
And little Ḥaydar, he ran away as fast
as a bucket falling down a well.
Whayyib the wimp bolted to the east
like an ostrich under fire.
I do not know the name of the fifth brave hero;
he scrammed, firing farts from his ass.[156]

~ ٣٢ ~

الدِين الدِين اللي بَيِّن   بَيِّن مِثل الشَمْس القَيظِيَّه
الدِين بْعَيرٍ خِرج اربَع   والخامس دِين اباضِيَّه
ما هَمَّن ذيبٍ في الباطن   هَمَّن عَودٍ بالدِرْعِيَّه
قَولِه حَقّ وفِعْلِه باطل   وسْيوفِه كُتْبٍ مَطْوِيَّه
خَلَّى هذا يَذْبَح هذا   وهو نايم بالزُولِيَّه
ان جاك السَبْع ابو رِيشه   يلْعَب لِك لِعْب الحَوحِيَّه
فاقْدَح واعْلِق وارْكَب واوشِم   وحِطّ القاطع بَين لْحِيَّه

~ 32 ~

This is the faith that is as clear 32.1
as a midsummer sun at noon.[157]
It is like a camel laden with four bags,
and there is a fifth, the Ibāḍī school.
My concern is not the wolf in al-Bāṭin—
it is al-Dirʿiyyah's wolf I keep my eye on.[158]
He speaks the truth but his deeds are wrong,
his swords are scrolls of scripture.
He has endorsed killing among the people, 32.5
while he sleeps serenely on his carpet.
Should the bogeyman come to play his games
like the lion in the story,
Attack with flintlock and spear,
and plant your sword right in his throat.[159]

~ ٣٣ ~

طالبٍ للقِصَب يوم انا بالجِنوب   والي العَرْش يِسْقِيه وَسَمِيّه
ياهَبيل العَرَب لا تِكِدّ القِصَب   لَين سَيله يَعَقْب الرقيبِيّه
اِكْتِب الغَرْس من قَبل دَينٍ يِجيه   اِرْسِمه للعييّل بِطَلْحِيّه
عن عييّلك لا تِدُور النِقاد   في هَمال القِصَب من جِنوبِيّه
ان بِقَنّ الزَرانيق لِك هاالسَنه   فاجْغَط الدين وِالْعَب به البيّه
وِخذ مِن ما طَرى لِك على ما ترى   وِاذْخَرِه فاللَيالي لَها نيّه
واوْدِعِه مع وقيّان لك ناقةٍ   خِلِّيَت في نفود الشماسِيّه
ربّي مساليك لا تُوزِني حارِث   الحَراريث قَومٍ شِقاوِيّه
غابَت الشَمْس ما فَكّ عن مِحْزِمه   والفَرايض قِضاها العشاوِيّه

~ 33 ~

If you head for al-Qaṣab you'll find me to its south— 33.1
may the Lord of the Throne irrigate it with rains.
You fool, don't think of working al-Qaṣab's soil
until torrents come coursing past al-Rgēbiyyah.
Secure the date harvest before the debt's collected
by putting it in your child's name.
Do not search the ground for dates to feed your little one
among the uncultivated palms south of al-Qaṣab.[160]
If you keep the well's supports ready this year, 33.5
gobble up the debt and start to have some fun;[161]
Grab anything that strikes your fancy
and cherish it: the dark nights lurk, waiting to spring their trap.
Take a gamble—like entrusting a camel to a Bedouin,
like getting Wugayyān to pasture it in al-Shimāsiyyah's dunes.[162]
My Lord, I beg you, do not force me to till the soil,
for I know no greater misery than the life of a peasant:
The sun sets, yet still your loins are girded up;
and you have to combine your last two prayers at night.[163]

~ ٣٤ ~

هُون الامور مـبـاديهـا   قَـدْحٍ ولهـيـبٍ تاليها
الفِـتْنِه نايمـةٍ دايـم   مَـير الاشـرار توعّيها
يِشِبّ الفِتْـنِه مَـقْـرود   يِعَلِّقـها مِن لا يطّـفـيـها
فـالَى عَـلْقَتْ ثُمّ اشـتَبّت   بالحَرْب انحاش مشاريها
تِلْحَق بـرجـالٍ واجْواد   دَومٍ تِـنْـصـا قَـهاويها
اِدْفَع الشَـرّ دامِك تَقْدَر   حَـتّى تِنْـصَـر بتـاليها
وانْظِـر رَبٍّ يِنْـظِر فَوقك   يِميت النَـفس ويحْيِيها
وارْدَع نَفْسِك عن العَـيلَه   حـاذور الزود تهـقْويها
فان جَتْك الطَلْبَه في حَلْقك   فاضْرِب بالسَيف مْعَدّيها
حـاذور الذلّه والمَـدّه   لو نِصْف اموالك تِعْطِيها
والسَيف القاطع والعَزْمَه   لارقاب الضِدّ يْهَدّيها
الارْنَب تَـرْقِد ما تُوذي   ولا شِفْت الناس تخَلّيها
والسَبْع المُوذي مـا يَرْقِد   ولا يُوطا بارضٍ هو فيها
خوفٍ من خَبْـطه بِكْفوفِه   كِلٍّ يِبْـعِد مَنـاحيها
مـا يَقْـرَب حَولِه بِدْياره   والذَلّه مـا هو ناسيها

~ 34 ~

Things are simple and easy at the start; 34.1
sparks and flames follow in their wake.
Discord and strife slumber
until roused by mean rascals.
Some bastard sets the riot alight,
starting a fire he cannot quench:
As the kindling bursts into the flames
of raging war, the culprit makes off,
Leaving it to brave and generous men, 34.5
hosts of the coffee-drinking crowd.
Quell evil at the beginning while you can
so as to gain the upper hand in the end.
Remember, the Lord watches from above;
He causes the soul to die and resurrects us.
Fend off all incentives to wrong behavior;
stay away from pride and arrogance!
If anyone comes to get you by the throat,
smite the attackers with your sword.
Mind you don't appear meek or ready to settle, 34.10
or you'll pay more than half of your wealth.
Let the swish of blades and a will of steel
be aimed at the necks of your foes.
A rabbit lies down and does not fight,
yet you don't see people leave it alone;
Ferocious lions do not crouch and hide;
no one ventures into their domain:
In fear of being torn apart by their paws,
all prefer to give them the widest berth.
The timorous do not approach his lands, 34.15
unable to forget the terror he struck in them.

Notes

1 This *hamziyyah*, a poem that rhymes on the letter *hamzah*, has generated a debate on its attribution to Ḥmēdān and on the question of whether he was literate, given the fact that the *hamzah* has disappeared from the vernacular: al-Fawzān, *Ra'īs al-taḥrīr Ḥumaydān al-Shuwayʿir*, 225–48. Both questions are undecided. Some of the images and wording recur in other poems by Ḥmēdān, and so does Ibn Nḥēṭ, the ruler of al-Ḥuṣūn. It is difficult to see who else could have composed this poem.

2 The meaning of the last two words of the second hemistich in the Arabic text is not clear, and neither word has been included in the translation. Such obscurity may be due to a mistake in transmission.

3 See p. xlv, n. 46.

4 The same classical word for "a beauty" (*kāʿab*), following a prelude about the ravages of old age with many similarities to Ḥmēdān's imagery and vocabulary, occurs in a poem by Jabr ibn Sayyār: Sowayan, *al-Shiʿr al-Nabaṭī*, 481.

5 The interpretation of the second hemistich is based on a communication from Dr. Saad Sowayan.

6 The "Egyptian tinge" is similar to the Ottoman Turkish one in Jabr ibn Sayyār's line, where *rūmiyyah*, literally "Byzantine," stands for Ottoman Turks, as is customary in Arabian poetry: "A Turkish beauty."

7 Eve may have been selected because of the rhyme: in Arabic the name ends on the letter *hamzah*.

8 I.e., he is a parvenu who cannot boast of a respected, ancient lineage that would put him on a par with most of the ruling clans in the area. The person denounced in these verses might be identical to the shaykh ridiculed in poem 11.

9 Ibn Nḥēṭ is praised by means of a contrast with the shaykh lampooned in §§1.21–23. He recovered his family's position as chiefs of al-Ḥuṣūn after his grandfather Māniʿ ibn ʿUthmān al-Ḥdēthī (al-Ḥudaythī) al-Timīmī had been expelled in 1673 with the assistance of the town of Julājil: Sowayan, *al-Shiʿr al-Nabaṭī, sulṭat al-naṣṣ wa-dhā'iqat al-shaʿb*, 484–85; al-Bassām, *Tuḥfat al-mushtāq fī akhbār Najd wa-l-Ḥijāz wa-l-ʿIrāq*, 132. The beautiful girl given to him as a present is a stereotypical motif in this poetry: she symbolizes the poem itself and its preciousness: cf. Sowayan, *Nabaṭi Poetry*, 179.

When this motif is the theme of an entire poem it is called *ʿarūs al-shiʿr*, "the bride of poetry," implying that it is a beautiful poem. According to Sowayan, "in Nabaṭi poetry, *al-ʿarūs* is also a panegyric poem addressed to a friend or patron."

10 It is questionable whether this request for material support should be taken literally. Ḥmēdān was not known for soliciting rewards in exchange for his verses. Content and tone rather imply irony shared with Ibn Nḥēṭ, with whom he appears to have been on friendly terms, see p. xix.

11 It was the custom to keep a victim of snakebite awake all night in the belief that sleep would prove fatal. Hence the saying: "Longer than the night of someone bitten by a snake" to indicate the severity of an ordeal: al-Juhaymān, *al-Amthāl al-shaʿbiyyah fī qalb al-jazīra al-ʿarabiyyah*, 1, 183–84.

12 See p. xxi.

13 The men of the pariah tribe of al-Ṣalab were renowned for their hunting skills (see Glossary).

14 These verses are said to refer to the beginning of Ibn ʿAbd al-Wahhāb's preaching (the "Wahhābī movement") but there is no proof or consensus that the poet lived to witness these events. In one MS these verses are included as part of the next poem, which has the same meter and rhyme.

15 In the rutting season camel studs produce large quantities of lather from their mouth, blobs of which often land on their withers. The reference would be to Muḥammad ibn ʿAbd al-Wahhāb and Muḥammad ibn Suʿūd.

16 Qur'anic verses are read to ward off evil, such as the danger posed by a scorpion's venom. Intriguingly, this piece and a second one on the subject (poem 32) might represent expressions of a rare skeptical view of the Wahhābī movement preserved in Najdī tradition.

17 A well-known saying, as are many other lines in this poem: al-Juhaymān, *al-Amthāl*, 7, 158, "Money covers up blemishes." "In season," i.e., when products are available at relatively low prices. On days like these, those who cannot afford such things are made even more conscious of their disadvantage.

18 Here five verses in the manuscripts have been excised because they are so enigmatic as to be wholly unintelligible. The printed editions offer no explanation. Perhaps other verses that would explain them have gone missing or perhaps these verses have been transposed from another, no longer extant, poem with the same meter and rhyme.

19 To lift heavy buckets and empty them into the basin at the well, and to hoe the earth around the palm trees and the irrigation channels, is backbreaking work done with one's robe girded up under the belt.

20 In this poem "chicken feed," as in English, means something utterly insignificant. In Ḥmēdān's stylistic use of binary phrasing, it is the opposite of war, one of the weightiest matters. The poem inveighs against those who take it lightheartedly.

21 A small matter, like a speck of dust, can bring pretensions crashing down.

22 The last word of the first hemistich of the poem's first verse, *hamāj* ("brackish-tasting water"), is repeated in the rhyme word of the last line, where it follows an antonym, *garāḥ* ("sweet water"), to reinforce the contrast between ruinous war and the pleasant calm of peace.

23 In houses of some standing the room where guests are received is on the second floor, called *rōshan* (from Persian *rowshan*). "A *dīwān* or coffee-room, or even an ordinary room, but always on the first floor, from where those seated in it have a view of what is outside at ground level": Huber, *Journal d'un voyage en Arabie*, 123; and Euting, *Tagbuch einer Reise in Inner-Arabien* , 2, 23. At certain times of the day, after afternoon and sunset prayers, it should be open for the hospitable entertainment of visitors. If the door is always shut, it is a sure sign that its inhabitants are mean-spirited and they may therefore expect to be held in contempt by the townsfolk.

24 A common image, e.g., "A bird without wings will not soar, your wings are camel herds on desert pastures"; or the opposite, "whoever had a wing to fly, took off," Sowayan, *al-Ṣaḥrā' al-ʿarabiyyah*, 350, 601, and "A poem and its narrative by Riḍa ibn Ṭārif al-Shammarī."

25 After grazing on rich pasture, sheep produce great quantities of droppings. This guest, a peasant, was hosted on the flat roof of the mud house and given a large bowl of dates, in the absence of the house's owner. Politeness demands moderation, not that the whole bowl be devoured. This is what the visitor managed to do, and then departed, leaving the roof terrace covered with date pits like sheep droppings. That dates were not a cheap commodity, in spite of the groves of date palms around the towns, is made clear in §18.4. The vengeful host, the poet, then fantasizes how the visitor will be flayed and his skin treated in the way he handled the dates.

26 The *sarrāḥ* of the Arabic text is a craftsman who makes leather thongs for various uses such as the straps of a camel saddle. If the leather made from the peasant visitor's skin is too flaky there is no choice but to discard it, like "limestone dust."

27 Clearly, the lazy fellow is Mānīʿ, the son who is on the receiving end of this kind of sarcasm in other poems.

28 This is a Najdī saying. In explanation it is said that locusts often settle in this tree that is known for its sharp needles so that the only way to catch them is for men to beat their sticks blindly at the tree, as hard as they can. The meaning would be "to act with random

violence": al-Juhaymān, *al-Amthāl*, 3, 89; also 2, 186; 10, 126. Roasted locusts are still eaten as a delicacy in Najd; their taste is comparable to that of shrimp.

29 As in the line of the poet Khalaf Abū Zwayyid, "Instead of you let death take all misers who throw a fit if a moth lands in their melted butter": Sowayan, *Ayyām al-ʿarab*, 611, al-Suwaydā'; *Min Shuʿarā' al-jabal al-ʿāmmiyyīn*, 2, 66.

30 This was indeed normal practice in Najd: Al Juhany, *Najd*, 154–55, "The judges derived part of their income from litigants (. . .) These expenses appear to have been so considerable and controversial that they created discussion, (. . .) expressed in the poetry of Humaydan al-Shuwayʿir, who accused the judges and ulema of his time of abusing their social position and accepting payments and gifts that influenced their legal judgments."

31 According to al-Juhaymān, *al-Amthāl*, 1, 368, a thing held together with metal clasps to keep it from falling apart, i.e., inherently weak and unreliable; al-ʿUbūdī, *Muʿjam al-uṣūl al-faṣīḥah li-l-alfāẓ al-dārijah*, 8, 276, explains that the saying refers to a story about a chief who was seized by his kinsmen and whose feet were shackled together with iron or brass rings. When he was asked to provide a piece of information, he said, "How can I be a chief and expected to act like one while I am shackled?"

32 Literally "rotten maternal uncle," as in the saying, "Every fellow resembles his maternal uncle": Snouck Hurgronje, *Mekkanische Sprichwörter und Redensarten*, 65. See also p. xxvii.

33 As described in the nineteenth century by the traveler Charles M. Doughty, the lances held by Arabian horsemen were very long, and therefore when on foot they had to drag them along: Charles M. Doughty, *Travels in Arabia Deserta*, 1:379.

34 The reference is to feather lice or mites that may impair a bird's plumage and its ability to fly. Such a lice-ridden bird is not fit for hunting, cf. §7.15.

35 The expression *ṯārat bi-ghēr ʿyār* is explained by al-Juhaymān, *al-Amthāl*, 2, 151, as: "A shot fired without precise aiming at the target; a shot fired at random;" and, by extension, "an action taken without due consideration, without measure."

36 The star Aldebaran, in Najd called al-Twēbiʿ, is one of the stars of the hot season and as such it follows the Pleiades. Like the other stars, it rules for thirteen days: al-ʿUbūdī, *Muʿjam al-anwā' wa-l-fuṣūl*, 30–31.

37 The Arabian spiny-tailed lizard, also called *dabb*, see p. xxiv. Jabr ibn Sayyār ridicules a self-important chief in similar terms, as a "rooster" who struts in his fancy dress, a fop who keeps perfuming himself with incense, as in §14.21: Sowayan, *al-Shiʿr al-Nabaṭī*, 486.

38 This is the type of woman recommended in the poet's marriage counseling in poem 19.

39 The word *ʿayārah* denotes playful impudence, an unconventional demeanor that tests the limits of what society can tolerate by confronting it with intentional irreverential and jocular ridicule of appearances. It is similar in meaning to *tajwīrah* in the first line of poem 18, and demonstrates the poet's fondness for puncturing vain pretensions.

40 Jabr ibn Sayyār gives the same definition of good and bad political leaders: Sowayan, *al-Shiʿr al-Nabaṭī*, 489.

41 See n. 37.

42 Cf. the verse of Ḥātim al-Ṭāʾī (see also §§21.53 and 30.32): "A miser's ill repute sticks to him after death, and his wealth is gathered up by a heir" (*inna l-bakhīl idhā mā māta yatbaʿuhu / sūʾu l-thanāʾi wa-yaḥwī al-wārith al-ibilā*). *Dīwān Ḥātim al-Ṭāʾī*, 76; *Dīwān Shiʿr Ḥātim ibn ʿAbd Allāh al-Ṭāʾī wa akhbāruhu*, 192.

43 The sayyid (i.e., a descendant of the prophet Muḥammad) is al-Zubayr ibn al-ʿAwwām, a companion of the Prophet who gave his name to the city of al-Zubayr, near Basra, and whose tomb is mentioned in this verse. According to tradition he is one of the Ten who were promised Paradise by the Prophet (*al-ʿasharah al-mubashsharūn bi-l-jannah*).

44 Famine is personified by Abū Mūsā, a pun on the word for a barber's razor, *mūs* and *mūsā*: al-ʿUbūdi, *Muʿjam al-uṣūl*, 12, 218–19; it is used for someone who fleeces people and works against their interests. See also p. xiii.

45 In another version: "The men of ʿUshayrah are 'sons of al-Manīʿī,'" i.e., a branch of Banū ʿAmr of Tamīm.

46 This verse is only found in the King Saud MS.

47 This poem is particularly thick with proverbs and sayings that have entered the Najdī collections: I counted fifty-two items in the collections that can be linked to verses in this poem. They start with this verse.

48 Literally "richly endowed with regard to his smaller part (*aṣgharih*)": "the smaller part" refers to one's tongue, i.e., eloquence, while one's "two smaller parts" refer to the tongue and the heart: al-Suwaydāʾ, *Faṣīḥ al-ʿāmmī fī shamāl Najd*, 1, 526, and Ibn Manẓūr, *Lisān al-ʿArab*, s.v. *ṣ-gh-r*.

49 "Morning brings profit": Snouck Hurgronje, *Mekkanische Sprichwörter*, 42–43.

50 The "little shaykh," the butt of Ḥmēdān's mockery, is the subject of poem 11. Night birds, like owls, who hunt under the cover of dark, are contrasted with noble falcons, as in §16.49. "Knight of the coffee cups," see also §§11.16 and 17.1–3. Cf. Khiyār al-Kātib's verse: "I am not chased away by every dog that barks, nor am I scared by every fly that buzzes" (*wa-mā kullu kalbin nābiḥin yastafizzunī / wa-lā kullamā ṭār al-dhubābu urāʿu*). Abū Bakr al-Ṣūlī, *The Life and Times of Abū Tammām*, 55.

51 Urine was used for the treatment of wounds and sores because of a belief that it can act as a disinfectant.

52 See p. xxiv.

53 This popular proverb is reflected in six items in the collections: in addition to this verse, "caution does not save you from fate," al-Juhaymān, *al-Amthāl*, 2, 261; "caution is useless against fate," ibid., 6, 260; "caution is of no avail against the arrows of fate," ibid., 7, 238, 249; "caution does not repel fate," al-ʿUbūdī, *al-Amthāl al-ʿāmmiyyah fī Najd* , 1, 394. It is similar in meaning to al-Mutanabbī's verse: "A man trying to dodge an arrow may run from a miss straight into a hit" (*wa-muttaqin wa-l-sihāmu mursalatun / yaḥīdu ʿan ḥābiḍin ilā ṣārid*).

54 "The land of al-Daʿm," i.e., the subtribe to which Ḥmēdān's clan of al-Sayāyirah belongs, see p. xiii.

55 According to al-Faraj, *Dīwān al-Nabaṭ*, 29, note 8, al-Dākhilah is meant, a town near Ibn Māḍī's al-Rawḍah.

56 Āl Migḥim is a family of the Qaḥṭān tribe whose members settled in Sudayr and al-Washm. Ibn Shakir is unknown to me.

57 The contrast is between the falcon that hunts during the day and night birds like the owl: the first is noble and honorable, the second despicable and foul. It is the nature of the "world" to turn things topsy-turvy, with the result, in the words of Rumayzān ibn Ghashshām, that "I observe that the owl is allowed to live in security, while the falcon lives in fear of its blows": Sowayan, *al-Shiʿr al-Nabaṭī*, 460.

58 A *dakkah* is the outdoor area of a house for sitting. In the Gulf it is a stone bench. In Central Arabia it could either be a carpeted area adjoining the house, with a parapet running around the other three sides, or a raised platform. In old al-Qaṣab it was a small terrace on the first floor (of the sort that I saw on my visit to the half-ruined mud dwelling that was said to have been the poet's house), although it could have been on the roof. This is consonant with the line in which this poem's protagonists look down from the top of the house to the street below.

59 Cf. §11.18 for the same topos.

60 See n. 39.

61 See p. xv.

62 They are perennially thirsty from working at al-Qaṣab's salt evaporation pools.

63 Similar in meaning to the verse of al-Ḥuṭayʾah: "Barefooted and naked, they did not have a loaf to eat, / Nor did they ever taste barley since they were born" (*ḥufātun ʿurātun mā ghtadhū khubza mallatin / wa-lā ʿarafū li-l-burri mudh khuliqū ṭaʿman*). Al-Ḥuṭayʾah, *Dīwān*, 178.

64 His daughter, i.e., his daughter-in-law, the wife of his son Māniʿ. In the poet's theatrical cast of characters she stands for the type of shameless, lewd, and unpractical woman one should avoid like the plague: see next poem and p. xxi. He includes himself in the scene of mockery as the poet who gained notoriety for his irreverence and relish for scandalous revelations, as vaunted in §26.3, see also p. xviii. The authenticity of the attribution of these verses in this and the previous poem is disputed by Saudi commentators.

65 His private parts, because of wear and tear, are in need of repair at the town's blacksmith shop. The first hemistich is literally: "He uses the file to take from my little dick" (i.e., to restore it in better shape; the diminutive is used for endearment). Underlying this image is the traditionally low social regard in which craftsmen like the blacksmith, *ṣāniʿ*, are held in tribal society.

66 In these verses the poet contrasts the austere Najdī peasant ethos, which he champions, with a pleasure-seeking mentality unsuited to the region's environment and ruinous to one's chances of survival. Cf. Jabr ibn Sayyār's description of a buxom girl (*kāʿab*), "the scent of sandalwood and musk wafts from her": Sowayan, *al-Shiʿr al-Nabaṭī*, 481.

67 The simile is about digging a well or a trench. The mounds of dug-up earth are the size of the hole that has been opened in the ground. Similarly, the curvaceous shape of this lady should warn Mānīʿ that sexually he may come in for a disappointment: her insides, i.e., her vagina, may turn out to be as wide and cold as the outside features that attracted him to her.

68 On sexual symbolism of the well and its equipment, see §§1.10 and 5.15.

69 A woman who frequently leaves the house to go visiting and gossiping, for which she needs to put on her black cloak, *ʿabāh*.

70 Al-Juhaymān, *al-Amthāl*, 1, 283–84, "attach the donkey rope," i.e., a rope thrown over the donkey's back and tied under his tail, where it is fouled by the animal's droppings. The donkey driver who handles this dirty rope must himself be regarded as impure and contemptible.

71 See §23.6. The man sitting behind the rider on a camel's back used to carry a gun and would slip off the camel's back to take aim. In order not to fall off he had to hold on to the rider in front. It is used here metaphorically, to refer in a derogatory manner to a woman's links to a previous marriage, principally children, and, through them, contacts with a former husband and his kin.

72 The *tarāwīḥ* prayers after the last evening prayer in the month of Ramadan may last for over an hour, and long sections of the Qur'an are read following the prayer leader. These readings are rounded off by a *witr* prayer. Hence, once the imam is heard intoning the formulas of the *witr*, one knows that people will start leaving the mosque soon.

"Cough, cough" occurs in a Najdī saying: al-Juhaymān, *al-Amthāl*, 6, 30, "cough and I cough to you," as a sign among lovers; al-ʿUbūdī, *al-Amthāl*, 1009–10, "Cough in your sleeve," i.e., do something with stealth.

73 Each time her husband has a new key made for the wooden lock to the storeroom to stop her from plundering it, she makes sure to get a copy of the key from the carpenter.

74 First she scares him off, and when he has left she sends him word, pretending that it was not meant as he thought—in the full knowledge that he will probably never return.

75 Q Ṭā Hā 20:85–97.

76 She is postmenopausal, yet on the lookout for an affair.

77 The fellow rider also occurs in §23.6, for a divorced woman, "saddled with fellow riders," i.e., the physical legacy from a previous marriage, the children, and, through them, their father, the former husband.

78 This poem occurs in one edition and two manuscripts. There is some doubt whether it is to be attributed to Ḥmēdān. For instance, the reference in §20.3 to writing the verses on paper is not found elsewhere in his work. Its somewhat ornate style is more characteristic of Jabr ibn Sayyār. On the other hand, its indignation at the disrespect shown him by kinsmen, in spite of his contributions to the common good of the group, and his determination to accept any hardship rather than suffer this humiliation, is a theme in other poems by Ḥmēdān, in particular poem 22, on his self-imposed exile from al-Qaṣab to Uthayfiyah. Its prelude on the art of poetry is reminiscent of the opening verse of poem 26. Some images occur in other poems as well, such as his fame reaching beyond the stars, Arcturus in this poem, Sagitta in §26.28. On balance, therefore, there seems to be no overwhelming argument against the inclusion of the poem.

79 There are doubts about this hemistich's wording. It may have been distorted in the course of transmission.

80 This Bedouin trope of a "world turned upside down" expressed in terms of the animal kingdom is very common: see for instance Holes and Abu Athera, *The Nabaṭī Poetry of the United Arab Emirates*, 24–29.

81 The next verse in the MS has not been included. It proved difficult to make sense of, also for other experts. It may have been distorted in the course of transmission.

82 Cf. the Najdī saying *al-būmah ṣārat girnāsah* "the owl became a peregrine falcon," i.e., a weak person became strong; more often the meaning is a complaint about a world (*al-dinya*) in which things have turned topsy-turvy, with the result that undeserving men have attained better positions and become more powerful than their good and noble fellows.

83 The Arabic text mentions the eleventh century specifically. There are more instances of such mistakes and commentators are in agreement that the poet must have meant a date that begins with the number eleven hundred, that is, the twelfth century hijri.

84 ʿAbd Allāh ibn Muʿammar, the prince of al-ʿUyaynah.

85 The word for "drunk" (*sakrān*), is used for any kind of mental intoxication that leads to loss of control or exuberant behavior. In the poems of Jabr ibn Sayyār vivacious coquettes and their slow, swaying gait are called *sakrānah*: Sowayan, *al-Shiʿr al-Nabaṭī*, 461–63.

86 Explained in the next verse: his mentor, ʿUthmān ibn Sayyār, fears that a man like Ibn Muʿammar, who terrifies his opponents in battle, will not be appeased by a show of contrition. In §21.64 the poet gainsays Ibn Sayyār's premonition.

87 ʿĪsā is a common name for "So-and-so," a servant charged with fetching the riding camel.

88 See n. 23 above.

89 In Arabic: *kāf* and *nūn*, the letter "k" and "n," for *kun*: "Be!" as in the Qurʾanic verses that declare that as God speaks a thing, it comes into being.

90 The reference is to Fāris ibn Bassām, whose poem in praise of ʿAbd Allāh ibn Muʿammar is found in manuscripts of Nabaṭī poetry. Sowayan, *al-Shiʿr al-Nabaṭī*, 569.

91 This poem has been compared to the poem of apologies (*iʿtidhāriyyah*) of the famous pre-Islamic bard al-Nābighah al-Dhubyāni addressed to al-Nuʿmān ibn Mundhir, the king of al-Ḥīrah: see al-Fawzān, *Raʾīs al-taḥrīr*, 4–31, for a perspicacious and detailed comparison between these poems of apology. In this verse Ḥmēdān improves on al-Nābighah's image of vultures following al-Nuʿmān's armies in expectation of feasting on enemy corpses: *idhā mā ghazaw bi-l-jayshi ḥallaqa fawqahum, aʿṣāʾibu ṭayrin tahdtadī bi-aʿṣāʾibī / yuṣāḥibnahum ḥattā yughirna mughārahum, min al-ḍāriyāti bi-l-dimāʾi l-dawāribī* (al-Nābighah al-Dhubyānī, *Dīwān*, 10). Ḥmēdān takes the same image of vultures and scavengers following the prince on the prowl, but ties it to Ibn Muʿammar's hospitality towards his guests. For further comparisons between the two poets, see my forthcoming article in *Quaderni di Studi Arabi*, "Politics and the art of eulogy in Najdī Nabaṭī poetry: Ḥmēdān al-Shwēʿir's (al-Shuwayʿir) apologies to Ibn Muʿammar and Ibn Sbayyil's Ode on Ibn Rashīd."

92 This verse echoes the verses of Abū Tammām: "ʿAmr's bold advance, Ḥātim's munificence, Aḥnaf's insight, and Iyās's wit" (*iqdāma ʿAmrin fī samāḥati Ḥātimin, fī ḥilmi Aḥnafa fī dhakāʾi Iyāsi*); and "You have become Ḥātim in generosity, Aḥnaf in sagacity, and Kayyis and Daghfal in knowledge." Abū Bakr al-Ṣūlī, *The Life and Times of Abū Tammām*, 261, 167. For Abū Tammām, shrewdness is exemplified by Iyās ibn Muʿāwiyah ibn Qurrah al-Muzanī (d. 121/739); Ḥmēdān cites ʿAmr ibn al-ʿĀṣ for cunning. In Abū Tammām's verse, boldness is exemplified by the poet and warrior ʿAmr ibn

Maʿdīkarib (d. after 16/637), ibid. 347, 359, 370. Al-Faraj mentions in a note that ʿAmr ibn al-ʿĀṣ was famous for his *makr*, "craftiness," *Dīwān al-Nabaṭ*, 47.

93 Cf. al-Farazdaq's verse: "It makes no difference to the Taghlib Wā'il whether you lampoon them or piss where the two seas clash" (*mā ḍarra Taghliba Wā'ilin ahjawtahā / am bulta ḥaythu tanāṭāḥa al-baḥrāni*). Abū Bakr al-Ṣūlī, *The Life and Times of Abū Tammām*, 55.

94 Cf. the Najdī saying *ṭēḥat jdārin mrāwis* "crashing down like a high wall," i.e., a collapse or disastrous event that has been in the making for a long time and then occurs all of a sudden without warning. Al-Juhaymān, *al-Amthāl*, 4, 267–68; and *ṭāḥ ṭēḥat jdār* ("he collapsed like a wall"). Al-ʿUbūdī, *al-Amthāl*, 762.

95 "Tabāraka" and "Hal Atā" here refer to to the Qur'anic suras al-Mulk (Q 67) and al-Insān (Q 76) respectively, using the opening words of each.

96 The poet argues that a ruler who instills such fear in his opponents in battle can afford to be generous toward supplicants and forgive them—contrary to the opinion given by the chief of al-Qaṣab, ʿUthmān ibn Sayyār, in §21.29.

97 The second hemistich is quoted as another example of the poet's pluckiness—as if he felt he had almost gone too far in eating humble pie in the previous lines. An alternative translation might be: "If he rejects it, no one knows what his life has in store."

98 The expression in the first hemistich is similar to the saying, "his deceit stuck in his throat," meaning that he became the victim of his own treachery: al-Juhaymān, *al-Amthāl*, 6, 179, and al-ʿUbūdī, *al-Amthāl*, 1073–74. It occurs in the poetry of Rumayzān ibn Ghashshām, the chief of al-Rawḍah with whom Jabr ibn Sayyār corresponded: "When sword is true to a heart on the prowl, the enemy's troops will choke on their deceit": Sowayan, *al-Shiʿr al-Nabaṭī*, 461.

99 Another reading of the second hemistich might be: "While I reckoned that there would always be another week."

100 During the hot season of ninety days in summer, *al-qayẓ*, the Bedouin and their herds stay fixed at wells, where they interact socially with other Bedouin and the villagers, as described romantically in the poetry of ʿAbdallah ibn Sbayyil. Spring, when the Bedouin and their herds are spread out in pasture, is the time for raiding, as noted by Euting, *Tagbuch*, 146: "This lovely winter and spring season also has a less appealing side. True, the owner of camel herds roams the desert pastures at will, without having to worry about food and drink. But then the same holds true for his enemies. Therefore spring is the heyday for countless raiding expeditions by individual robbers or gangs of honorable marauders."

101 Ṣalab, see Glossary.

102 The groves are evoked in the same words by Jabr ibn Sayyār: "I wish for a shady palm grove at a gushing well": Sowayan, *al-Shiʿr al-Nabaṭī*, 490.

103 A conventional motif: Jabr ibn Sayyār speaks in similar terms about sending his undaunted son on a mission: Sowayan, *al-Shiʿr al-Nabaṭī*, 492.

104 He exhorts his son by reminding him that he is not a woman from whom such feats are not to be expected, but a man who must undertake demanding tasks without hesitation.

105 Many verses mention the tendency of riding camels, once they leave the open desert spaces behind and have entered a town, to be startled by the sight of dark shapes in their vicinity, such as their own shadow, mud walls, palm trees, and houses. Musil, *The Manners and Customs of the Rwala Bedouins*, 299: "The Bedouin she-camels are easily scared by the shade and the rustling of palm groves, as well as by the high walls enclosing them." Similarly, Euting, *Tagbuch*, 48, 156; Palgrave, *Personal Narrative of a Year's Journey through Central and Eastern Arabia (1862–63)* , 72.

106 This prince's generosity makes it superfluous to go in search of real pastures. Muḥammad is mentioned in only one manuscript, listed in the index as MS Shiʿr Nabati; the others have ʿAbd Allāh. If it is ʿAbd Allāh ibn Muʿammar who is addressed, then this raises a question about dating, because he died before Muḥammad ibn Māḍī (§22.52) came to power. He was succeeded by his grandson Muḥammad ibn Ḥamad ibn ʿAbd Allāh, nicknamed Khirfāsh, who was killed in 1729. Reading Muḥammad for ʿAbd Allāh is also more in conformity with the meter.

107 Normally men would not part with their fillies, their most prized possessions. In times of famine and hardship they may be forced to do so. The meaning of this second hemistich is not certain : it might also mean that in addition the ruler gives fillies as presents. The word for "filly," *bint al-ḥṣān*, is explained by Lady Anne Blunt in *A Pilgrimage to Nejd*, 351, as "what the Anazeh would call 'beni' or 'banat hossan'; that is to say, animals with a stain in their pedigree, and therefore not asil, though often nearly as good and as good-looking."

108 A standard expression, see §28.14.

109 The town of Shaqrā' must be meant, the largest settlement of Banū Zayd in al-Washm: Juhany, *Najd*, 118–19. The unflattering judgments of the places in §§22.45–48 are reminiscent of Ḥmēdān's poem 15, in which he attaches mostly derisive labels to a series of towns in Sudayr.

110 The literal meaning of the last two words of the verse is "the sweepings of the threshing floor," or, in another version, "the chaff of a threshing floor." Al-Junaydil, *al-Sānī w-al-sāniyah*, 118.

111 The expression *gibābīn ṣaḥṣaḥ*, literally "darkling beetles (sg. *gbūn*, CA *qubūn*) on a barren plain," is used to indicate the impossibility of getting hold of something because its parts scatter in all directions and keep eluding one's grasp, i.e., "an ungovernable lot," al-Juhaymān, *al-Amthāl*, 5, 272.

112 With Canopus at his back, the messenger sets out in northerly direction toward Ibn Māḍī's town, Rawḍat Sudayr.

113 It is unknown which town is meant. Al-Ḥātam mentions Ibn Mu'ammar, but the date he gives for Muḥammad ibn Māḍī's death, 1644, is impossible. The incident he mentions was the killing of Māḍī ibn Muḥammad in 1647.

114 Q Ghāshiyah 88:6. It is the thorny shrub fed to those in Hell.

115 An expression often encountered in Najdī poetry: mountain such-and-such would sooner fly away than so-and-so would be to act in a certain way. See for example, Hess, *Von den Beduinen des Innern Arabiens*, 1–2, the tale of the love affair between the mountains Ṭimiyyah and Giṭan. Here the mountain and the tribe of the town Julājil are meant.

116 Julājil used to be the dominant military power in Sudayr, see p. xii.

117 After having been divorced by her brutish husband, it is implied, she returns to her parents' house with her little children and pregnant with another child by her former husband, thereby imposing the burden of care on her parents and other kin. Literally, the Arabic word translated as "burdened with a family of their own" reads "saddled with a rear-rider."

118 Al-'Ubūdī, *al-Amthāl*, 726–27: "The young ones in the group should act as the servants." In the Arabic text the word for "servant" has a double diminutive. The intention is to underline the dangers inherent in an abundance of good and to stress the opportunities hardship offers. The first hemistich may assert that if famine reigns, generous men become even more of a shining example and acquire added prestige and power; or it may mean that hospitable men are also forced by their "servant," famine, to reduce their entertainment of guests. The same meaning is expressed in §14.5. This poem is particularly rich in proverbs and sayings.

119 Similar to the shaykh who is the main subject of poem 11 and also features in poem 1, §12.6, and §16.23.

120 Al-Juhaymān, *al-Amthāl*, 8, 94, cites the story of an otherwise unknown man, called Ibn Dirmah, who was killed in an act of revenge and left to die a painful death, his sweat mixing with his blood, as an exemplary punishment.

121 One wonders if this verse was added in a later era. It does not sound typical of Ḥmēdān.

122 The lives of men fallen in war are the price to be paid for successful mediation to restore peace.

123 The same image, but in a negative sense, in §24.17.

124 The dish, *duwayfah*, is made of wheat mixed with milk or water, and kneaded into a thick paste and boiled. It is a poor man's version of *ʿaṣīdah*, which is the same but uses less water and contains clarified butter and seeds.

125 One of the poet's editors, al-Ḥamdān, who is from al-Bīr, the town lampooned in this piece, believes that it has been mistakenly attributed to Ḥmēdān. According to him, there is no indication that the poet visited the town. Also, he notes, this poem has a double rhyme, unlike Ḥmēdān's other poetry: al-Ḥamdān, *Dīwān Ḥumaydān*, 131–32. In fact, the use of double rhyme has been attested even earlier than Ḥmēdān's compositions. In any case, the tone is very much that of Ḥmēdān. Its verses are also much quoted as popular sayings: I counted fourteen items in the collections for this piece's seven verses, the highest ratio among his poems. The individuals named are not known and could well be fictional. The piece might be considered part of the poet's peasant burlesque: in this case as he makes fun of the paltry hospitality on offer among those who have a hard time just scraping by.

126 Boasting about one's reckless exploits also occurs in early Arabic poetry as part of the poet's amorous encounters. An immediate predecessor of Ḥmēdān in this regard was Rumayzān ibn Ghashshām, e.g., the verses in which he boasts about evading "the sleeping enviers and the informer" (*al-ḥussād w-al-wāshi*), sword in hand, "O Jabr, the blade of my sword is my key to happiness" (*ya-Jabr ḥadd al-sēf miftāḥ al-faraj*). Sowayan, *al-Shiʿr al-Nabaṭī*, 458. On Rumayzān as a predecessor of Ḥmēdān, see p. xiv.

127 A standard expression for "kissing" in this poetry is "to drink the honey-like saliva from the beloved's lips."

128 Like the laborers in al-Qaṣab's salt evaporation pools, men who make their living by cutting fire bush (*Calligonum comosum*, Arabic *irṭā*, an excellent smokeless fuel) in the belt of sands to the town's southwest are presented in §18.2 as among the poorest peasants. Here they are contrasted with wealthy men who own great herds of camels: the peasants' hand gestures express their amazement at this spectacle.

129 In poetry God is praised as the healer of fractured bones. To have knowledge of ways to heal broken bones is therefore held in high regard. The second hemistich is a well-known proverb, see p. xxix, meaning that money is the solution for many of life's problems.

130 Literally, "enters [the house] but does not venture forth."

131 See p. xvi and n. 30.

132 A similar image occurs in a poem by Rumayzān ibn Ghashshām: "Times are always pregnant, never sterile; their vicious and evil camel calves sicken the hearts of men," Sowayan, *al-Shiʿr al-Nabaṭī*, 426. The last word of the hemistich, *ʿawān*, occurs in a

similar line by the first/seventh century poet Muzarrid ibn Ḍirār al-Dhubyānī: "When time becomes pregnant and gives birth to continuous war, and the air is heavy with foreboding of coming disaster" (*wa-ʿindī idhā l-ḥarbu al-ʿawānu talaqqaḥat, wa-abdat hawādīhā l-khuṭūbu l-zalāzilu*), where *ʿawān* is an "epithet of war, long-continued trouble," Lyall, *The Mufaḍḍalīyāt*, 1:164; 3:28. See also Zuhayr ibn Abī Sulmā: *idhā laqiḥat ḥarbun ʿawānun muḍirratun* ("When times become pregnant with a grinding, devastating war"), *Dīwān*, 103–4.

133 In the first hemistich, Birrīt is a deep well from which water is drawn with long ropes and much toil. The second hemistich mentions al-Khudūd, an abundant well in al-Aḥsāʾ oasis where the water gushes at the surface almost like a running stream.

134 Here Ḥmēdān is outdone by his predecessor Jabr ibn Sayyār, who is not driven by concern for his self-esteem but by infatuation. For him love is worth more than "the Hijaz and Syria and Egypt / and Sanaa and Damascus and Iraq and India, the kingdoms of the Christians, and the lands of the Jews": Sowayan, *al-Shiʿr al-Nabaṭī*, 461.

135 See n. 30.

136 See p. xxvi.

137 This gate is unknown to the commentators. In Saudi Arabia old towns made of mud brick have been abandoned in favor of new cities built in their proximity.

138 The word translated as "camel plundered" (*ʿrāfah*) is used for a camel that is recognized by its branding marks to belong to a certain family or clan, for instance when it is offered for sale. If this comes to the attention of the rightful owner, he may claim it. That should be easy in this case, according to the poet, because its ownership is known to all and it is the owners' legitimate right to retrieve it.

139 From §28.40 on, printed editions and manuscripts differ in the order of verses and in which verses are included, see p. xxxix. It is not clear how this verse and the next should be interpreted: do they refer to the men addressed by the messenger and their response? If it is the poet speaking, on what occasion did he receive this response from them? Do the verses belong somewhere else in the poem, or have some verses gone missing? These questions must remain unanswered for lack of information or until better alternatives are discovered.

140 Here the poet speaks of al-Qaṣab, his hometown situated to the northeast of a strip of sands named ʿUrayq al-Buldān or Nafūd al-Washm.

141 Here the poet resumes the messenger's speech to al-ʿAzāʿīz.

142 This place is not known to the commentators and does not occur in the geographical dictionaries.

143 ʿAlī ibn Zāmil was killed in battle against ʿAbd al-ʿAzīz ibn Muḥammad ibn Suʿūd, fighting on the side of Tharmadāʾ, in 1750; ʿAbd al-Karīm ibn Zāmil was taken prisoner in another battle waged by ʿAbd al-ʿAzīz against Tharmadāʾ and its allies in 1754–55: al-Bassām, *Tuḥfat al-mushtāq*, 199 and 201. It is most unlikely that this poem refers to these events: it cannot have been composed at such a late date. It must be placed in the context of Ḥmēdān's self-exile to Uthayfiyah and Uthayfiyah's refusal to pay tribute to Tharmadāʾ, which can only have taken place many years earlier. Therefore, these verses probably represent a later addition, possibly by transmitters who wished to insert some flattering words about the Ibn Zāmil clan from Uthayfiyah, a fairly normal practice in the case of famous poets whose verses were widely quoted and could redound to or detract from the reputation of personalities, families, and clans. At that time poems were the only effective way of self-advertisement, so few individuals were averse to riding piggyback on so powerful a vehicle for attaining high repute. See also Glossary under Uthayfiyah and Tharmadāʾ.

144 See p. xxiv. The enemy is the town of Julājil, the most powerful in Sudayr. In 1673 the chief of Julājil, Ibrāhīm ibn Sulaymān, expelled Ibn Nḥēṭ's grandfather Māniʿ ibn ʿUthmān of the Ḥudaythah (Ḥdēthah) clan and installed another group: al-Fākhirī, *al-Akhbār al-Najdiyyah*, 76.

145 A reference to Moses's unintended killing of an Egyptian, Q Qaṣaṣ 28:15.

146 The phrase "Bedouin and settled folks" is another way of saying, "all men; everyone."

147 Cf. the saying, "Starve your dog so that he will follow you" (*ajiʿ kalbak yatbaʿk*); Ibn Manẓūr, *Lisān al-ʿArab*, s.v. *j-w-ʿ*. In the Najdī vernacular, the proverb is similar, with a slight linguistic difference (*jawwiʿ kalbik yatbaʿk*). Al-Juhaymān, *al-Amthāl*, 2, 224.

148 These are standard descriptions of a riding camel's qualities and body parts that are as old as the pre-Islamic poet Ṭarafah's famous camel ode. See Geiger, "Die Muʿallaqa des Ṭarafa." Here the breastbone does not rub against the leg muscles—which is why the camel is praised for having widely spaced axillae. The soft soles of a camel's feet are ideally suited to sand but will easily bleed on rocky ground and sharp stones: bleeding soles will be swaddled in cloth for protection but the animal's gait will be impaired. In Ḥmēdān's work there is no effort to make the messenger motif sound like a scene derived from lived reality. It is a nod to literary convention.

149 Uthayfiyah, the messenger's destination, lies to the southwest of al-Qaṣab. It is not clear, therefore, why the poet sends him in an easterly direction. Possibly he traveled by a roundabout way on a path that first veered a little east before bending west toward al-Marāh and then on to his destination. The last word of the hemistich, *ʿawān*, occurs in a similar line by the first/seventh century poet Muzarrid ibn Ḍirār al-Dhubyānī:

"When time becomes pregnant and gives birth to continuous war, and the air is heavy with foreboding of coming disaster" (*wa-ʿindī idhā l-ḥarbu al-ʿawānu talaqqaḥat, wa-abdat hawādīhā l-khuṭūbu l-zalāzilu*), where *ʿawān* is an "epithet of war, long-continued trouble," C.J. Lyall, The Mufaḍḍalīyāt, 1:164; 3:282. See also Zuhayr ibn Abī Sulmā: *idhā laqiḥat ḥarbun ʿawānun muḍirratun* ("When times become pregnant with a grinding, devastating war"), *Dīwān*, 103–4.

150 The poet is Ḥātim al-Ṭāʾī. The printed editions do not mention which verse is meant. In the collected poetry of Ḥātim, or poetry attributed to him, a verse that comes somewhat close in meaning to the next two verses in this poem is: "Even when death stares me in the eye, I do not shrink and keep my composure" (*wa-innī idhā mā al-mawtu lam yaku dūnahu / qidā al-shibri aḥmī al-anfa an ataʾakhkharā*). Similarly, Ḥātim prefers to keep his self-respect intact by living up to the code of chivalry even if it results in poverty: "Riches do not raise my standing among kinsmen, nor does poverty scar my reputation" (*fa-mā zādanā baʾwan ʿalā dhī qarābatin / ghinānā wa-lā azrā b-aḥsābinā al-faqru*). Ḥmēdān uses the same verb, *azrā*, with the meaning "to bring disgrace, shame," in §30.33. *Dīwān Ḥātim al-Ṭāʾī*, 51, 53; *Dīwān Shiʿr Ḥātim*, 203, 257.

151 One is reminded of Dolores Ibarruri's maxim, "It is better to die on your feet than to live on your knees." This verse echoes the saying of the Prophet: "Whoever is killed in defense of his possessions is a martyr" (*man qutila dūna mālihi fa-huwa shahīdun*).

152 An ʿIngirī is a member of al-ʿAnāgir, the ruling clan of al-Tharmadāʾ.

153 A frequently used expression: al-Juhaymān, *al-Amthāl*, 9, 198; al-ʿUbūdī, *al-Amthāl*, 122, "to cut the breast that fed you," a jocular expression similar to "biting the hand that feeds you." Here it sends the message that the ruler of Tharmadāʾ should forcibly be deprived of his tribute from Uthayfiyah, just as he forced others to part with sustenance they tried to hold on to.

154 A playful allusion to the old custom among warring tribes of having their beauties ride in a howdah carried by a strong, brightly festooned camel in order to shout encouragement to the fighters, occasionally even baring their breasts. It adds to the comic effect to think that these village clodhoppers imagine themselves performing in a heroic display with such time-honored chivalrous overtones.

155 The Arabic word *magrūn* here has the meaning of "a fancy dress like a cloak (*bisht*) or headdress," communication from Dr. Saad Sowayan.

156 It is generally assumed by Saudi commentators that in this last verse the poet includes himself in the picture to round off the quixotic enterprise with a fitting touch of bathos.

157 See poem 3 and n. 14.

158 As in poem 3, these verses deploy camel imagery in their allusions to the rise of the religious reform movement of Muḥammad ibn ʿAbd al-Wahhāb, here likened to a wolf. The four bags are the four major schools of Islamic law, with the Ibāḍī school added as a fifth. According to al-Fawzān, *Raʾīs al-taḥrīr*, 199, al-Bāṭin here refers to a dry watercourse to the west of al-Qaṣab.

159 This element in the piece's enigmatic style was explained to me as deriving from a children's tale or game featuring a lion with big whiskers. Prof. Clive Holes has come across *al-ḥōḥiyyah*, the same expression, in Bahrain: "I have come across *ḥūḥū* (or *ḥūḥaw*) in Bahrain; it is the noise supposedly made by a bogeyman (*abū l-ʿuyūn il-ḥumur*, 'the one with the red eyes') who comes in the night and 'gets' children if they are disobedient," (personal communication). And in the glossary of Holes's *Dialect, Culture, and Society in Eastern Arabia*, 1, we find: "*ḥūḥū* 'woof woof' sound supposedly made by bogeymen used to frighten children."

160 Dates of uncultivated trees can be picked by anyone. It is also customary to allow the poor to pick up any dates that have fallen from cultivated date palms before the harvest. The implication is that he should postpone payment of his debt for another year instead of paying it straightaway and thus be left without means.

161 Literally "and play the game of *al-biyyih*." This is one of the oldest traditional games, also called *al-mangalih*. It consists of two wooden boards, each with seven holes, and with a total of seventy small balls. In the early days the holes were made in the ground and the game played with pebbles. It is played by two participants who are encouraged by their friends. See http://www.rwlh.net/vb/t52045-6.html. In al-Qaṣīm it is played with pebbles or date pits in small holes in the ground, Sowayan, *al-Thaqāfah al-taqlīdiyyah*, 12, *al-Alʿāb*, 131–32.

162 This refers to a proverb: al-Juhaymān, *al-Amthāl*, 4, 425; 8, 85: "To keep a she-camel with Wugayyān." The explanation is that anything given to the care of this poor, wandering Bedouin should be considered as lost. Such a she-camel is therefore a purely imaginary possession. It is used to express doubts about the promises an individual makes.

163 When peasants and Bedouin are hard at work watering their camels or working their fields, they pull up their robes and keep them in place with their belts. Because they are forced to continue working until after sunset, they combine the last two prayers of the day in the evening prayer.

Glossary

Aḥnaf al-Aḥnaf ibn Qays, an influential leader of the major tribe of Tamīm who was instrumental in convincing his fellow tribesmen to embrace Islam. Later he became one of the generals who led the Muslim armies in Persia. He worked tirelessly as a moderate force and mediator in tribal and other conflicts. For this reason his quality of *ḥilm*, forbearance and intelligence, became proverbial: *aḥlam min al-Aḥnaf*, "more understanding than al-Aḥnaf."

ʿAjfat al-Gūr an unknown location. Perhaps ʿAfjah is meant, a wadi with various kinds of shrubs, and the name of three different locations in al-Yamāmah.

ʿĀmir one of the ruling families in Julājil, which was in the seventeenth and eighteenth centuries the regional powerhouse in Sudayr. Its members belong to the subtribe of al-Badārīn of al-Dawāsir. Originally from Wādi al-Dawāsir in southern Najd, they migrated to central Najd in the fifteenth century. This family appears for the first time in the Najdī chronicles as the rulers of this town in 1667.

ʿAmr [ibn al-ʿĀṣ] leader of the Muslim armies in some of their most spectacular early victories. He is especially known for the conquest of Egypt, where he acquired a reputation as an exceptionally able administrator. He sided with Muʿāwiyah against Muḥammad's son-in-law ʿAlī in the First Civil War, and avoided defeat by the ruse of attaching Qur'an pages to lances. The poet cites him as a symbol of shrewdness and political cunning.

al-ʿAnāgir (al-ʿAnāqir) a tribe of Banū Saʿd of Tamīm. It is concentrated in the regions of al-Washm, al-ʿĀriḍ, and al-Qaṣīm. The branch of Āl Khanāfir ruled in Tharmadā', the dominant regional power that levied tribute from Shaqrā' and Uthayfiyah in the north to Ḍurmā in the south. The singular is al-ʿIngirī, as in the name of the famous ruler and poet Bdāḥ al-ʿIngirī. Ibn Muʿammar of al-ʿUyaynah was descended from al-ʿAnāqir in Tharmadā', as were the families of some other chieftains in the area.

al-ʿĀriḍ the heart of the al-Yamāmah region, called "the barrier" after the Ṭuwayq escarpment that runs through it from north to south and rises like a wall of stone. It is traversed by Wādi Ḥanīfah, where there are important towns like al-ʿUyaynah, al-Dirʿiyyah, and Riyadh, the capital of Saudi Arabia.

al-ʿAṭṭār a town in the lower part of Wādi Faqī, inhabited by al-ʿUraynāt of Subayʿ whose chiefs were Āl Sayf.

al-ʿAwdah see *al-ʿŌdih.*

al-ʿAzāʿīz a branch of Banū Ḥanẓalah ibn Mālik ibn Zayd al-Manāh of Tamīm. According to the historian al-Fākhirī, in 1704 they became the masters of Uthayfiyah (now Uthaythiyah). They gave Ḥmēdān asylum and he praised them in his poetry.

Bini Zēd (Banū Zayd) a Najdī tribe which originally had its center in the High Najd and al-Washm. They are strongly represented in the towns of Shaqrāʾ (it is they whom Ḥmēdān mentions), al-Quwayʿiyyah, al-Shaʿrāʾ, and al-Dawādimī.

al-Bīr a town whose name means "well," situated south of al-Washm in the region of al-Miḥmal, not far from Thādiq. Before 1616 it was a well of the Subayʿ tribe. It has since been settled by families of al-Dawāsir in southern Najd. It is the birthplace of Muḥammad al-Ḥamdān, an editor of Ḥmēdān's poetry, who also wrote a book about his town.

Chosroes (Ar. Kisrā, from the Persian name Khusraw) the Sasanid rulers in general. It is remarkable that Ḥmēdān employs the Persian kings as a symbol for justice; in Arab lore they stood for extravagance and despotism.

al-Dahnāʾ a range of sands in eastern Arabia that connects the Nafūd desert in the north with the Empty Quarter in the south over a length of more than a thousand kilometers. From the perspective of the poet these block the view to the east from the regions of al-Washm and Sudayr. The word means "desert" and also "a red-leaved shrub that is used as a color agent." The poet uses it as a symbol of great fortune, in terms both of the immensity of the sands and the red gleam associated with gold (§1.3).

al-Dākhlah (al-Dākhilah) a prosperous village to the northeast of al-Rawḍah and very close to it. Its inhabitants are from al-Nuwāṣir of Tamīm. There is said to be a poet called Rāʿ al-Dākhlah whose invective is as caustic as Ḥmēdān's but he has not been published nor do I have information concerning any manuscript where his work may be found.

al-Dir'iyyah the original capital of the Suʿūd dynasty, now a suburb of Riyadh. The town was destroyed in 1819 at the orders of Ibrāhīm Pasha of Egypt after his successful siege of the town.

Ḍruma (Ḍurmā') a town in al-ʿĀriḍ about sixty kilometers to the west of Riyadh, known as an agricultural center on the old road from Riyadh to the Ḥijāz. Its fortunes were always interwined with al-Dirʿiyyah across the Ṭuwayq escarpment.

al-Ghāṭ a town overlooked by two promontories of the Ṭuwayq escarpment, Khashm al-Shāsh from the south, and Khashm al-ʿIrniyyah from the north. It is the town of the famous family of al-Sidārā (singular: al-Sudayrī), originally from al-Dawāsir, who became affiliated to the Suʿūd family. Its inhabitants are from different tribal backgrounds.

Ḥātim [al-Ṭā'ī] a symbol of prodigious hospitality, the pre-Islamic Bedouin poet Ḥātim al-Ṭā'ī is one of the most widely known ancient figures in Saudi Arabia today. He is synonymous with the traditional virtues of generosity and the lavish entertainment of guests, similar to the huge sculptures of coffeepots that adorn the entrance to many Najdī towns. A popular Najdī saying runs, "more generous than Ḥātim." He is especially associated with the region of Ḥā'il, whose inhabitants claim him as one of their own. The tribe may have gone but the mountain ranges are still called Jabal Ṭayyi'.

al-Ḥawṭah see *al-Ḥōṭah*.

Ḥizwa (Ḥuzwā) an area of dunes in the al-Dahnā' sands near Maʿqalah, where the early Bedouin poet Dhū l-Rummah is buried.

al-Ḥjarah a place north of the old village of Līnah and its deep wells on the pilgrim road to Iraq in the northeastern part of Saudi Arabia, about one hundred kilometers from the border with Iraq. South of Līnah lie the sands of al-Dahnā'.

al-Ḥōṭah (al-Ḥawṭah) a town at the center of Wādi al-Faqī in Sudayr, inhabited by various clans of Tamīm and other tribes.

al-Ḥrayyig (al-Ḥurayyiq) an isolated village on the flanks of the Ṭuwayq escarpment. It had strong ties with Ushayqir, where the founders of al-Mashārifah (Āl Musharraf) branch of al-Wahabah of Tamīm came from. Al-Qaṣab became involved in this village's internecine struggles: the chief Ibn Yūsuf fled, and returned in 1700 with the help of al-Qaṣab.

al-Ḥṣūn (al-Ḥuṣūn) a town with many palm groves that was settled by Āl Tumayyim with the permission of al-Qārah, another village near al-Janūbiyyah in Sudayr. Its chiefs, the Ibn Nḥēṭ clan, were dislodged and then returned. Later they were succeeded by Āl Yaḥyā of al-Wahabah of Tamīm.

Ḥuzwā see *Ḥizwa.*

Ibn ʿAbd al-Wahhāb, Muḥammad (1703–92) preacher of a rigorous version of Islam. In 1745 he concluded a religio-political compact with Muḥammad ibn Suʿūd, the ruler of al-Dirʿiyyah. The armed campaigns that followed brought the town of al-Yamāmah and others further afield under Saudi dominion, one after the other. This became the foundation of modern Saudi Arabia.

Ibn Māḍī, Muḥammad ruler of al-Rawḍah. The earliest mention of the Ibn Māḍī family of Āl Rājiḥ of Banū ʿAmr of Tamīm as a ruling house in al-Rawḍah dates from the first half of the seventeenth century. They were frequently involved in internecine struggles with the other families who traced their descent from the same ancestor, with involvement from Julājil and other towns in Sudayr. Māḍī ibn Jāsir ibn Māḍī died in 1726–27 and it is probable that he was succeeded by his son Muḥammad. He was murdered in the mosque of al-Rawḍah in 1745 by his brothers Māniʿ and Turkī; the latter came with armed assistance from Julājil, where he had found refuge.

Ibn Muʿammar, ʿAbd Allāh (d. 1725, during the plague) chief of al-ʿUyaynah from 1684. The period of his rule is considered the town's golden era: it became the undisputed cultural, religious, and political center of al-Yamāmah. His high standing, and the fear he inspired, are reflected in Ḥmēdān's long and poignant poem of apology to him (poem 21). The exact reason for this poem is not known, and it is unlikely to be something he said in one of the other poems in this collection. The poem itself refers to "words" Ḥmēdān was supposed to have said and that were reported to Ibn Muʿammar by his enemies at the court. "Words" in this context must be understood as "verse."

Ibn Nḥēṭ ruler of al-Ḥuṣūn. In spite of an insulting description of Ibn Nḥēṭ in one poem, Ḥmēdān appears to have been on friendly terms with him if one goes by the other poems, especially the one in which he addresses him in the first line (see §29.1). Jabr ibn Sayyār lavished great praise on Ibn Nḥēṭ's brother Suʿūd ibn Māniʿ ibn ʿUthmān (it is assumed that it is he who is meant by "Ibn Māniʿ"), describing him as "the jewel of all Arab lineages" in an exchange of poems. Therefore, the Sayāyirah of al-Qaṣab seem to have traditionally had good relations with this family. In 1699 ʿUthmān ibn Nḥēṭ returned from al-Aḥsāʾ to the town of al-Ḥuṣūn and defeated Āl Tumayyim of Banū Khālid. ʿUthmān's grandfather Māniʿ ibn ʿUthmān al-Ḥudaythī (Āl Ḥudaythah) of Tamīm had been forced out by Āl Tumayyim in 1672, along with his sons Suʿūd and Nḥēṭ. ʿUthmān was later turned out of the town (but it is not known when) by his sons Māniʿ and Suʿūd, in collusion with the ruler of Julājil, an event described by Ḥmēdān in a poem that compares his opponents' tactics to a ruse whereby the dabb, the large Arabian lizard, is enticed out of its underground hole. Ḥmēdān says that he warned Ibn Nḥēṭ repeatedly about this very danger.

Ibn Sayyār, Jabr Jabr ibn Ḥazmī (or according to another source, Jabr ibn Ḥzēmī) ibn Sayyār, considered one of the outstanding Najdī poets of his time. He exchanged many poems with colleagues, foremost among them the ruler of al-Rawḍah, Rumayzān ibn Ghashshām. It is assumed that Ḥmēdān may have known him as a young man and that he was influenced by his work. He died in approximately 1708 at a great age, after the death of Ibrāhīm ibn Rāshid al-Sayyārī, his successor as chief of al-Qaṣab.

Ibn Sayyār, ʿUthmān a relative of the famous poet Jabr ibn Sayyār whose family belongs to al-Sayāyirah of Banū Khālid. In 1725–26 ʿUthmān ibn Ibrāhīm ibn Rāshid ibn Māniʿ killed his son Ibrāhīm, who had succeeded him as the town's chief. Ḥmēdān's respect for ʿUthmān is clear from the advice he asks him for in his poem of apology to Ibn Muʿmmar.

Ibn Zāmil a family of the ʿĀʾidh branch of the Qaḥṭān tribe in Uthayfiyah and al-Kharj. The chronicles mention ʿAlī and ʿAbd al-Karīm ibn Zāmil, who were killed or captured in fighting between Tharmadāʾ and al-Dirʿiyyah and its allies.

al-ʿIrniyyah a mountain peak towering over al-Ghāṭ.

Jazrah see *Jzerah*.

Jlājil (Julājil) a major town in Sudayr. In the seventeenth century it is mentioned in connection with a visit by the sharif of Mecca, Zayd ibn Muḥsin, and with armed conflict with al-Tuwaym, another powerful town in Sudayr. It also clashed repeatedly with clans in Rawḍat Sudayr. Its rulers belonged to Āl ʿĀmir of al-Dawāsir tribe. In 1763–64 it was subdued by the Saudi rulers of al-Dirʿiyyah. As with the dominant town in al-Washm, Tharmadā', once Julājil submitted, all resistance in the region disappeared.

Jzerah (Jazrah) a tributary to the wadi of Julājil.

al-Khīs a village in Sudayr northwest of al-Majmaʿah.

al-Majmaʿah a regional center founded in 1427 by ʿAbd Allāh al-Shammarī with permission from Ibn Mudlij al-Wā'ilī from nearby al-Ḥarmah, a town that was subsequently eclipsed by the new settlement. The ʿUthmān family, whose ancestor is mentioned by Ḥmēdān, are his descendants.

Mecca, valley of (Ar. al-Bāṭḥa) the lower part of the valley (*baṭḥā'*) of Mecca where the Kaaba stands. It is used as a synonym for the Meccan sanctuary.

Mghērā (Mughayrā) a well fifteen kilometers south of al-Zulfī.

al-Miḥmal an area on the western side of the Ṭuwayq escarpment south of Sudayr and al-Washm. Thādiq and al-Bīr are included among its townships.

Mughayrā see *Mghērā*.

Musaylimah belonged to the Banū Ḥanīfah kings of Tamīm in al-Yamāmah, many of them Christians and allied with the Persian kings. He seems to have been ambitious to set up a political system based on prophethood, as Muḥammad had done successfully in Medina. After Muḥammad's death, he married the prophetess Sajāḥ and was eventually defeated and killed in a fierce battle.

al-Nābighah al-Dhubyānī one of the great pre-Islamic poets whose works were included among the prestigious al-Muʿallaqāt, "the suspended odes" said to have been hung in the Kaaba. He frequented the courts of the Lakhmid rulers of al-Ḥīrah and of the Banū Ghassān. Some of his best compositions are the poems of apology he composed after having angered al-Mundhir III of al-Ḥīrah. This is why it is said that his genius became especially inspired when gripped by fear. Parallels with the poem of apology by Ḥmēdān to Ibn Muʿammar, and a similarity in source of inspiration, have been pointed out. See n. 91 to §21.52.

Najd generally understood as the central part of the Arabian peninsula—the plateau area roughly situated to the east of the mountain ranges of al-Ḥijāz, south of the Nafūd desert, west of the al-Dahnā' sands, and including Wādi al-Dawāsir in the south but not beyond it to the south and southwest. This enormous region is subdivided into many areas that differ greatly in character. Historically and environmentally it has been characterized by a division of its inhabitants into sedentary and Bedouin groups, a division at once symbiotic and antithetic. Nabaṭī poetry is essentially a Najdī phenomenon with roots in classical Arabian culture—a pedigree shared by many of the sedentary and Bedouin tribes in the Najd.

al-ʿŌdih (al-ʿAwdah) an agricultural town in lower Wādi Faqī with a mixed population, among them Āl Dubās and Banū ʿAnbar of Tamīm.

Qaḥṭān traditionally tribes of South Arabian descent, as opposed to ʿAdnān, the northern Arabian tribes. For centuries it has denoted a large tribal group in areas southwest of Najd, like Wādi Tathlīth and Bīshah, and in parts of southern Najd, especially the desert lands known as Ḥaṣāt Qaḥṭān, "Qaḥṭān Rocks," where the Qaḥṭān frequently clashed with the Bargā division of ʿUtaybah. They also migrated farther north and settled in many Najdī towns. They are mentioned in Najdī chronicles for the first time in the second half of the sixteenth century as an ally of the Dawāsir tribe. It is not clear where or when Ḥmēdān took part in a raid against the tribe. The episode may be purely fictional or it may refer to a camp of migrating Qaḥṭān tribesmen in relative proximity to al-Washm.

al-Qaṣab the hometown of the poet Ḥmēdān al-Shwēʿir. It is situated in a fertile agricultural area with more than a hundred wells and a large number of homesteads producing dates and wheat. Its wadi comes down from the Ṭuwayq escarpment via the little town of al-Hurayyiq and al-Ruqaybiyyah. The nearby salt evaporation ponds supply al-Yamāmah and areas beyond with salt. Its population was very mixed, with only a few representatives of the Sayyār clan to which the poet belonged.

Quraysh the Meccan tribe to which the prophet Muḥammad belonged.

al-ʿRēnāt (al-ʿUraynāt) a large subdivision of the Subayʿ tribe. The chiefs of the groups that founded the town of al-ʿAṭṭār in Sudayr, near al-Ḥawṭah, are from the Āl Sayf branch of al-ʿRēnāt.

al-Rgēbiyyah (al-Ruqaybiyyah) a village upstream from al-Qaṣab in the wadi that comes down from the headlands of Ṭuwayq.

al-Rigʿī a well just south of the Saudi border with Iraq in al-Bāṭin, where it meets Wādi al-ʿAwjā.

al-Rijm may refer to the al-Rijm mountains west of al-Dawādimī in the High Najd, which is famous for its excellent camel pastures.

al-Rōḍah (al-Rawḍah) a famous old town in Sudayr, situated in the upper reaches of Wādi al-Faqī, which means that it is the first location to receive floodwaters after rainfall. Under the leadership of Rumayzān ibn

Ghashshām, a prolific poet with whom the poet Jabr ibn Sayyār of al-Qaṣab was in poetic correspondence, a dam was built to store the floodwaters for the town. This created tension with the other towns farther downstream. Rumayzān was killed in 1669 by a member of the Abū Hilāl clan. In 1647 the Sharīf of Mecca killed Māḍī ibn Muḥammad, the ancestor of the Ibn Māḍī family who enjoyed prominence in the town. The rulers of Julājil frequently intervened in the internal struggles among the leading clans of Rawḍah.

al-Ruqaybiyyah see *al-Rgēbiyyah.*

Sajāḥ a prophetess who tried to convert her tribe, Tamīm, to her version of the faith following the death of the prophet Muḥammad. When she failed and her followers were defeated in battle, she joined the prophet Musaylimah, whom she is said to have married. She later returned to her tribe, and little is known about her except that she embraced Islam and died in Basra as a Muslim.

Ṣalab (also *ṣlēb*, singular *ṣlubi*) regarded as a pariah tribe by other tribes, with whom intermarriage is regarded as taboo. In the past they used to perform various services for the Bedouin, such as shoeing their horses and other ironwork. They had a reputation as skilled hunters and were renowned for the beauty of their women.

Sāmirī in the Qur'an, the person who created the Golden Calf during Moses's absence and who tried to lead people from the faith by persuading them to worship this idol (Q Ṭā Hā 20:85–97).

Sanām an elevation of 150 meters (more like a little hill, but still called a "mountain," Jabal Sanām), a salt dome, in an otherwise flat land forty-five kilometers southwest of Basra on the border with Kuwait.

Sardiyyah a woman from Sardiyyah, a small tribe in Ḥawrān, which until about 1800 had the right to accompany the pilgrim caravan from Damascus. See Burckhardt, *Notes on the Bedouins and Wahabys*, 16–17.

al-Shamāsiyyah see *al-Shimāsiyyah.*

Shaqrā' a town in al-Washm that served as a trading post for the Bedouins of the High Najd. The inhabitants are descended from Banū Zayd (Binī Zēd), a group that traces its descent from Qaḥṭān.

'Shērah ('Ushayrah) a town in Sudayr founded by Māni' of 'Amr of Banū Tamīm, a group called al-Manī'āt or al-Man'āt. According to one tale, the

name is derived from the *'ushar* tree. Its fields are irrigated from Wādi al-Miyāh. Its chiefs came traditionally from Āl Nāṣir of Tamīm.

al-Shimāsiyyah (al-Shamāsiyyah) an agricultural district in al-Qaṣīm, twenty kilometers from the city of Buraydah. To its west lie sand dunes.

Sudayr a populous agricultural region about 180 kilometers north of Riyadh. It encompasses most of Wādi al-Faqī. Among its many towns are Julājil, al-Majma'ah, al-Ghāṭ, al-Rawḍah, al-Tuwaym, al-Ḥawṭah, and al-Ḥuṣūn.

al-Ṭēri (Wādi al-Ṭayrī) a wadi to the east of Sudayr, near Ḥafr al-'Atk and the sands of al-Dahnā'.

Tharmadā' an ancient town in al-Washm, mentioned in pre-Islamic poetry. Its inhabitants belong to al-'Anāqir of Banū Sa'd of Tamīm. It used to be the dominant town of al-Washm and its influence extended to neighboring towns, like Uthayfiyah, al-Marāh, and Shaqrā'. An eighteenth-century chief, Bdāḥ al-'Ingiri, composed a famous poem on what separates and unites sedentary people and Bedouin (see Sowayan, *Nabaṭi Poetry*, 21–22). Tharmadā' stubbornly resisted absorption into the Saudi state until the death of its capable leader, Ibrāhīm ibn Sulēmān al-'Ingiri, in 1767/68.

Timīm (Tamīm) a large tribal group that before Islam was centered in al-Yamāmah and fanned out through Najd, the Gulf, and Iraq. They included nomadic and sedentary sections, the latter in al-Washm and eastern Arabia. The most important branch of the 'Amr ibn Tamīm was the Banū l-'Anbar, a name that occurs frequently in the more recent Najdī chronicles.

Tmēr (Tumayr) a village with palm groves in the southeastern part of Sudayr at the wadi and the heights of Mujazzal. Its inhabitants are from Tamīm, al-Dawāsir, 'Utaybah, and other tribes.

al-Twēm (al-Tuwaym) a town in Sudayr, abandoned and then resettled by Mudlij ibn Ḥusayn al-Wā'ilī from Ushayqir after a conflict there with al-Wahabah of Tamīm. In 1699/1700 al-Tuwaym's Wā'il rulers ousted Āl Tumayyim of Banū Khālid from the town of al-Ḥuṣūn and installed Ibn Nḥēṭ of Banū l-'Anbar ibn 'Amr as the new chief. In the same year Māḍī ibn Jāsir, the chief of the Āl Rājiḥ of Banū 'Amr in al-Rawḍah appealed for al-Tuwaym's help against their fellow tribesmen Banū Hilāl, who were then ousted from the town by Āl Mudlij of al-Tuwaym. Both events set in motion a chain of reprisals and counterattacks that played out over a long time. Al-Tuwaym is the birthplace of two famous Najdī poets: Ibrāhīm al-Juʿaythin and Muḥammad ibn Ḥamad ibn Laʿbūn, whose father, Ḥamad ibn Muḥammad, was a famous Najdī historian and genealogist.

Umm ʿNēg (Umm ʿUnayq) a prominent, solitary peak that looms over Julājil from the southeast. Its name, "Little Neck," refers to its shape.

ʿUrayʿir the family of chiefs of Banū Khālid, a tribe in the eastern part of present-day Saudi Arabia with its center at the large palm oasis of al-Aḥsāʾ. In 1670 they ousted the Ottoman Turks and established themselves as independent rulers. In 1795 their rule was ended in al-Dirʿiyyah by the Saudi state.

al-ʿUraynāt see *al-ʿRēnāt.*

Ushaygir (Ushayqir) an ancient town in al-Washm named after a mountain and wadi. In classical times it was the town of Banū ʿIkl. It played an important role in the region. After a conflict in the town between al-Wahabah of Banū Tamīm and Banū Wāʾil, many groups of the latter left and founded new towns, such as al-Ḥarmah, al-Tuwaym, al-Majmaʿah (together with Abd Allāh al-Shammarī), and Ḥuraymilāʾ.

ʿUshayrah see *ʿShērah.*

Uthayfiyah a town named after three rocky outcrops that resemble the three vertical pieces of stone used to suspend the cooking pot above the fire (*athāfī*). Its modern name is Uthaythiyah. It was the town inhabited by the Banū Kalb of the Banū Tamīm tribe of the Umayyad poet Jarīr (d. AD 728). Until well into the last century its inhabitants were said to have preserved elements of the ancient dialect of Tamīm. In the early eighteenth century its headmen came from al-ʿAzāʿīz of Tamīm. They accepted Ḥmēdān's request for asylum and gave him a plot of land, called Mulayḥ. He incited them to rise up against Tharmadāʾ and to stop paying tribute to its rulers.

al-ʿUyaynah the "little well" that belonged to Banū ʿĀmir of Banū Ḥanīfah in the wadi of the same name, in the district of al-ʿĀriḍ, the ancient heart of al-Yamāmah region. In 1446 Banū Ḥanīfah was forced to sell it to Ḥasan ibn Ṭawq of Banū Saʿd of Tamīm from the town of Malham, the forefather of the Ibn Muʿammar dynasty that turned the town into the most powerful and successful township in this part of Najd, especially during the long rule of ʿAbd Allāh ibn Muʿammar. The religious reformer Muḥammad ibn ʿAbd al-Wahhāb was born here in 1703. In 1768 he had the palace of Ibn Muʿammar destroyed and ordered the end of their rule in the town.

Wādi Ḥanīfah a valley in the heart of al-Yamāmah named after the tribe of Ḥanīfah ibn Lujaym.

Wādi Khlayyif one of two wadis between Tharmadā' and Uthayfiyah. Its upper course joins another wadi and they join Wādi Uthayfiyah. It may also refer to a place between Ushayqir and Shaqrā'. According to another source it is a wadi near Rawḍat Tinhāt close to the northwestern edge of the al-Dahnā' sands, which would fit better with its mention in conjunction with al-Ṭēri.

Wahhābī a term currently widely used as a description of the doctrine and practices elaborated by the religious reformer Muḥammad ibn ʿAbd al-Wahhāb, and later established as the foundational principles of the Kingdom of Saudi Arabia, where it is perceived as a pejorative term. The preferred description of this movement is Salafī, a movement that believes in a return to the purity of early religion practiced by the salaf, the early generations of Muslims. From the point of view of doctrine, its adherents call themselves "those who profess the unicity of God" (*al-muwaḥḥidūn*).

al-Washm in the early Islamic period, a region with villages and towns mainly inhabited by tribesmen of Tamīm who had left their nomadic life behind, and as a consequence were looked down upon by their Bedouin kinsmen. It is the region where Ḥmēdān lived. Among its towns are Tharmadā', Shaqrā', Ushayqir, al-Qaṣab, Marāh, and Uthayfiyah.

Wāyil (Wā'il) a tribal group said to be related to the ancient Bakr ibn Wā'il that included the Ḥanīfah tribe after which Wādi Ḥanīfah is named. They lived in al-Yamāmah and its ancient capital al-Ḥajr, near modern Riyadh.

al-Yamāmah in pre- and early Islam, the region of Wādi Ḥanīfah and its capital al-Ḥajr. Nowadays it is used as a loose, general term that may comprise the entire region that runs parallel to Ṭuwayq's escarpment from al-Kharj south of Riyadh to the northern part of Sudayr, where it is bordered by al-Qaṣīm.

al-Zilfī (al-Zulfī) in the late seventeenth and early eighteenth centuries this town's ownership was disputed by Āl Muḥdith of Banū l-ʿAnbar of Tamīm, al-Farāhīd, a branch of the ʿUtaybah tribe, and Āl Mudlij from the town of al-Ḥarmah. It is the last town of al-Yamāmah before the desert crossing to Kuwait and Iraq.

al-Zyerah (al-Ziyarah) a place identified with the ancient town of al-Ḥarmah, established by Banū Wā'il in 1368, near al-Majmaʿah. The poet Ibn Laʿbūn belonged to al-Ḥarmah's family of chiefs, Āl Mudlij of Banū Wā'il. The inhabitants of al-Ziyarah (the name comes from its ancestor al-Zīr) are of al-Rāshid of Āl Ḥamad from the town of al-Ḥuraymilā', a town founded in 1635 by a clan of Banū Wā'il from al-Tuwaym. Al-Tuwaym itself was founded by Āl Mudlij of Banū Wā'il, who had left Ushayqir.

Bibliography

Al-ʿAjmī, Mursil Fāliḥ. *Al-Nakhlah wa-l-jamal: ʿIlāqāt al-shiʿr al-Nabaṭī bi-l-shiʿr al-jāhilī*. Kuwait: Maktabat al-Āfāq, 2012.

Al-Bassām, ʿAbd Allāh ibn Muḥammad. *Tuḥfat al-mushtāq fī akhbār Najd wa-l-Ḥijāz wa-l-ʿIrāq*. Edited by Ibrāhīm Ḥāmid al-Khālidī. Kuwait: Sharikat al-Mukhtalif li-l-Nashr wa-l-Tawziʿ, 2000.

Blachère, Régis. *Histoire de la littérature arabe des origines à la fin du XVe siècle de J.-C.*, 3 vols. Paris: A. Maisonneuve, 1952.

Blunt, Lady Anne. *A Pilgrimage to Nejd*. Reprint of the first edition in 1881 by John Murray. London: Century Publishing, 1985.

Burckhardt, John Lewis. *Notes on the Bedouins and Wahabys*. Reprint of the first edition in 1830 by Colburn and Bentley. Cambridge, UK: Cambridge University Press, 2010.

Al-Dakhīl, Sulaymān ibn Ṣāliḥ. *Kitāb al-Baḥth ʿan aʿrāb Najd wa-ʿammā yataʿallaqu bihum*. MS on the website of Dr. Saad Sowayan, http://www.saadsowayan.com/html/manuscripts.html.

Doughty, Charles M. *Travels in Arabia Deserta*. 2 vols. Reprint of the third edition in 1936 by Jonathan Cape. New York, NY: Dover, 1979.

Euting, Julius. *Tagbuch einer Reise in Inner-Arabien*. 2 vols. Leiden: Brill, 1896–1914.

Al-Fākhirī, Muḥammad ibn ʿUmar. *Al-Akhbār al-najdiyyah*. Edited by ʿAbd Allāh ibn Yūsuf al-Shibl. Riyadh: Lajnat al-Buḥūth wa-l-Taʾlīf wa-l-Tarjamah wa-l-Nashr, Imam Muhammad ibn Saud University, n.d.

Al-Faraj, Khālid. *Dīwān al-Nabaṭ, majmūʿah min al-shiʿr al-ʿāmmī fī Najd*, vol. 1. Damascus: n.p., 1952.

Al-Fawzān, ʿAbd Allāh Nāṣir. *Raʾīs al-taḥrīr Ḥumaydān al-Shuwayʿir: ṣaḥāfat Najd al-muthīrah fī l-qarn al-thānī ʿashar*. Riyadh: Markaz al-Ḥarf, 1988.

Geiger, Bernhard. "Die Muʿallaqa des Ṭarafa." *Wiener Zeitschrift für die Kunde des Morgenlandes*, 19 (1905): 323–70.

Al-Ḥamdān, Muḥammad ibn ʿAbd Allāh. *Dīwān Ḥumaydān al-Shuwayʿir*. Riyadh: Dār Qays li-l-Nashr, 1417/1996–97 (first ed. 1409/1988–89).

Al-Ḥaqīl, ʿAbd al-Karīm ibn Ḥamad ibn Ibrāhīm. *Alfāẓ dārijah wa-madlūlātuhā fī l-jazīrah al-ʿarabiyyah*. Riyadh: Maṭābiʿ al-Farazdaq, 1989.

Al-Ḥātam, ʻAbd Allāh ibn Khālid. *Khiyār mā yulṭaqat min al-shiʻr al-nabaṭ*, vol. 2. First edition Damascus: al-Maṭbaʻah al-ʻUmūmiyyah, 1968. Third edition Kuwait: Dhāt al-Salāsil, 1981.

Ḥātim al-Ṭāʼī. *Dīwān Ḥātim al-Ṭāʼī*. Edited by Mufīd Muḥammad Qumayḥah. Jedda: Dār al-Maṭbūʻāt al-Ḥadīthah, 1987–88.

———. *Dīwān Shiʻr Ḥātim ibn ʻAbd Allāh al-Ṭāʼī wa akhbāruhu*. Edited by ʻĀdil Sulaymān Jamāl. Cairo: Maṭbaʻat al-Khānji, 1990.

Hess, J. J. *Von den Beduinen des Innern Arabiens*. Zürich-Leipzig: Max Niehaus Verlag, 1938.

Holes, Clive. *Dialect, Culture, and Society in Eastern Arabia*, vol. 1, glossary; vol. 2, *Ethnographic Texts*; vol. 3, *Phonology, Morphology, Syntax, Style*. Leiden: Brill, 2001–16.

———. "The Language of Nabaṭi Poetry." In *Encyclopaedia of Arabic Language and Linguistics On-Line Edition*. Edited by R. De Jong and L. Edzard. Leiden: Brill, 2012.

Holes, Clive, and Said Salman Abu Athera. *The Nabaṭī Poetry of the United Arab Emirates*. Reading, UK: Ithaca Press, 2011.

Huber, Charles. *Journal d'un voyage en Arabie (1883–1884)*. Paris: Société Asiatique et la Société de Géographie, 1891.

———. "Voyage dans l'arabie central." *Bulletin de la Société Géographique*, 7e série, 5(1884): 304–63, 468–530; 6(1885):92–148.

Al-Ḥuṭayʼah. *Dīwān al-Ḥuṭayʼah bi-riwāyah wa-sharḥ ibn al-Sikkīt*. Edited by Mufīd Muḥammad Qumayḥah. Beirut: Dār al-Kutūb al-ʻIlmiyyah, 1993.

Ibn Bishr, ʻUthmān. *ʻUnwān al-majd fī taʼrīkh Najd*. Riyadh: Maktabat al-Riyaḍ al-Ḥadīthah, n.d.

Ibn Bulayhid, Muḥammad ibn ʻAbd Allāh. *Ṣaḥīḥ al-akhbār ʻammā fī bilād al-ʻArab min al-āthār*. 5 vols. Riyadh: n.p., 1972.

Ibn ʻĪsā, Ibrāhīm ibn Ṣāliḥ. *ʻIqd al-durar fī-mā waqaʻa fī Najd min al-ḥawādith*. Riyadh: Dār al-Yamāmah, 1966.

Ibn Junaydil, Saʻd ibn ʻAbd Allāh. *Al-Muʻjam al-jūghrāfī li-l-bilād al-ʻarabiyyah al-suʻūdiyyah ʻāliyat Najd*. 3 vols. Riyadh: n.p., 1978.

———. *Al-Sānī wa-l-sāniyah*. Riyadh: Maṭābiʻ Jāmiʻat al-Imām Muḥammad ibn Suʻūd, 1988.

———. *Min aʻlām al-adab al-shaʻbī, shuʻarāʼ al-ʻāliyah*. Riyadh: Al-Maktabah al-Suʻūdiyyah, al-Jamʻiyyah al-Suʻūdiyyah li-l-Thaqāfah wa-l-Funūn, Maṭābiʻ al-Farazdaq, 1980–81.

Ibn Khamīs, ʻAbd Allāh ibn Muḥammad. *Al-Muʻjam al-jūghrāfī li-l-bilād al-ʻarabiyyah al-suʻūdiyyah, muʻjam al-Yamāmah*, 2 vols. Riyadh: Maṭābiʻ al-Farazdaq, 1980.

———. *Al-Majāz bayn al-Yamāmah wa-l-Ḥijāz*. Riyadh: Dār al-Yamāmah, 1970.

Ibn Mandīl, Mandīl ibn Muḥammad, Āl al-Fuhayd. *Min ādābinā al-shaʻbiyyah fī l-jazīra al-ʻarabiyyah, qiṣaṣ wa-ashʻār*. 4 vols. Riyadh: n.p., 1981–84.

Ibn Manẓūr. *Lisān al-ʿArab*. Cairo: Dār al-Maʿārif, n.d.

Ibn Qutaybah. *The Excellence of the Arabs*. Edited by James E. Montgomery and Peter Webb. Translated by Sarah Bowen Savant and Peter Webb. New York, NY: Library of Arabic Literature, New York University Press, 2017.

Ingham, Bruce. *Bedouins of Northern Arabia: Traditions of the Al Dhafir*. London–New York–Sydney: Kegan Paul, 1986.

Al-Iṣfahānī, Abū l-Faraj. *Kitāb al-Aghānī*. Cairo: Maṭbaʿat Dār al-Kutub al-Miṣriyyah, 1928.

Jones, Alan. *Early Arabic Poetry, Select Poems*. 2nd ed. Reading, UK: Ithaca Press, 2011.

Al Juhany, Uwaidah M. *Najd before the Salafi Movement: Social, Political and Religious Conditions during the Three Centuries preceding the Rise of the Saudi State*. Reading, UK: Ithaca Press, 2002.

Al-Juhaymān, ʿAbd al-Karīm. *Al-Amthāl al-shaʿbiyyah fī qalb al-jazīrah al-ʿarabiyyah*. 10 vols. Riyadh: n.p., 1982.

Al-Jundī, Darwīsh. *Al-Ḥuṭay'ah al-badawī al-muḥtarif.* Cairo: Maktabat Nahḍat Miṣr, 1962.

Al-Kamālī, Shafīq. *Al-Shiʿr ʿind al-badū*. Baghdad: n.p., 1964.

Kurpershoek, P. Marcel. *Oral Poetry and Narratives from Central Arabia*. 5 vols. Leiden: Brill, 1994–2005.

———. "Praying Mantis in the Desert." *Arabian Humanities*, 5, 2015.

———. "Two manuscripts of Bedouin poetry in Strasbourg National and University Library and the travels of Charles Huber in Arabia." *Revue de la BNU*, n.s., 2018.

———. "Politics and the art of eulogy in Najdi Nabaṭi poetry: Ḥmēdān al-Shwēʿir's (al-Shuwayʿir) Apologies to Ibn Muʿammar and Ibn Sbayyil's Ode on Ibn Rashīd." *Quaderni di Studi Arabi*, n.s. (2017).

———. "Ḥaywānāt Ḥmēdān al-Shwēʿir wa-ḥulm Ibn Sbayyil," in *Layālī al-shiʿr al-nabaṭī*, 21–29. Riyadh: Markaz al-Malik Fahd li-l-Thaqāfah, 2017.

Lyall, C. J. *The Mufaḍḍalīyāt: Volume 1*. Oxford: Clarendon Press, 1921; *Volume 3*. Leiden: Brill, 1924.

Musil, Alois. *The Manners and Customs of the Rwala Bedouins*. Oriental Explorations and Studies No. 6. New York, NY: American Geographical Society, 1928.

Al-Nābighah al-Dhubyānī. *Dīwān*, ed. Karam al-Bustānī. Beirut: Dār Bayrūt, 1986.

Palgrave, William Gifford. *Personal Narrative of a Year's Journey through Central and Eastern Arabia (1862–63)*. London and New York: Macmillan, 1871.

Papoutaskis, Nefeli. *Desert Travel as a Form of Boasting: A Study of Ḏū r-Rumma's Poetry*. Wiesbaden: Harrassowitz, 2009.

Snouck Hurgronje, Christiaan. *Mekkanische Sprichwörter und Redensarten*. Reprint, Bremen: Unikum Verlag, 2012.

Sowayan, Saad Abdullah. "A poem and its narrative by Riḍa ibn Ṭārif al-Shammarī." *Zeitschrift für arabische Linguistik*, 7(1982):69.

———. *Nabaṭī Poetry. The Oral Poetry of Arabia*. Berkeley, CA: University of California Press, 1985.

———. *The Arabian Oral Historical Narrative. An Ethnographic and Linguistic Analysis*. Wiesbaden: Otto Harrasowiz, 1992.

———. *Al-Shiʿr al-nabaṭī: dhāʾiqat al-shaʿb wa-sulṭat al-naṣṣ*. Beirut: Dār al-Sāqī, 2000.

———. *Fihrist al-shiʿr al-nabaṭī*. Riyadh: self-published, 2001.

———. *Al-Ṣaḥrāʾ al-ʿarabiyyah, thaqāfatuhā wa-shiʿruhā ʿabra al-ʿuṣūr, qirāʾah anthrūbūlūjiyyah*. Beirut: Arab Network for Research and Publishing, 2010.

———. *Ayyām al-ʿarab al-awākhir: asāṭīr wa-marwiyyāt shafahiyyah fī l-taʾrīkh wa-l-adab min shamāl al-jazīrah al-ʿarabiyyah maʿ shadharāt mukhtārah min qabīlat āl Murrah wa-Subayʿ*. Beirut: Arab Network for Research and Publishing, 2010.

Al-Ṣūlī, Abū Bakr. *The Life and Times of Abū Tammām*. Edited and translated by Beatrice Gruendler. New York, NY: New York University Press, 2015.

Al-Suwaydāʾ, ʿAbd al-Raḥmān ibn Zayd. *Faṣīḥ al-ʿāmmī fī shamāl Najd*. 2 vols. Riyadh: Dār al-Suwaydāʾ, Maṭābiʿ al-Farazdaq, 1987.

———. *Min Shuʿarāʾ al-jabal al-ʿāmmiyyīn*. 3 vols. Riyadh: Dār al-Suwaydāʾ, 1988.

Al-ʿUbayyid, Muḥammad al-ʿAlī. *Al-Najm al-lāmiʿ li-l-nawādir jāmiʿ*. MS on the website of Dr. Saad Sowayan, http://www.saadsowayan.com/html/manuscripts.html.

Al-ʿUbūdī, Muḥammad ibn Nāṣir. *Al-Amthāl al-ʿāmmiyyah fī Najd*. 5 vols. Riyadh: n.p., 1979.

———. *Muʿjam al-anwāʾ wa-l-fuṣūl*. Riyadh: n.p., 2011.

———. *Muʿjam al-uṣūl al-faṣīḥah li-l-alfāẓ al-dārijah*. 13 vols. Riyadh: n.p. 2008.

Von Oppenheim, Max Freiherr. *Die Beduinen*. 5 vols. Leipzig: Otto Harrassowitz, 1939.

Wallin, Georg August. *Travels in Arabia*. Cambridge, New York: The Oleander Press, 1979.

Zuhayr ibn Abī Sulmā. *Dīwān*. Cairo: Dār al-Kutub, 1944.

Further Reading

Holes, Clive. *Dialect, Culture, and Society in Eastern Arabia*, vol. 1, glossary; vol. 2, *Ethnographic Texts*; vol. 3, *Phonology, Morphology, Syntax, Style*. Leiden: Brill, 2001–16.

Holes, Clive, and Said Salman Abu Athera. *The Nabaṭī Poetry of the United Arab Emirates*. Reading, UK: Ithaca Press, 2011.

Honvault, Juliette, ed. "Nouveaux accents de la poésie dialectale en péninsule Arabique" [Vernacular "Poetry in the Arabian Peninsula Today"]. Special issue, *Arabian Humanities* 5 (2015). URL: https://cy.revues.org/2952.

Kurpershoek, P. Marcel. *Oral Poetry and Narratives from Central Arabia*. 5 vols. Leiden: Brill Publishers, 1994–2005.

———. *Arabia of the Bedouins*. London: Saqi, 2001.

———. *Al-Badawī al-akhīr: al-qabā'il al-badawiyyah fī l-ṣaḥrā' al-'arabiyyah*. N.p.: Dār al-Sāqī, 2002.

Sowayan, Saad Abdullah. *Nabaṭī Poetry. The Oral Poetry of Arabia*. Berkeley, CA: University of California Press, 1985.

Index of Poems, Editions, and Manuscripts Used for this Edition

This edition is based on published collections and manuscripts, specifically the ones listed below. The poems have been ordered by rhyme according to the position of the rhyming consonant in the Arabic alphabet, as is customary in editions of classical Arabic poetry (the only other edition to do so is the one by al-Ḥamdān; other editions and the manuscripts are haphazard in how they arrange the poems). The first line of each poem is given with an indication of the meter; for the meter that consists exclusively of long syllables the designation "long" is used.

The shorthand references in bold at the start of each source listed below indicate where a particular poem can be found. These references are followed by page numbers and the relevant number of verses of the poem in that edition or manuscript. The versions in a published edition are listed first, followed by the manuscript versions on a separate line.

Printed Editions

FK refers to Khālid al-Faraj's *Dīwān al-Nabaṭ, majmūʿah min al-shiʿr al-ʿāmmī fī Najd*, vol. 1, published in Damascus in 1952.

Faw refers to ʿAbd Allāh Nāṣir al-Fawzān's *Raʾīs al-taḥrīr Ḥumaydān al-Shuwayʿir: ṣaḥāfat Najd al-muthīrah fī l-qarn al-thānī ʿashar*, published by Markaz al-Ḥarf in Riyadh in 1988.

Ham refers to Muḥammad ibn ʿAbd Allāh al-Ḥamdān's *Dīwān Ḥumaydān al-Shuwayʿir*. The first edition was published in 1409/1988–89, by Dār Qays li-l-Nashr in Riyadh, with a subsequent edition in 1417/1996–97.

Hat refers to the third edition of ʿAbd Allāh ibn Khālid al-Ḥātam's *Khiyār mā yulṭaqat min al-shiʿr al-nabaṭī*, vol. 2, published by Dhāt al-Salāsil in Kuwait in 1981.

Mandil refers to Mandīl ibn Muḥammad ibn Mandīl al-Fuhayd's *Min ādābinā al-shaʿbiyyah fī l-jazīrah al-ʿarabiyyah, qiṣaṣ wa-ashʿār*, in four volumes, published in Riyadh between 1981 and 1984.

Manuscripts

The best available description of all known manuscripts that contain Nabaṭī poetry, and the challenges they pose to researchers, is the chapter on this subject in Sowayan, *al-Shiʿr al-Nabaṭī, sulṭat al-naṣṣ wa-dhāʾiqat al-shaʿb*, 196–206.

The Manṣūr al-Ḥusayn al-ʿAssāf [**Assaf**] manuscript can be found on the website www.saadsowayan.com.

The al-Dāwud [**Dawud**] manuscript is also on the Sowayan website.

The ʿAbd al-Raḥmān ibn ʿAbd al-Muḥsin al-Dhukayr [**Dhukayr**] manuscript, also on the Sowayan website, has many ink-blotted pages and is partly unreadable.

The al-Ḥasāwī manuscript [**Hasawi**] opens with the note that these "Bedouin songs," (*Beduinenlieder*) were acquired by Professor Socin, and gives the date of 1901. It can also be found on the Sowayan website.

Huber refers to two manuscripts on the Sowayan website acquired by Charles Huber, with a few of Ḥmēdān's poems missing. I received a complete copy of the manuscripts from the National and University Library in Strasbourg, where I also examined the manuscripts.

King Saud refers to a *dīwān* owned by King Saud University. I was given a copy of the *dīwān*, which is in fact more a series of handwritten notebooks than a manuscript proper. These are from the collection of Muḥammad al-Ḥamad al-ʿUmarī. (See the entry "al-ʿMiri" in the index for Sowayan's *Nabaṭi Poetry*.)

MS Shir Nabati *Makhṭūṭat al-Shiʿr al-Nabaṭī (1)*. Sowayan website.

The ʿAbd al-Raḥmān al-Ibrāhīm al-Rābīʿī manuscript [**Rabii**] is on the Sowayan website. I also received a printed copy from Muḥammad al-Ḥamdān, who published an annotated edition of the diwan and is the learned proprietor of the Qays Library in Riyadh. In ʿUnayzah I copied some of al-Rābīʿī's collection of notebooks in the Ibn Ṣāliḥ Library.

Lāfī ibn Shabbāb al-Shurayyiṭī's *Makhṭūṭah li-shuʿarāʾ al-Jabal wa-shuʿarāʾ min Najd* [**al-Shurayyiṭī**], based on notes by ʿAbd Allāh ibn ʿAlī ibn Sālim al-Dāwud and collected by al-Shurayyiṭī.

The Muḥammad Nāṣir al-ʿUbūdī manuscript [**Ubudi**] is a copy of a manuscript given to me by Muḥammad al-Ḥamdān.

لاح المِشيب وبان في عَرضائي   ونعَيت من بعد المِشيب صَبائي

Poem 1, p. 2.
Meter: *rajaz*.
Faw 230; Mandil 3, 34–35; Ham 53–55, 28 vv.
Rabii 174, 9 vv.; King Saud 26, 7 vv.

يامجَلّي تِسَمَّع لعَودٍ فِصيح   فاهمٍ عارفٍ في فنون العرب

Poem 2, p. 6.
Meter: *mutadārik*.
Ham 64, 15 vv.; Hat 172, 14 vv.; Faw 175 15 vv.; KF 51, 20 vv.
King Saud, 12, 15 vv.; Rabii 193, 23 vv.; Ubudi, 3–4, 15 vv.

شِفْت جَمَلينٍ بالعارض   زِبَدها فوق غوارِبها

Poem 3, p. 8.
Meter: long.
Ham 59, 5 vv (as part of next poem); Faw 200, 5 vv.
Assaf 98, 8 vv.; King Saud, 30, 9 vv. (as part of next poem).

النَفْس ان جت لِمْحاسبها   فالدين خيار مْكاسبها

Poem 4, p. 10.
Meter: long.
Faw 152, 28 vv.; Ham 59, 33 vv.; Hat 145, 33 vv.; KF 32, 27 vv.
Assaf 184, 30 vv.; Dhukayr 155–56, 29 vv.; King Saud 30, 27 vv (combines two poems with same rhyme and meter).

بالعَون منيفٍ قاله لي   يقول غَلاك يوم انت صِبي

Poem 5, p. 14.
Meter: long.
Faw 188, 15 vv.; Ham 62, 15 vv.; Hat 162, 11 vv.; KF 34, 15 vv.
Assaf 97, 11 vv.; Dhukayr 154, 12 vv.; King Saud 74, 15 vv.; Rabii 198, 18 vv.; Ubudi 2–3, 15 vv.

مَوارِد حِيضان الحروب هَماج   ترِزجّه حِيران الرِبيع رِزجاج

Poem 6, p. 16.

Meter: irregular, it seems to be a mixture of different meters.

Ham 68, 9 vv.

King Saud 40, 11 vv.; Rabii 195, 9 vv.; Ubudi 4–5, 9 vv.

طالب الفَضْل من عند الشحاح   مِثل من اهْدَى زِمان الصَرام اللِقاح

Poem 7, p. 18.

Meter: *mutadārik*.

Faw 180, 17 vv.; Ham 71, 19 vv.; Hat 170, 16 vv.; KF 36, 17 vv.

Assaf 97, 18 vv.; Dhukayr 148, 18 vv.; King Saud 35, 18 vv.; Rabii 199, 18 vv.

ادِعو للخاطر يامانع   بافْعَىً بالدَرْب الَى راحِ

Poem 8, p. 22.

Meter: long.

Faw 198, 7 vv.; Ham 69, 8 vv.; Hat 159, 7; KF 61, 6 vv.

Assaf 98, 7 vv.; King Saud 76, 6 vv.; Rabii 179, 6 vv.

انا سَهْرٍ بِمْنَيحيّتي   وهو مِجْلنْطٍ بِسْطوحِه

Poem 9, p. 24.

Meter: long.

Faw 195, 8 vv.; Ham 73, 8 vv.; Hat 171, 8 vv.; KF 49, 8 vv.

King Saud 13, 8 vv.; Rabii 194, 8 vv.; Ubudi 5, 8 vv.

لقيت انا بالناس عَيٍ جاهل   ما لحْق والقادي بنُصّ مراده

Poem 10, p. 26.

Meter: *rajaz*.

Faw 161, 21 vv.; Ham 76, 21 vv.; Hat 147, 17 vv.; KF 25, 21 vv.

Assaf 99, 17 vv.; King Saud 33, 17 vv.; Rabii 161, 21 vv.; Ubudi 8–9, 17 vv.

اسباب ما فاجى الضِمير وذار   كَرى العَين ودْموع النِظَير نِثار

Poem 11, p. 30.
Meter: *rajaz.*
Faw 171, 30 vv.; Ham 79, 33 vv.
King Saud 7, 30 vv.; Rabii 169, 31 vv.; Ubudi 11, 33 vv.

ياذا افْتِهم مِنّي جُوابٍ يِشْتَرَى   مِثْل اللُوالو من عقودٍ تِنْثرا

Poem 12, p. 34.
Meter: *rajaz.*
Faw 145, 29 vv.; Ham 109, 29 vv.; Hat 150, 29 vv.; KF 30, 28 vv.
Assaf 97, 27 vv.; King Saud 79, 28 vv.; Rabii 204, 29 vv.

احدٍ مبسوطٍ ومْكَيَّف   ياكِل وِيِنْعِم في داره

Poem 13, p. 38.
Meter: long.
Ham 112, 10 vv.
King Saud 75, 10 vv.

يقول الشاعر الحَبْر الِفهيم   حْمَيدان المِتَّهَم بالعَياره

Poem 14, p. 40.
Meter: *hazaj.*
Faw 126, 45 vv.; Ham 83, 46 vv.; Hat 162, 46 vv.; KF 41, 45 vv.
Assaf 93, 44 vv.; Dhukayr 153–54, 23 vv.; Rabii 186, 46 vv.; Ubudi 12–13, 46 vv.

ظَهَرْت من الحَزْم اللي به   سِيد السادات من العشَره

Poem 15, p. 46.
Meter: long.
Faw 158, 23 vv.; Ham 86, 23 vv.; Hat 168, 22 vv.; KF 19, 22 vv.
King Saud 43, 21 vv.; Rabii 175, 22 vv.; Ubudi 7–8, 20 vv.

قال عَودٍ زَلَف له سـنينٍ مِـضَت   زلّ عَصرِ الصِبا والمِشيب حْضَـره

Poem 16, p. 50.
Meter: *mutadārik.*
Faw 105, 52 vv.; Ham 94, 41 vv.; Hat 148, 49 vv.; KF 26, 49 vv.
Assaf 92, 49 vv.; Dhukayr 147–49, 54 vv.; King Saud 27, 54 vv.

مـانع خَيّـالٍ ـفي الدكّه   ظَفـرٍ في راس المَقْصوره

Poem 17, p. 56.
Meter: long.
Faw 155, 24 vv.; Ham 104, 24 vv.; Hat 146, 24 vv.; KF 52, 24 vv.
Assaf 98, 13 vv.; King Saud 71, 24 vv.; Rabii 180, 25 vv.

يقول حمَـيدان الشـاعر   ايْضـا وبْجُوّر تجَويـره

Poem 18, p. 60.
Meter: long.
Faw 186, 18 vv.; Ham 107, 20 vv.; Hat 159, 14 vv.; KF 54, 18 vv.
Assaf 98, 13 vv.; King Saud 70, 15 vv.; Rabii 181, 15 vv.; Ubudi 6, 15 vv.

يوم دَلّوا زَراريعـنا للحَـريث   رَوّحَتْ بِـه سويَـره عن العَيـثَرِ

Poem 19, p. 64.
Meter: *mutadārik.*
Faw 118, 74 vv.; Ham 89, 76 vv.; Hat 156, 68 vv.; KF 55, 72 vv.
Assaf 95–96, 70 vv.; King Saud 45, 77 vv.; Rabii 182, 75 vv.

نِشـا من غَرامِ القيل بالقلب هاجس   بـدُولاب فِكرٍ للقُوافي مـعايس

Poem 20, p. 74.
Meter: *ṭawīl.*
Ham 117, 41 vv.
King Saud 13, 43 vv.; Rabii 166, 43 vv.

الاموال تـرْفع من ذَراريه خـانسِه   والقِلّ يِهْفِي ما رِفَع من مَغارْسِه

Poem 21, p. 80.
Meter: *ṭawīl.*
Faw. 111, 65 vv.; Ham 113, 66 vv.; Hat 142, 64 vv.; KF 44, 61 vv.
Assaf 94–95, 71 vv.; Huber 2–3, 52 vv.; King Saud 9, 61 vv.; Rabii 170, 61 vv.; Ubudi 15–16, 41 vv.

الايامِ مـا يِـرْجَى لِهِن رْجوع   غـَدَتْ بخِلاّنٍ لنـا ورْبوع

Poem 22, p. 88.
Meter: *ṭawīl.*
Faw 164, 54 vv.; Ham 120, 58 vv.; Hat 139, 57 vv.
Assaf 91–92, 54 vv.; Dawud 121–22, 39 vv.; Dhukayr 149–51, 47 vv.; Huber 30–32, 35 vv.; King Saud 20, 55 vv.; MS Shiʿr Nabati 1, 45 vv.; Rabii 155, 56 vv.; Shurayyiṭī 121–22, 39 vv.

لا جا ثوَرٍ يَخْطِب بِنْتِك   فاضْرِب رِجْله قِلْ له قَفّ

Poem 23, p. 96.
Meter: long.
Faw 197, 6 vv.; Ham 124, 6 vv.; Hat 171, 6 vv.; KF 48, 6 vv.
King Saud 78, 6 vv.; Rabii ms 179, 6 vv.; Ubudi 4, 6 vv.

النِعْمِه خَمْرٍ جَيّاش   ما يَمْلِكْها كُود الوْثِقِه

Poem 24, p. 98.
Meter: long.
Faw 149, 22 vv.; Ham 126, 22 vv.; Hat 160, 15 vv.; KF 63, 21 vv.
Assaf 176, 15 vv.; King Saud 42, 17 vv.; Rabii 176, 22 vv.; Ubudi 6–7, 17 vv.

امْس بالبِير يَنْشِدْني خَلَيفه   يِقول وَين انْت بِه مِن ذا النخيل

Poem 25, p. 102.
Meter: *mumtadd.*
Faw 196, 6 vv.; Ham 131, 6 vv.; Hat 172, 6 vv.; KF 50, 6 vv.
King Saud 78, 6 vv.; Rabii 193, 7 vv.; Ubudi 5–6, 6 vv.

يا صِبَيّ اِفْتِهِمْ من عْوَيدٍ فِهيم   وفي كلّ غِبّه من الفِكْرْ عايِمْ

Poem 26, p. 104.
Meter: *mutadārik*.
Faw 142, 29 vv.; Ham 133, 33 vv.; Hat 160, 29 vv.; KF 39, 28 vv.
Assaf 100, 6 vv.; Assaf 183, 30 vv.; King Saud 81, 30 vv.; Rabii 189, 30 vv.

والله دِينٍ باشَرْ دِين   من باب الغاط الى ضَرِما

Poem 27, p. 108.
Meter: long.
Faw 184, 13 vv.; Ham 135, 13 vv.; Hat 152, 12 vv.; KF 62, 12 vv.
Assaf 99, 12 vv.; King Saud 32, 12 vv.; Rabii 178, 13 vv.; Ubudi 10, 11 vv.

الايامْ حُبْلى والامورْ عَوان   فهَل يا تَرى ما لا يِكون وكان

Poem 28, p. 110.
Meter: *ṭawīl*.
Faw 131, 54 vv.; Ham 138, 62 vv.; Hat 166, 62 vv.; KF 21, 53 vv.
Assaf 90–91, 59 vv.; Dawud 213–15, 53 vv.; Dhukayr 151–53, 56 vv.; Hasawi 22–24, 62 vv.; Huber 1–2, 58 vv.; King Saud 16, 57 vv; Rabii 158–61, 57 vv.

يابن نحَيط اِفْهَمْ جواب مْهَذَّب   جا من صِديقٍ واضحٍ عِنوانَها

Poem 29, p. 118.
Meter: *rajaz*.
Faw 178, 17 vv.; Ham 143, 18 vv.; Hat 169, 17 vv.; KF 35, 17 vv.
Assaf 187, 18 vv.; Dhukayr 145, 18 vv.; Rabii 198, 18 vv.

قال عَودٍ كِبِرْ واعِتِلاه المِشيب   وانْحَنَى مِثل قَوسٍ يتالي عَصاه

Poem 30, p. 122.
Meter: *mutadārik*.
Faw 138, 38 vv.; Ham 147, 41 vv.; Hat 164, 36 vv.; KF 37, 38 vv.
Assaf 93–94, 38 vv.; King Saud 28, 37 vv.; Rabii 191, 39 vv.

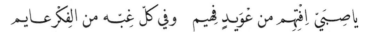

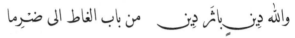

ابا اوَصّيكم ياالذّهَنا   عَن نَطّحَة قوَمٍ بتْحِيّه

Poem 31, p. 128.
Meter: long.
Ham 151, 13 vv.; Hat 173, 13 vv.; KF 60, 13 vv.
King Saud 77, 13 vv.; Rabii 178, 13 vv.; Ubudi 9, 13 vv.

الدِين الدِين اللي بَيّن   بَيّن مِثل الشَمْس القَيظِيّه

Poem 32, p. 130.
Meter: long.
Faw 199, 7 vv.; Ham 153, 7 vv.; Hat 158, 7 vv.
Assaf 98, 7 vv.

طالبٍ للقِصَب يوم انا بالِجنوب   والي العَرْش يِسْقِيه وَسْمِيّه

Poem 33, p. 132.
Meter: *mutadārik*.
Faw 190, 9 vv.; Ham 157, 9 vv.; Hat 171, 7 vv.; KF 49, 7 vv.
King Saud 54, 7 vv.; Rabii 205, 7 vv.; Ubudi 5, 7 vv.

هُون الامور مباديها   قَدْحٍ ولهيبٍ تاليها

Poem 34, p. 134.
Meter: long.
Faw 182, 15 vv.; Ham 154, 15 vv.; Hat 151, 14 vv.; KF 33, 15 vv.
Assaf 98, 15 vv.; Dhukayr 155, 15 vv.; King Saud 34, 15 vv.; Rabii 197, 15 vv.; Ubudi 1, 15 vv.

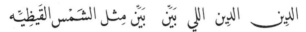

Index

ʿAbd al-ʿAzīz, King, xlix n107, 151n143
ʿAbd al-Wahhāb, Muḥammad ibn, ix, xii, xxv, 138n14, 138n15, 153n158
Abū Mūsā, xiii, §15.3, 141n44
Abū Zwayyid, Khalaf, 140n29
abuse, §13.8, §28.24; tongue-lashing, ix, §19.39; vile speech, §21.19
adversary. *See* enemy
advice, xii, xviii, xx, xxi, xxii, xxvii, xxix, xxx, xl, xliv n47, xlvi n55, §4.11, §19.6, §19.15, §24.7, §26.12, §28.15, §30.6, §30.31, §31.1; counsel, x, xvii, xviii, xxix, xxx, xxxi, xliv n42, §12.1, §16.5, §16.44, §18.19, §19.14, §22.56, §24.5, §26.3, §28.44, §30.357, 140n38; wisdom poems, §§2.1–15, §§7.1–17, §§16.1–51; §§19.1–74, §§26.1–29, §§30.1–38, §§33.1–9. *See also* wisdom
agriculture, xi, xiii, §10.20, §§33.1–4, §33.8. *See also* crops, harvest, irrigation, palm trees, peasant
Aḥnaf ibn Qays, §21.53, 145n92
al-Aḥsāʾ, xiii, §12.21, 150n133
ʿAjfat al-Gūr, §28.55
Ajwad ibn Zāmil, xlviii n89
Aleppo, §2.15
ally, §28.19, 151n143. *See also* enemy
alms, §24.21
alms tax, §16.25
ambition, xv, xlv n46, §11.25, §20.16, §20.39, §28.11
Āl ʿĀmir, xxvi, §§11.19–20, §22.58
al-ʿĀmirī, Abu Ḥamzah, xxxvii, xlviii n88
ʿAmr ibn al-ʿĀṣ, xxvi, §11.19, §16.42, §21.53, 141n45, 145n92
al-ʿAnāgir, §28.38, 152n152
al-ʿAnāqir. *See* al-ʿAnāgir
ancestors, xxvi–xxvii, §4.21, §10.9, §§11.19–23, §12.3, §16.6, §29.2, §30.16; boasting about, xxvi–xxvii, §1.24, §4.21, §10.9, §§11.19–23, 137n8. *See also* genealogy
animals, xxiii–xxiv, 144n80; bestiary, xxiii, xxxiv; bull, §17.16; cat, xxxi, §17.4, §20.37; cow, xxv, §6.5, §14.42, §15.17, §16.48, §23.3, §25.2, §31.8; dog, xxx, §6.3, §19.54, §24.13, §27.5, §30.19, 141n50, 151n147; donkey, §11.17, §14.39, §15.23, §19.26, §24.4, 143n70; fox, §21.38; ewe, §29.7; gazelle, xxiv, §2.13; goat, xxix, §7.2; hyena, xxii, xxiv, §13.6, §14.6, §19.5, §26.7; lamb, xiv, §6.7; leopard, §14.6; lion, xxiv, §6.7, §14.26, §21.44, §32.6, §34.13, 153n159; lizard, xxiv, §12.11, §15.11, §16.30, 140n37; oryx, §16.40; ostrich, §16.41, §28.35, §31.12; ox, xxiv, xxx, xxxi, xxxiv, §1.23, §10.3, §23.1, §25.6, §26.27; rabbit, xxiv, §34.12; rat, §14.44; rock badger, §22.47; sheep, §8.3, §14.18, §19.54, §30.22, 139n25; wolf, xxxvii, §28.26, §29.7, §32.3, 153n158. *See also* birds, camel, horse, scorpion, snake

apology, x, xii, xvi–ii, xlvi n52, §§21.1–69, 145n91; poem of apology to ʿAbd Allāh ibn Muʿammar, §§21.1–69
al-Aʿrāf, §21.61
al-ʿĀriḍ, xxi, §3.1, §19.5
arms, xxiii, xliii n12, §28.49; coat of mail, §20.26; flintlock, §7.9, §9.5, §32.7; gun, §7.9, §24.19, §31.8, 143n71; lance, §7.11, §11.8, §11.11, §19.64, 140n33; spear, xlvi, §7.8, §21.49, §32.7; sword, xxiv, xxv, xxvi, xlvi, §6.5, §7.11, §7.15, §14.24, §15.21, §18.9, §22.33, §28.17, §28.46, §32.4, §32.7, §34.9, 146n98, 149n126
arsenic, §8.7
al-Aʿshā, xlvi n56
ashes, xxvi, §10.10. *See also* fire
aspiration. *See* ambition
assemblies, §16.2, §21.20
asylum, xi, xiv, xxii. *See also* refuge
al-ʿAṭṭār, §15.19
al-ʿAzāʿīz, §22.49, §28.38, §30.29, 150n141

Baghdad, xxiii, §28.14
Banū Khālid, xiv, xxxi–xxxii
Banū Zayd. *See* Bini Zēd
Basra, xiii, xxiii, §22.44, §28.14, 141n43
battle, xxiv, §10.8, §§11.14–16, §13.9, §17.1, §18.3, §21.29, §21.44, §21.64, §24.13, §28.21, §28.31, §28.55, 145n83, 146n96, 151n143; battlefield, §14.43, xxiv, §14.29, §21.52; battle cry, §11.18, §16.43; dust of, §13.9
beauty, xxviii, §4.7, §17.8, §21.37, 137n4, 137n6; beautiful girl, xlii n4, 137n9; beautiful girl symbolizing poem, 137n9
Bedouin, xi, xvi, xxvi–xxvii, xxviii, xxxii, xlvi n59, xlvii n63, xlix n101, xlix n106, xlix n107, §14.27, §28.49, §29.17, §30.17, §33.7, 144n80, 146n100, 147n105, 151n146, 153n162, 153n163; anti-Bedouin bias, xliii n6. *See also* sedentary
beetle, §20.34, §22.48, 148n111
beloved. *See* love
bereaved. *See* death
bestiary. *See* animals, birds
bewitch, §16.32
Bini Zēd (Banū Zayd), §22.45, 109n147, 147n109
al-Bīr, xxxvi, xxxvii, §25.5, 149n125
birds, xxiii, xxiv, xxv, xxix, §7.15, §11.27, §16.8, §16.23, §16.49, §21.35, 139n24, 140n34, 141n50, 142n57; bustard, §30.23; chicken, §6.6, 139n20; dove, xxviii, §14.46, §20.40, §21.65, §26.20; eagle, xlvi n55, §20.33; falcon, xxiii, §16.7, §16.49, §20.30, §30.23, §30.36, 141n50, 142n57, 144n82; kite, §17.5, §20.33; nocturnal, §16.23, §16.49, 141n50, 142n57; owl, §14.43, §22.54, 142n57, 144n82, xlii n9, 141n50; peregrine, §16.8, §21.3, §30.23, 144n82; pigeon, §11.11; rooster, §12.10, 140n37; sparrow, xxiv, §12.12; sparrowhawk, §16.7, §21.3; vulture, §20.33, §21.52, §22.46, 145n91; wingless, xxv, §7.15, 139n24
blacksmith (*ṣāniʿ*), §18.19, §20.10, 143n65; bellows, §18.20, §20.10
blame, x, xviii, §21.20, §24.21, §26.3. *See also* censure
boasting, xv, xvii, xxvi, xxix, xlv n43, xlv n46, §1.24, §10.9, §16.26, 137n8, 149n126; bragging, §10.9, §24.4

family (cont.), son. *See* Māniʿ, Mjalli; uncle, §11.30, 140n32; wife, x, xx, xxi, xxvii, xlii n3, xlv n43, xlv n46, xlv n47, §1.3, §7.17, §16.2; wife, advice on choosing, §§19.1–74, §30.15, 143n64

famine, xiii, §15.3, 141n44, 147n107, 148n118. *See also* drought

al-Faraj, Khālid, xxxvii, xliii n15, xlix n98, 142n55, 146n92

al-Farazdaq, xxxii, 146n93

Fāris ibn Bassām, 145n90

fart, x, §18.14, §18.17, §31.13. *See also* shit

fasting, xxix, §16.25

fate, xii, xv, xvi, xviii, xxiii, xxiv, xxix, xxxvii, xlv n46, §2.2, §11.12, §11.14, §16.36, §16.39, §19.9, §19.12, §28.11, 142n53; arrows, blows of, xviii, xxiv, xxix, §2.2, §16.36, §19.9, 142n53; destiny, §14.45, §22.29

al-Fawzān, ʿAbd Allāh Nāṣir, xlv n44, 137n1, 145n91, 153n158

fear, x, xviii, xxii, xxiv, xxx, xliii n8, xli n56, §5.13, §11.15, §12.7, §16.12, §17.7, §19.51, §21.44, §21.59, §22.9, §26.3, §27.3, §30.23, §34.14, 142n57, 145n86, 146n96; of censure, x, xviii, §26.3; of death, §5.12, xlvi n56; fearless, xviii, xlvi n56, §14.27; fear as poor counselor, xxiv, §22.28. *See also* vices (cowardice), virtues (courage)

feast, §9.1, §12.15, §19.50, §28.55, 145n91

fellow rider. *See* co-rider

fire, xxv, xxvi, xlvii, §4.18, §6.4, §10.10, §18.2, §24.8, §28.52, §29.9, §31.12, §34.3; firewood, xv, §26.22; friendly fire, §29.9; fires of Hell, §11.4, §14.37

fire bush, xliii, 149n128

firewood collectors, xv, §26.22, 149n128. *See also* poverty

flattery, §29.15, 151n143; unflattering, xxxvii, 147n109

floods, xv, §21.36

flower, xxii, §4.3, §14.10, §19.7, §26.5

fly (insect), §10.7, 141n50

flying, xxv, §7.15, §9.4, §21.49, §22.58, §30.12, 139n24, 140n34, 148n115

foe. *See* enemy

food, xx, xxii, xxiv, xxviii, §9.5, §10.7, §11.26, §14.6, §14.21, §14.32, §18.8, §19.20, §19.35, §20.23, §22.27, §23.3, §28.45, §30.4, §30.9, 146n100; butter, xxx, xlviii n97, §17.15, §25.4, 140n29, 149n124; cow's and camel's hooves, §23.3; dinner, §16.28, §30.8; fatal morsel, §16.47; flour and butter paste, xlviii n97, §25.4; locusts, roasted, 140n28; meat and broth, xxv, §19.50, §24.8; meat, roast, §14.40, §15.21, §28.57; pastry, §17.12; store, supplies, §§19.35–36; supper, §12.8, §16.25,§21.52; wheat gruel (*ʿaṣīdah, duwayfah*), §25.3, 149n124. *See also* dates, eat, fasting

foolishness. *See* stupidity

fooled, §16.14, §19.22. *See also* deceit

footwear: barefoot, §11.12, 142n63; sandals, §19.53

forbearance. *See* patience

fortress, xxiv, §28.19, §28.22. *See also* castle

fortune, xxii, §28.10; luck, x, §1.13, §16.39, §19.41

fragrant, §15.12, §16.17, §22.44. *See also* perfume

rain (cont.), prayer for, xix, §1.19, §25.5, §30.29, §33.1; thunderclouds, §28.36
rajaz. *See* meter
razor, barber's, 141n44
realism, xiii; unrealistic expectations, xxix
rear-rider. *See* co-rider
refuge, xii, xv, §20.26, §20.34, §22.5, §22.49; refugee, xiii, §21.39. *See also* asylum
religion, ix, xii, xiv, xvi, xvii, xxii, xxxii, xxxviii, xliii n6, §3.2, §12.13, §21.63, §21.65, §27.2, §27.9, 153n158; religious establishment, criticisms of, ix, xvi, xvii, xxii, §3.2, §12.13, §27.2, §§27.5–13, 140n30, 153n158
al-ʿRēnāt (al-ʿUrayniyyāt), §15.19
repute, reputation. *See* honor
respect, xx, xlvii, §19.74, §20.18, §21.43, §22.10; disrespect, xvii, 144n78; less-respectable, xxviii, respectable, xxxii, 137n8; self-respect, xxiii, §28.11, 152n150. *See also* honor
retaliation. *See* revenge
revenge, xxi, xxv, xxx, §2.11, §4.18, §16.13, §28.51, 148n120
al-Rgēbiyyah (al-Ruqaybiyyah), §33.2
rhyme, xviii, xxxiii–iv, xxxviii, xxxix, xlix n100, §20.1, §20.6, §26.2, 137n1, 137n7, 138n14, 138n18, 139n22, 149n125; hamziyyah, 137n1
rich. *See* wealth
rights, xxvi, xlvi n58, §14.26, §§28.17–18, §28.41, §30.5, 150n138
al-Rijm, §21.31
al-Rigʿī, §21.58
Riyadh, ix, xi, xxi, xxxii, xxxv–vi, xxxvii
robbery, xxxi, §10.8, §11.6, §13.5, §14.24, §22.42, 146n100
rock, xv, §16.7, §16.30, §19.68, §20.16, §20.40, §22.35, §22.47, §26.7, §28.30, 151n148; as pillow, xxiii, §28.12
al-Rōḍah (al-Rawḍah), §15.16, xiv, xliv n42, xlv n45, 142n55, 146n98
rope, xxi, xlv n48, §1.10, §1.12, §1.14, §2.10, §19.26, §28.7, 143n70, 150n133
ruin, xxii, §1.19, §8.8, §14.25, §18.18, §29.10, 139n22, 143n66; disaster, xxviii, §3.4, §10.19, §26.19
ruins, xiv, §22.54, 142n58
rule, ruler, x, xiii, xxiii, xxiv, xxv, xxvi, xxvii, xxx, xli n3, xlii n5, xlvi n59, xlviii n82, xlviii n89, xlix n104, §7.15, §§14.13–29, §16.6, §21.42, §21.60, §22.13, §§27.2–3, §28.28, §28.35, §§30.20–21, 137n1, 140n36, 146n96, 152n153. *See also* tyranny

Ṣafā, §21.17
sage, xvii–iii, §2.1, §30.6. *See also* old
Sajāḥ, xvii, xxix, xlvii n67, §7.16
Ṣalab, §2.13, 138n13, 146n101
salt, xxxvi, xliii n9, §16.27, §18.2; digestive salts, xliii n9, §18.2; evaporation pools, 142n62, 149n128; salt flat, §16.19, §22.24
Sanaa, §2.15, §16.51, 150n134
Sāmirī, §19.65
Sanām, xxxv, §15.2
Sārah (Swērah), xx, xxi, xxxiv, xlviii n97, §18.7, §19.1, §§19.5–10. *See also* Mānīʿ
al-Sardiyyah, §31.5
satire, xiii, xxxiv. *See also hijāʾ*
Saudi, ix, xii, xiii, xiv, xxii, xxv, xxviii, xxxviii, xliii n8, xlvii n63, 143n64, 150n137, 152n156; commentators, xvi, xxviii, 143n64, 152n156;

About the NYU Abu Dhabi Institute

The Library of Arabic Literature is supported by a grant from the NYU Abu Dhabi Institute, a major hub of intellectual and creative activity and advanced research. The Institute hosts academic conferences, workshops, lectures, film series, performances, and other public programs directed both to audiences within the UAE and to the worldwide academic and research community. It is a center of the scholarly community for Abu Dhabi, bringing together faculty and researchers from institutions of higher learning throughout the region.

NYU Abu Dhabi, through the NYU Abu Dhabi Institute, is a world-class center of cutting-edge research, scholarship, and cultural activity. The Institute creates singular opportunities for leading researchers from across the arts, humanities, social sciences, sciences, engineering, and the professions to carry out creative scholarship and conduct research on issues of major disciplinary, multidisciplinary, and global significance.

About the Typefaces

The Arabic body text is set in DecoType Naskh, designed by Thomas Milo and Mirjam Somers, based on an analysis of five centuries of Ottoman manuscript practice. The exceptionally legible result is the first and only typeface in a style that fully implements the principles of script grammar (*qawāʿid al-khaṭṭ*).

The Arabic footnote text is set in DecoType Emiri, drawn by Mirjam Somers, based on the metal typeface in the naskh style that was cut for the 1924 Cairo edition of the Qur'an.

Both Arabic typefaces in this series are controlled by a dedicated font layout engine. ACE, the Arabic Calligraphic Engine, invented by Peter Somers, Thomas Milo, and Mirjam Somers of DecoType, first operational in 1985, pioneered the principle followed by later smart font layout technologies such as OpenType, which is used for all other typefaces in this series.

The Arabic text was set with WinSoft Tasmeem, a sophisticated user interface for DecoType ACE inside Adobe InDesign. Tasmeem was conceived and created by Thomas Milo (DecoType) and Pascal Rubini (WinSoft) in 2005.

The English text is set in Adobe Text, a new and versatile text typeface family designed by Robert Slimbach for Western (Latin, Greek, Cyrillic) typesetting. Its workhorse qualities make it perfect for a wide variety of applications, especially for longer passages of text where legibility and economy are important. Adobe Text bridges the gap between calligraphic Renaissance types of the 15th and 16th centuries and high-contrast Modern styles of the 18th century, taking many of its design cues from early post-Renaissance Baroque transitional types cut by designers such as Christoffel van Dijck, Nicolaus Kis, and William Caslon. While grounded in classical form, Adobe Text is also a statement of contemporary utilitarian design, well suited to a wide variety of print and on-screen applications.

Titles Published by the Library of Arabic Literature

For more details on individual titles, visit www.libraryofarabicliterature.org.

Classical Arabic Literature
Selected and translated by Geert Jan Van Gelder

A Treasury of Virtues: Sayings, Sermons and Teachings of ʿAlī, by al-Qāḍī al-Quḍāʿī with the **One Hundred Proverbs** attributed to al-Jāḥiẓ
Edited and translated by Tahera Qutbuddin

The Epistle on Legal Theory, by al-Shāfiʿī
Edited and translated by Joseph E. Lowry

Leg over Leg, by Aḥmad Fāris al-Shidyāq
Edited and translated by Humphrey Davies (four volumes)

Virtues of the Imām Aḥmad ibn Ḥanbal, by Ibn al-Jawzī
Edited and translated by Michael Cooperson (two volumes)

The Epistle of Forgiveness, by Abū l-ʿAlāʾ al-Maʿarrī
Edited and translated by Geert Jan van Gelder and Gregor Schoeler (two volumes)

The Principles of Sufism, by ʿĀʾishah al-Bāʿūniyyah
Edited and translated by Th. Emil Homerin

The Expeditions: An Early Biography of Muḥammad, by Maʿmar ibn Rāshid
Edited and translated by Sean W. Anthony

Two Arabic Travel Books

Accounts of China and India, by Abū Zayd al-Sīrāfī
Edited and translated by Tim Mackintosh-Smith

Mission to the Volga, by Aḥmad ibn Faḍlān
Edited and translated by James Montgomery

Disagreements of the Jurists: A Manual of Islamic Legal Theory, by al-Qāḍī al-Nuʿmān
Edited and translated by Devin J. Stewart

Consorts of the Caliphs: Women and the Court of Baghdad, by Ibn al-Sāʿī
Edited by Shawkat M. Toorawa and translated by the Editors of the Library of Arabic Literature

What ʿĪsā ibn Hishām Told Us, by Muḥammad al-Muwayliḥī
Edited and translated by Roger Allen (two volumes)

The Life and Times of Abū Tammām, by Abū Bakr Muḥammad ibn Yaḥyā al-Ṣūlī
Edited and translated by Beatrice Gruendler

The Sword of Ambition: Bureaucratic Rivalry in Medieval Egypt, by ʿUthmān ibn Ibrāhīm al-Nābulusī
Edited and translated by Luke Yarbrough

Brains Confounded by the Ode of Abū Shādūf Expounded, by Yūsuf al-Shirbīnī
Edited and translated by Humphrey Davies (two volumes)

Light in the Heavens: Sayings of the Prophet Muḥammad, by al-Qāḍī al-Quḍāʿī
Edited and translated by Tahera Qutbuddin

Risible Rhymes, by Muḥammad ibn Maḥfūẓ al-Sanhūrī
Edited and translated by Humphrey Davies

A Hundred and One Nights
Edited and translated by Bruce Fudge

The Excellence of the Arabs, by Ibn Qutaybah
Edited by James E. Montgomery and Peter Webb
Translated by Sarah Bowen Savant and Peter Webb

Scents and Flavors: A Syrian Cookbook
Edited and translated by Charles Perry

Arabian Satire: Poetry from 18th-Century Najd, by Ḥmēdān al-Shwēʿir
Edited and translated by Marcel Kurpershoek

English-only Paperbacks

Leg over Leg, by Aḥmad Fāris al-Shidyāq (two volumes)
The Expeditions: An Early Biography of Muḥammad, by Maʿmar ibn Rāshid
The Epistle on Legal Theory: A Translation of al-Shāfiʿī's Risālah, by al-Shāfiʿī
The Epistle of Forgiveness, by Abū l-ʿAlāʾ al-Maʿarrī
The Principles of Sufism, by ʿĀʾishah al-Bāʿūniyyah
A Treasury of Virtues: Sayings, Sermons and Teachings of ʿAlī, by al-Qāḍī al-Quḍāʿī with **The One Hundred Proverbs**, attributed to al-Jāḥiẓ
The Life of Ibn Ḥanbal, by Ibn al-Jawzī
Mission to the Volga, by Ibn Faḍlān
Accounts of China and India, by Abū Zayd al-Sīrāfī
Consorts of the Caliphs: Women and the Court of Baghdad, by Ibn al-Sāʿī
A Hundred and One Nights
Disagreements of the Jurists: A Manual of Islamic Legal Theory, by al-Qāḍī al-Nuʿmān

About the Editor–Translator

Marcel Kurpershoek is a senior research fellow at New York University Abu Dhabi and a specialist in the oral traditions and poetry of Arabia. He obtained his PhD in modern Arabic literature at the University of Leiden. He has written a number of books on historical, cultural, and contemporary topics in the Middle East, including the five-volume *Oral Poetry and Narratives from Central Arabia* (1994–2005), which draws on his recordings of Bedouin tribes. In 2016, Al Arabiya television broadcast an eight-part documentary series based on the travelogue of fieldwork he had undertaken in the Nefud desert of northern Arabia for his book *Arabia of the Bedouins* (in Arabic translation *The Last Bedouin*). He spent his career as a diplomat for the Netherlands, having served as ambassador to Pakistan, Afghanistan, Turkey, Poland, and special envoy for Syria until 2015. From 1996 to 2002, he held a chair as professor of literature and politics in the Arab world at the University of Leiden.